AF572124

IMAGES OF FAITH

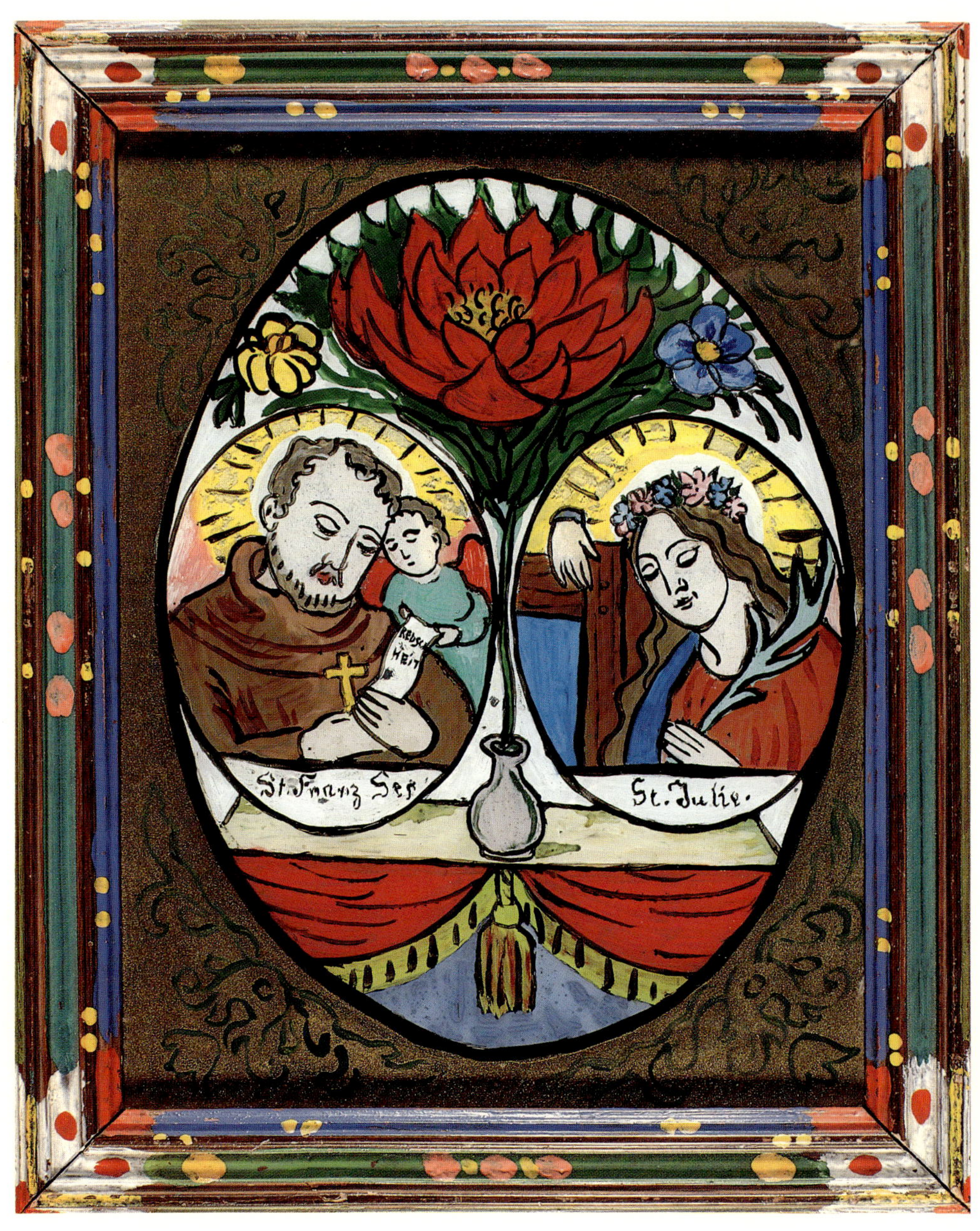
REUSC
HEIT
St. Franz Se
St. Julie.

IMAGES OF FAITH

Expressionism, Catholic Folk Art, and the Industrial Revolution

Helena Waddy Lepovitz

THE UNIVERSITY OF GEORGIA PRESS
Athens and London

Designed by Mary Mendell Set in 10½/13 Sabon
The paper in this book meets the guidelines for permanence and durability of the Committee on Production Guidelines for Book Longevity of the Council on Library Resources.
Printed in the United States of America
95 94 93 92 91 5 4 3 2 1

Library of Congress Cataloging in Publication Data

Lepovitz, Helena Waddy, 1945–
Images of faith : expressionism, Catholic folk art and the industrial revolution / Helena Waddy Lepovitz.
p. cm.
Includes bibliographical references.
ISBN 0-8203-1256-8 (alk. paper)
1. Glass underpainting—Germany—History.
2. Holy cards—Germany—History. 3. Expressionism—Germany. 4. Glass underpainting—Germany—History—20th century. 5. Folk art—Germany—Influence.
I. Title.
NK5435.G3L4 1991
760'.04482'094336—dc20 90-33630 CIP
British Library Cataloging in Publication Data available

Frontispiece: Gabriele Münter's glasspainting
Die Heiligen Franz Seraph und Julie.
(Städtische Galerie im Lenbachhaus, Munich)

TO MY FAMILY

Contents

Illustrations

Tables

Preface

The vibrant color and luminosity of stained glass windows delighted the medieval visitors to churches and cathedrals all over Europe. Not surprisingly, these special qualities of decorative glass also inspired its transferral from the sacred space of the churches to the private homes of the well-to-do. By the sixteenth century, smaller windows or roundels and paintings on glass had begun to enliven living quarters or enhance family shrines. This practice in turn encouraged middle- and lower-class Europeans to display framed paintings executed on the reverse side of glass panes as inexpensive substitutes for oil paintings. The result was the translation of the elite medium of stained glass into a folk art.[1]

This folk glasspainting—known as *Hinterglasmalerei*—caught the attention of artists associated with the Munich-based Blue Rider circle in the years before World War I when they were developing an abstract expressionist style. Visiting Alpine villages where mountain vistas inspired their magnificent landscape paintings, group members also drew inspiration from local folk crafts, of which glasspainting became a particular favorite. Indeed, one authority argues that it "influenced the views and styles of the Munich group more than any other kind of folk art."[2] A large part of their fascination for this peasant medium derived from the spiritual messages of most glasspaintings; for they had retained the predominantly religious iconography of stained glass. Popular glasspaintings were usually sold on the international Catholic market for biblical and doctrinal images during the eighteenth and nineteenth centuries, and even middle-class consumers frequently preferred religious themes for their paintings.

To be sure, the middle-class purchasers of glasspaintings also favored secular subjects; as a result, traditional favorites like the Four Seasons or Continents, hunting scenes, and patriotic portraits appear regularly in glasspaintings aimed at this middle-class clientele. Moreover, the producers of glasspaintings were flexible enough to adapt their iconographical offerings to the secular demands of a growing colonial market that came to include the United States. Consequently, portraits on glass of George Washington and other famous American leaders, or of formulaic female images such as southern belles, crossed the Atlantic during the nineteenth century, while glasspainting was sometimes adopted by American folk artists as well. Visitors to museums located all over the United States can therefore find examples of native work in the medium, including some examples attributable to such artists as William Matthew Prior and Benjamin Greenleaf. Seldom are these paintings religious in theme, however, so they remain unrepresentative of the emphasis on religious iconography that typified the craft in Europe.[3]

These European folk glasspaintings were marketed from production centers established in central Europe around 1750, when at the height of a wave of pilgrimage fervor, smallholders in a handful of rural locations took up the trade. Like many other European smallholders these families began to mix small-scale farming with the production and marketing of goods that linked them with the developing commercial networks of eighteenth-century Europe. The craft flourished until the mid-nineteenth century, when its practitioners increasingly began to face a lethal form of competition, the industrial production of chromolithographs as substitutes for oil paintings. The rural glasspainters did not make a transition to factory production themselves but conceded that initiative to the city-based lithographic industry, an offshoot of the graphic arts industry that had flourished for centuries in production centers like Augsburg. As industrialization proceeded, the glasspainters' villages became tourist centers, adapting their commercial activities to suit the new requirements for leisure opportunities of the growing urban population. Glasspainting became a tourist-oriented occupation within this context, a small part of the large transformative process by which the painters' communities adapted to twentieth-century industrial culture.

It was while this transformation was underway, and after it became clear that the craft of glasspainting was falling victim to the industrializing process taking place in European cities, that Blue Rider members came across the medium. They were visiting—as urbanites and tourists—one of the major Bavarian centers of production. Their romantic imagination fired by the spiritual context and formal simplicity of local glasspaintings, group members themselves painted on glass as a means of conveying their expressionist message. Their excitement about this dying folk art, with its symbolic resonances of a fading preindustrial culture, thus inspired a lasting intellectual interest in glasspainting that persists to this day. Their "discovery" also became mine as I followed their lead in studying these culturally rich artifacts and the rural craftsmen who created them.

In the first part and in the Epilogue of this book I examine the glasspainters as rural craftsmen who contributed to the transformation of their region from its "preindustrial" form to its modern role as tourist center. For this reason I consider not only the producers themselves in their social and economic context but also the distributors who wove the network of the trade and linked the producers with their markets. Moreover, since the glasspainters worked within the broader context of the city-based graphic arts industry, I also explore the interrelationship between the rural glasspainting workshops and the industrializing process taking place in nearby urban centers. In the second part of the book my focus shifts to the consumers of glasspaintings and lithographs, because it was their desire to own religious artworks that underlay the success of the rural glasspainting workshops and later helped to stimulate the development of industrial chromolithography. This exploration into the motivations behind the purchasing of religious paintings leads me to the heart of popular Catholic culture—to the shrines and pilgrimages of the original cult images from which the iconography of many glasspaintings was derived, and to the protective function of those images in the daily lives of believers. The dual focus of the book thus allows me to provide both a new look at the economic and social transformations brought about in rural Europe by the Industrial Revolution and an in-depth study of the cultural underpinnings of religious art production for the popular Catholic market. Of course, the Blue Rider artists were experiencing the social impact of the industrial transformation at first hand, and they found inspiration for their reaction against its materialist implications in the traditional culture about which the paintings spoke so eloquently to them. So, by examining the glasspainters' story and the cultural context of their work, I also illuminate the traditional roots of the group's expressionist message in this medium so enticingly linked to a spiritual past that had seemingly been discarded by the heady materialism of the industrial present.

Acknowledgments

The preparation of this book would not have been possible without the assistance and support of a great many people. In particular, I would like to thank my graduate advisor H. Stuart Hughes for his constant encouragement and guidance. My colleagues and teachers at the University of California at San Diego, the University of Oregon, and the State University of New York at Geneseo have also provided invaluable advice and assistance along the way: James Allen, Marilynn Board, Thomas Brady, Aline Hornaday, Ellen Kintz, Eunice Konold, Robert and Nerys Levy, David Luft, John Marino, Joyce Mastboom, Michael Meeker, Allan Mitchell, Moira Roth, Karen Shabetai, George Sheridan, Harriet Sleggs, David Tamarin, Julie Taylor, and Dana Tiffany. In addition, Steven Reynolds kindly prepared the map for me. The University of California at San Diego provided me with generous financial support through fellowships and teaching assistantships as I prepared the original dissertation manuscript. I was also privileged to take part in a summer National Endowment for the Arts seminar at Cornell University under the direction of Walter Pintner, at which time I was able to reformulate the theoretical foundations of the book. I thank both the NEH and my colleagues at the seminar for their support of this venture. More recently, I have gratefully received assistance from the Geneseo Foundation and the Geneseo Faculty Small Grants program. I am also particularly grateful for the Geneseo Presidential Research Development Grant that underwrote much of the cost of the color frontispiece.

In Germany I received valuable assistance from many kind people, among them Gislind Ritz in Munich, Ernst Krönner and Eckhart Feuchtmayr in Murnau, Axel Janeck in Nuremberg, Theo Hahn and Florian Lang in Oberammergau, Jakob Scheck in Uffing, and Herbert Fastner, Reinhard Haller, and Raimund Schuster in Zwiesel. I am grateful to them for their helpfulness and friendship. The Deutscher Akademischer Austauschdienst generously supported a summer's research trip in 1983, and I thank them also.

This book draws on and reproduces material from my article "The Industrialization of Popular Art in Bavaria," which appeared in *Past and Present* 99 (May 1983), pp. 88–122 (World Copyright: The Past and Present Society, Corpus Christi College, Oxford, England). Portions of Chapters 4 and 5 appeared as "Spiritual Insurance: A Strategy for Psychological Survival" in *Notebooks in Cultural Analysis* 1 (1984), edited by Norman F. Cantor and published by Duke University Press. A few paragraphs of Chapter 5 appear in my article "The Religious Context of Crisis Resolution in the Votive Paintings of Catholic Europe," *Journal of Social History* 23 (June 1990). The theoretical framing of the book has been provided in much greater detail in my article "Gateway to the Mountains: Tourism and Positive Deindustrialization in the Bavarian Alps," *German History* 7 (December 1989): 293–318 (World Copyright: The German History Society). I am grateful to the editors of these journals for their permission to incorporate this material into the present study. I am also grateful for the constructive comments provided by anonymous readers for the University of Georgia Press and for anonymous readings and comments by the editors of journals to which portions of this manuscript had been submitted. Helena Wright of the Division of Graphic Arts, Smithsonian Institution, also kindly provided me with very helpful comments. Finally, I would like to thank my editor, Nancy Grayson Holmes, for her faith in this project and her guidance in its successful completion.

IMAGES OF FAITH

Introduction: The "Discovery" and the Reality of Glasspainting

When Arnold Schönberg decided to spend the summer vacation of 1914 in Bavaria, he inspired a stream of correspondence from his friends Gabriele Münter and Wassily Kandinsky over the merits of available recreational lodgings in the Murnau area.[1] Münter and Kandinsky, who were leading figures in the Blue Rider artistic circle, had developed a strong affinity for this mountain retreat lying at the foot of the lovely Bavarian Alps. They had identified it in 1908 as yet another fascinating Alpine location, like the Kochel area that had inspired much of their earlier landscape work.[2] But this "find" held an even greater significance than Kochel for the pair.[3] They kept returning to Murnau, and it is hardly surprising that they would entice fellow artists such as Schönberg to their retreat. A painting by Münter of two Blue Rider friends, Alexej von Jawlensky and Marianne von Werefkin, stretched out on a mountain pasture in festive attire, sums up perfectly the recreational and inspirational nature of the group's Murnau experience.[4]

Murnau features in large numbers of Kandinsky's paintings and to a lesser extent in paintings by Münter in 1908 and subsequent years. These paintings read like a travel diary, recording the impressions of a pair of tourists enchanted both by small-town vistas and by the surrounding countryside. There was nothing unusual about this, of course, since the Bavarian countryside had attracted many nineteenth-century artists before them, as collections in Munich galleries attest.[5] But the two visitors' repeated examination of views of the town itself is intriguing. Kandinsky in particular paints Murnau street scenes over and over again, moving the viewer from the Johannisstrasse as seen from the window of the couple's inn, the Griesbräu, to the courtyard of the local castle, to the Kohlgruberstrasse, to the Pfarrgasse, to the Burggrabenstrasse, to the Peterskapelle, and so forth. His *Blick aus dem Fenster des Griesbräu* (1908) captures both the atmosphere of the town in the foreground and the brilliant green of its outlying fields broken by a couple of red barn roofs and set against the purply blue background of the Alps (figure 1). Kandinsky's focus from the center of town later shifts to reflect that in 1909 Münter was able to purchase a house on the edge of Murnau, in the Kottmüllerallee; a series of paintings record the view from the garden there across to Murnau's castle and central church (Saint Nicholas). For example, a stunningly beautiful painting from 1910 entitled simply *Murnau—Garten I* describes the onion-domed church and crenellated castle façade as they appear through the intervening trees and flowers. The rich and vibrant colors of this painting invest the landscape forms with a thrilling spiritual presence.[6]

The Blue Rider artists' intense interest in Murnau as a summer resort reflects the general growth of tourism so carefully fostered by Alpine Bavarians in this period when their older folk industries had given way to industrial competition.[7] Together with their fellow vacationers, the group's members contributed to the economic regeneration of this region of Upper Bavaria. But their intellectual and artistic focus was turned backward toward a "traditional" form of living that they encountered in local churches and homes. Münter and Kandinsky clearly found in Murnau a special source of inspiration that led them to adopt the town as one of their permanent living places in these years left to them before the outbreak of war. (Ainmillerstrasse Number 36 in the Schwabing section of Munich was the other.) Indeed, Peg Weiss argues that it was in Murnau that Kandinsky's "self-confidence" about his art took off. "As if a door had suddenly opened," she observes, "Kandinsky now experienced a stylistic release."[8]

Part of this inspiration clearly lay in the couple's decision to immerse themselves in a peasant life-style while staying in Murnau. To begin with, the decision to take up residence in the Kottmüllerallee house perforce included the adoption of a simple living environment—there were no modern conveniences.[9] To add to this rustic experience, Kandinsky painted the staircase in decorative folk style and the wooden

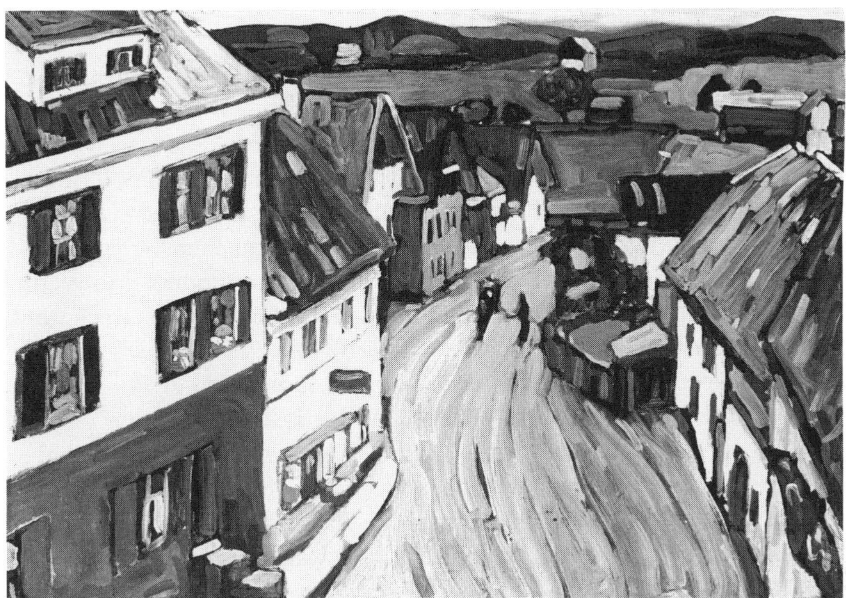

Figure 1. Wassily Kandinsky, *Blick auf dem Fenster des Griesbräu*. (Photograph by VG Bild-Kunst, Poppelsdorfer Allee 43, D-5300 Bonn; reproduced courtesy of Städtische Galerie im Lenbachhaus, Munich)

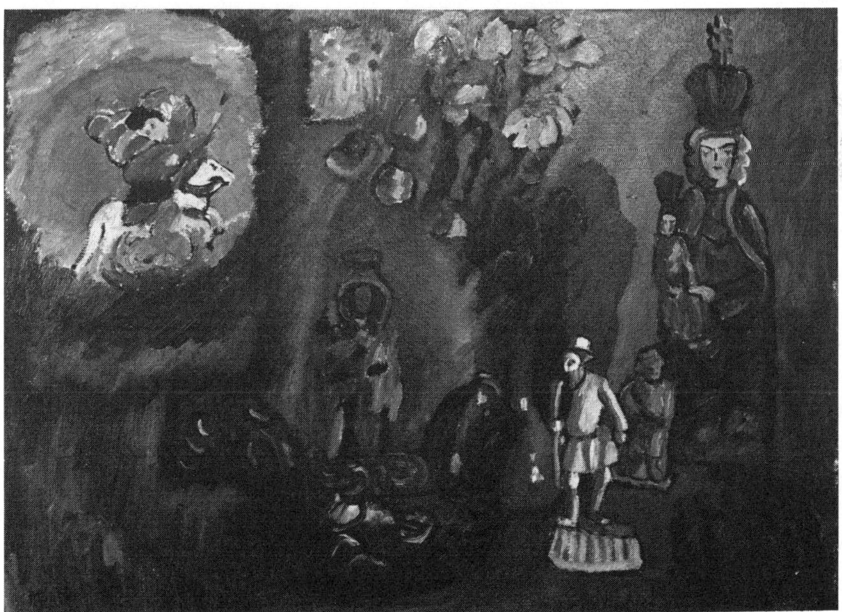

Figure 2. Gabriele Münter, *Stilleben mit Heil. Georg*, 1911. (Städtische Galerie im Lenbachhaus, Munich)

furniture to match.[10] One of Münter's most fascinating paintings describes the dining area of the Kottmüllerallee household. Kandinsky himself sits at a simple table decked festively with a white fringed tablecloth and blue-white striped peasant ware. The walls and floor are washed with strong colors, and the dining area is decorated with folk paintings and other objets d'art. To complete the homey effect, Kandinsky adopted peasant attire—blue jacket, white shirt, shorts, and green leggings. Photographs of him taken by Münter confirm his attraction for the leather shorts, leggings, sandals, and indeed the waistcoat, felt hat, and pipe of the mountaineer. One snapshot even catches him at work in the "peasant garden" attached to the house.[11]

This playing at peasant living was not, however, the major influence on Kandinsky's stylistic revolution provided by Murnau's "traditional" repertoire. For the town was one of the Bavarian centers of folk art production, in particular of the *Hinterglasmalerei* that inspired the Blue Rider artists at this time.[12] They collected examples and visited the extensive collection of a local brewer named Simon Krötz; they painted on glass (especially Kandinsky and Münter) and incorporated stylistic elements from glasspainting into their formal works. In particular, the heavy outlining typical of the glasspaintings found its way into the new style, and the intense, glowing colors of the glasspaintings must surely have encouraged the group in their experimentations with color symbolism as well.[13] The formal elements of glasspaintings, however, were merely the outward expression of mystical references to which these usually religious artifacts connected the viewer. In fact, they seemed to offer a direct, culturally unmediated vision of "eternal verities."[14] As such, they offered an ideal medium for a new art dedicated to spiritual awakening.[15]

Because of the central role played by glasspainting in the creativity of the Blue Rider artists, it is hardly surprising to find a variety of examples of the medium presented in *The Blue Rider Almanac,* their eclectic volume dedicated to the new art. Eleven glasspainting motifs appear there, including the frontispiece, a Saint Martin. Indeed, the group's identification with folk art was so complete that the cover figure of the *Almanac* originated as a Kandinsky glasspainting of Saint George, who was so popular in the Murnau area.[16] In addition, Kandinsky chose to illustrate his essay "On the Question of Form" with five votive paintings depicting wondrous interventions by the Murnau Madonna. He also used one of the glasspaintings and the Münter still life that includes a glasspainting of Saint George from her collection (figure 2). All these selections were juxtaposed with children's drawings, Rousseaus, and a mixture of other modern and traditional reproductions.[17] We can assume, then, that the painters of both glass and votive paintings used "form . . . to achieve the necessary expression of . . . inner experience." This exemplifies Kandinsky's principle that "when the conditions necessary for the maturation of a certain form are met, the yearning, the inner urge, the force is strengthened so that it can create a new value in the human spirit that consciously or unconsciously begins to live in man." In this process, "matter" becomes "a kind of larder from which the spirit chooses what is *necessary* for itself, much as a cook would."[18] Certainly, folk art seems to have provided the author and his colleagues with a tasty spiritual repast.[19]

Glasspainting became an active pursuit for the Blue Rider group through their direct encounter with one of the few remaining practitioners of the craft, which had been rapidly disappearing because of the competition offered by chromolithography. Heinrich Rambold had learned to paint behind glass as a substitute for painting on canvas or wood from a member of the Gege family, whose activities reached back to the origins of local production in the mid-eighteenth century.[20] A 1912 article describes the "laughing" color of Rambold's paintings; their spirit harked back to older and better days, according to Hans Kyser, in a way that his mentor Josef Gege's paintings had lost.[21] Rambold guided Münter's initiation into his craft after she had met him through Jawlensky, who seems to have been the first of the group to discover both the practicing Rambold and the magnificent collection of paintings gathered by Krötz in his *Haus am Burggraben*. Interestingly, Rosel Gollek argues that many of Rambold's paintings were left over from commercial stock.[22] Münter describes her reaction to this find: "At Rambold's I saw how one did it. I was the first in Murnau—so far as I know—who took glass panes and did something. First copies—then also various personal things. . . . I was entranced by the technique and how beautifully it went and kept telling Kandinsky about it, to stimulate him about it too—until he too began and then did many glasspaintings."[23] Gollek draws attention to an early effort, unquestionably a copy of a Rambold votive painting on glass; the motifs are identical, and the Münter version is reversed as one would expect. Gollek suggests that even the pane may have come from his own stock.[24]

Rambold provided the Blue Rider artists with a direct link back to the heyday of rural glasspainting, since his wares resembled the colorful, popularized paintings produced from 1750 to 1850 in Upper Bavaria and in many other areas of central Europe as well.[25] At the most complex stage of production development an "assembly line" of craftsmen would paint each pane of glass: initially, one worker would paint in the outlines of the subject matter in a dark color, then others would gradually add the colors required to complete subject, background, and decorative border. Frames, usually made of darkly painted or decorated wood, were constructed separately and attached to the finished painting. The framed painting was then ready to hang on the wall of a peasant or craftsman's living room, where in Bavaria it usually served a religious purpose as part of a holy corner or *Herrgottswinkel* centered above the dining area and dominated by a crucifix.[26] This is why the iconographical content of the paintings was usually concentrated on popular saints and biblical scenes and on numerous images of the Madonna, Christ, and the Holy Trinity. Paintings ranged in quality of style from the plastic, nuanced work of the urban Augsburg school to the simple, often schematized efforts of village painters from the remote Bavarian Forest.

Rambold also introduced the Blue Rider artists to the simple distribution methods adopted by his predecessors. Glasspainters had frequently sold their finished products through the agency of hawkers, who enabled the market of a production center to stretch far beyond the local confines normal for village craftsmen in these areas. Rambold too visited local festivals and pilgrimage sites with the rucksack on his back that he had inherited from his great-grandfather. Thus, his sales methods as well as his production techniques exemplified the "primitive" structure of his craft.[27]

In these ways Rambold's glasspainting business opened up the world of rural industry to the group. What the artists do not appear to have understood, however, was that practicing glasspainting had been a relatively recent economic stratagem in the region. In an interview with Edouard Roditi in 1960, Münter talked of "the glass paintings of the Bavarian peasants of the Murnau area, who had painted for centuries in this style."[28] Yet glasspainting had been introduced into rural European craft centers only in the mid-eighteenth century, at a time when an increase in the smallholding population was putting pressure on peasant proprietors to search for subsidiary occupations. Certainly, the expressive iconographical quality of the paintings drew from a much older tradition of Christian art; the consumers of glasspaintings bought them for that reason. But the Blue Rider artists' delight in the technical simplicity and spiritual sincerity of this "peasant" art, which contrasted so favorably with cognitive, Renaissance-based styles, led them to dehistoricize their new medium's past.

Nevertheless, the artists did recognize a key historical link between glasspainting and the graphic arts that resulted from the dependence of glasspainters on devotional prints as patterns for their paintings. For example, Münter's *Saints Franz Seraph and Julie* copies one such print identified by Gollek as a "handcolored woodcut," although the motifs are not reversed, suggesting that she did not lay the print beneath the glass as a guide (frontispiece and figure 3). The result is a heavily contoured and multi-colored work, enclosed both in a golden cartouche and in a painted wooden frame. As is common in glasspainting, the graphic original has dictated the style of the final product.[29] A strong sense of the possible relationship between prints and paintings also reveals itself in the use of contouring by Kandinsky and Münter at this time.[30]

In this way, the perceptiveness of the Blue Rider artists leads us back toward the graphic arts industry in search of an accurate historical account of the "peasant" glasspaintings they so admired. It is true that practice of the craft itself predates the invention of printing, since painting behind glass has a long history that reaches back into the antique world.[31] Indeed, the technique had been known in Germany for several centuries before it was adapted to the production of inexpensive oil paintings for the expanding European and colonial market in graphic art. An exquisite glasspainting dated as early as 1320–30, in which the intricately carved wooden frame and lozenge-shaped wooden inserts contain an abundant variety of biblical and animal scenes, has been identified as German.[32] By the eighteenth century rococo-style glasspaintings were providing a charming means of decorating such aristocratic retreats as the Hall of Mirrors in the archbishop of Würzburg's Palace.[33] More relevant to our story, however, is that in eighteenth-century Augsburg, then a great center for the production of graphic art, a guild of painters, glaziers, sculptors, and gold and silver craftsmen included glasspainters; the profession first appeared in the records in 1684.[34] The subsequent business activities of these Augsburg glasspainters led both to the popularization of their products and to the eventual adoption of their craft by rural artisans from the Murnau area.[35]

The Augsburg glasspainters' official connection with other artistic

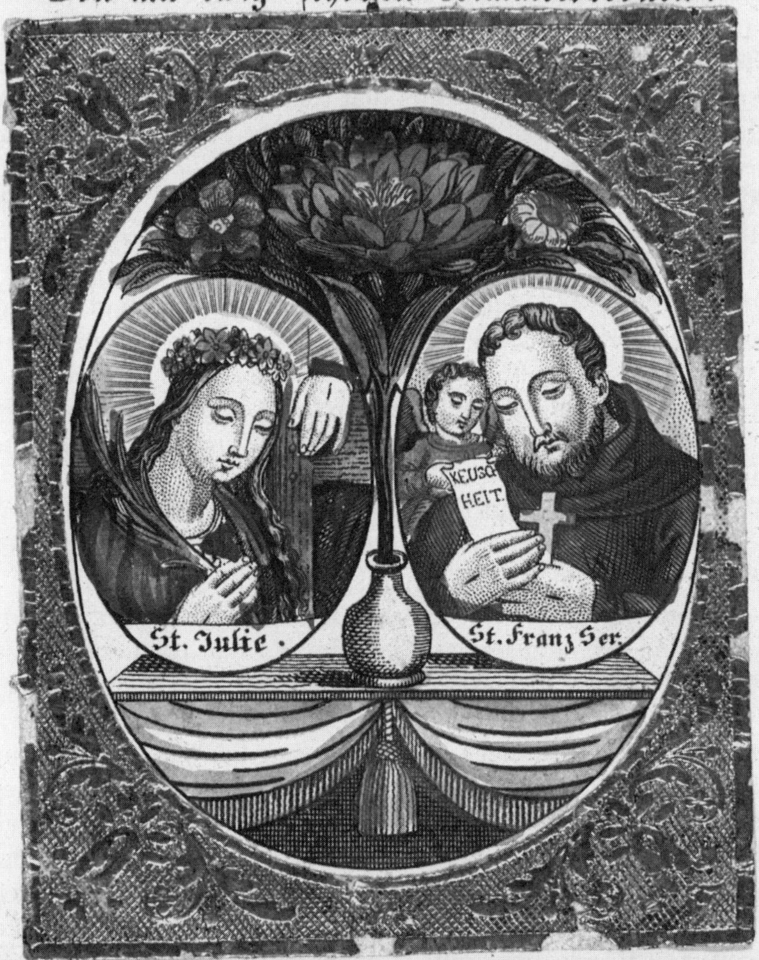

Figure 3. Print from which Münter's *Die Heiligen Franz Seraph und Julie* was copied. (Städtische Galerie im Lenbachhaus, Munich)

craftsmen, rather than with the many printers and engravers involved in the production of graphic art in Augsburg, tells only part of the story. While they were painters (and sometimes good ones), their product was to become a means of extending and reshaping the market for graphic prints.[36] Indeed, the connection was so close that Johann Wolfgang Baumgartner, the most prominent early eighteenth-century Augsburg glasspainter, also worked for engravers by drawing the original designs from which they created their plates.[37] During the early days of Augsburg glasspainting, Gabriel Bodenehr and others were known for their gold and silver engraved paintings, in which the addition of metallic ornamentation to the glass created a rich if not very colorful effect.[38] Moreover, the patterns placed under the glass or even transferred to it by Augsburg glasspainters as a guide in the execution of their work were normally prints; Paul von Stettin reported the use of "French, English and other engravings," with the consequence that "the individual artist was required only for the color."[39] The resulting paintings might even become reproductions of a famous work; Karl Ludwig Thuot, for example, copied Albrecht Dürer's 1504 engraving *Adam and Eve* as a glasspainting in 1686.[40] The reproductive and often propagandistic nature of graphic art and the standardization of its product was thus translated into a medium more directly competitive with the oil paintings patronized by the rich and more responsive to the artistic talents of the early glasspainters who were oil and fresco painters as well.[41] Augsburg glasspaintings provided unique qualities of color and luminosity that resulted from the viewing of the painting through glass. They therefore competed favorably with both tinted engravings, in which color had for the most part to be subordinated to draftsmanship, and popular woodcuts, in which the crude application of bright colors erased any sense of the finer points of design. As Horace Walpole put it, "Want of Colouring is the capital deficiency of prints." So the decorativeness of glasspaintings made them particularly suitable adornments for the rococo interiors of the period.[42] Consequently, with competitive business acumen the eighteenth-century Augsburg glasspainters exploited the possibilities for large-scale production inherent in their product's popular appeal, expanding their markets to include both European urban consumers and the colonial market in India and South America.[43]

Around 1780 there were at least six glasspainting masters active in Augsburg together with their apprentices; indeed, the Josef Mayr shop employed as many as seven helpers.[44] Much of their work was sold for them by well-connected merchant houses, of which three or four have been identified. Gislind Ritz further suggests that the production methods used in glasspainting workshops like Mayr's must have included a division of labor. Yet this substantial craft activity was by then being supplemented by the work of rural glasspainters from the surrounding countryside. The close relationship between printing and engraving workshops and the extensive use of machinery in the printing process discouraged the spread of graphic reproduction into the rural hinterland of Augsburg. But glasspainting was a craft sufficiently flexible that it could attract rural and small-town labor.[45] An enterprising merchant could even adopt the "putting out" system to tap the reserves of excess manpower available in rural areas.[46]

Such a merchant was the Augsburger Simon Schropp. With Johann Michael Hohenleitner, Schropp ran a business in glasspaintings that extended to Spain, Portugal, America, and India. To meet the demands of their customers, Schropp and Hohenleitner brought glass into the city in large quantities for painting by local glasspainters. But as early as 1771, these merchants had their eye on sources of labor outside the city, for they threatened to make use of out-of-town workers if their trading practices were disrupted by disgruntled glaziers looking for their business. By 1778 it was reported that Augsburg merchants were using the services of about five out-of-town glasspainters because the city workforce was not able to keep up with the demand. The Ursperger "ordinary" messenger made the statement that he "brings Antoni Walter, glasspainting apprentice in Krumbach, glass panes from the local merchant, Mr. Schropp, to Krumbach every eight days, and then he brings back the finished glasspaintings from him to Mr. Schropp weekly to Augsburg."[47] Yet the flow of goods appears to have been more complicated than this; in 1780 Bartholomäus März of Murnau's request for admission to the Augsburg guild as a master glasspainter was met by the complaint that Murnau merchants were ordering substantial amounts of glasspaintings from Augsburg because local craftsmen were not producing enough stock. The glasspainter Hubert Valentin reported supplying both Augsburg and out-of-town merchants with work when he made an appeal to the guild in 1777. Moreover, it seems to have been easier, more attractive, and perhaps more legal, for out-of-town men seeking to work for Augsburg businesses such as Schropp and Hohenleitner's or Mëyer and Handel's to become masters in the city. Several out-of-towners managed to attain this goal through judicious marriages into craft families.[48]

By the time Schropp had extended his employment network outside the city limits, several householders in the Murnau area had become glasspainters (in Murnau itself, in the villages of Seehausen and Uffing located on Murnau's Lake Staffel, and in nearby Oberammergau); all were able to draw their glass supplies from the local glass factory at Aschau. Moreover, a substantial trade in glasspaintings also existed in areas of Lower Bavaria and Bohemia that could draw upon the supplies of inexpensive glass provided by local glass factories, and there were glasspainters active in the Black Forest, Switzerland, the Tyrol, and other areas of central Europe as well.[49] In Lower Bavaria and Bohemia the decoration and marketing of glass objects such as drinking glasses and mirrors in the context of factory production seems to have been the decisive factor in encouraging families associated with the factories to take up glasspainting; however, it is almost certain that they knew about the painting activities of Augsburg and other city craftsmen as well.[50] In Upper Bavaria, on the other hand, the proximity of Augsburg seems to have been the decisive factor in persuading local families to take up the trade.

We may never know the extent of that connection. For there is no evidence to suggest that merchants like Schropp actually commissioned paintings from the first generation of Upper Bavarian craftsmen, establishing a basis for the independent workshops that emerged there. Yet, the apprenticing of villagers to Augsburg craftsmen did forge a substantial link between the urban and rural painters. One such trainee was Joseph Hohenleitner of Oberammergau, probably a relative of the merchant Hohenleitner who guaranteed his legitimacy. In 1760 he became the apprentice of the Augsburg glasspainter, Ignaz Baur, who had married an Oberammergau woman in 1748. Hohenleitner apparently did not remain in Augsburg; he may have returned to his village to work, as did Andreas Lang, also of Oberammergau, who is reported to have studied under Baur as well in the 1750s. Lang is recognized as the founder of the glasspainting business in his home village, but the entrepreneurial precocity of Oberammergau craftsmen in this period suggests that it was as an independent merchant, not as the hireling of Augsburg merchants, that he established his business.[51]

The first-generation Seehausen glasspainter Michael Kirchmayr may have had connections in Augsburg as well, although there is no evidence for the apprenticeship of any Seehausen craftsmen in the city. There was a painter, Johann Kirchmeyer, in Augsburg around the mid-eighteenth century who could have been related, although the name was a common one. A clearer connection can be made to the Augsburg bookseller, Matthias Rieger, possibly a relative and the neighbor of Kirchmayr's listed in a tax survey of 1752. In a glasspainting portrait of the bookseller, attributed to Kirchmayr, he holds a picture of the Seehausen church for which he donated money in 1774. Both endowment and painting suggest that Rieger retained an emotional, if not a material, bond to the village of his birth, and to his village relations, that must have facilitated the artistic connection between the two locations.[52] Furthermore, when Kirchmayr's son Johann Paul moved to Uffing and established a glasspainting business there in 1773, he was accustomed to ordering his painting supplies from Augsburg merchants such as "Josef Anton Mayer's widow."[53] Yet the earliest Seehausen glasspainter to order glass from the local Aschau glass factory, Johannes Noder, has left no proof of any connections with the city.

By contrast, the Bartholomäus März whose petition to the Augsburg guild in 1780 we noted above was the son of one of the first Murnau glasspainters, yet he chose to work in Augsburg and marry a local woman rather than return to Murnau. His father Jakob, a merchant with business connections to Oberammergau and possibly to Augsburg as well, may have been one of the Murnau merchants who were buying Augsburg glasspaintings rather than supplying a city middleman. Moreover, unlike Antoni Walter, the Upper Bavarian painters were entirely independent of any mercantile supply of glass, since they could order on their own account from Aschau.[54] On balance, it seems to me that there is no evidence for direct employment connections between Augsburg merchants and Upper Bavarian glasspainters, whereas there is some evidence that local merchants like Jakob März, or aspiring merchants like Andreas Lang, brough the practice of the craft to their home towns and persuaded other residents to take it up.

With the development of rural glasspainting centers both in the Murnau area and in other parts of central Europe by the late eighteenth century, a large productive effort was under way that did not depend to any noticeable extent on the city. Centers like Raimundsreuth in Lower Bavaria that were particularly influenced by the decoration of other popular glass products showed little sign of even a stylistic influence from Augsburg painterly standards; their orientation was from the start toward the popular country market. Upper Bavarian painters, however, reflected their connections with the city in working standards much closer to those acceptable in urban and colonial middle-class circles. Indeed, it is often difficult to tell whether a baroque painting of the late eighteenth century was executed in Augsburg or in the country. Yet even the Upper Bavarian painters became increasingly interested in the popular European market for paintings that Lower Bavarian schematized and rapidly executed work so readily filled. With the general disruptions of trade caused by the Napoleonic Wars, Augsburg's glasspainting activity declined, particularly since the middle-class market was lost in the early nineteenth century to other more attractive media. So it was left to the rural production centers to realign their trading goals toward a European mass market.[55] In this way they came to emphasize the religious themes still popular in the countryside, drawing from the wealth of iconography that centuries of Catholic worship and propaganda had perpetuated, as I explore in Part 2.

Sadly, however, as was so often the case with rural craftsmen, the glasspainters' successful exploitation of a large and specific market for their products within the graphic arts industry also led to their craft's decline. For the appeal of their colorful paintings helped to stimulate the industrial development of lithography, a new graphic procedure that had been invented in Munich during the 1790s by Alois Senefelder. Specifically, the transformation of lithography into its colorful "chromolithographic" form as a mechanized medium for the creation of affordable oil paintings was influenced by the already established success of glasspaintings in filling this need. At first Senefelder discovered that he could use the flat surface of a Solenhofen limestone to print images, musical notations, and script drawn in a specially prepared ink. No engraving or cutting was necessary, and his invention was therefore the first reproductive technique to be entirely planographic, "based not on mechanical but purely chemical properties."[56] The procedure offered immediate advantages over the other graphic reproduction techniques that had preceded it, for it could be used to print quickly and cheaply in a variety of styles. Indeed, the ease with which script and also cartography could be applied to the stone soon led to the use of lithography by government agencies as a form of early duplicating machine.[57] Lithography was also used to reproduce drawings, although in this field it faced a major competitor, particularly in the field of newspaper and book illustration, a wood-engraving technique that held the advantage of combining easily with type. For artists, however, lithography offered the possibility of working directly on the stone, without the need for an intermediary craftsman. Artists responded immediately to the challenge, and a great many early examples of artistic production on stone are still extant.[58] Because of lithography's advantages in the field of art reproduction, Senefelder and his followers soon began working on the more complicated procedure of color printing with several lithographic stones. Meanwhile, a hybrid system of lithographic printing and hand-colored, often stenciled embellishment was adopted by firms serving the popular market for the production of cheaper prints. The techniques used by lithographers became more and more clearly industrialized, and by the 1880s large factories full of steam-powered machines were printing chromolithographs for a huge mass public.[59]

Lithography emerged as a graphic technique out of the same matrix of the graphic arts and printing industries from which glasspainting had earlier evolved. Older graphic procedures like engraving and woodcuts had been used by city-based firms to fill a wide variety of demands from a public that included both the consumers of popular broadsheets or devotional materials and the wealthy collectors of "tasteful" prints. During the nineteenth century the multiple functions of the simple graphic sheets became diversified into separate branches of cultural interest such as newspapers, illustrated journals, advertising posters, and reproductive art. Meanwhile, lithography came to offer all classes the chance to enjoy colored, often framed reproductions of oil paintings usable as decoration for the home in a form comparable with the art "furnishings" of the well-to-do. However, the habit of hanging framed paintings on the living-room wall had been engrained in many of the peasants and craftsmen of central Europe by the glasspainting market, which already provided the poorer consumer with a substitute for the more expensive art of middle- or upper-class drawing rooms. Together with the common habit of pinning popular broadsheets on a wall or into the lid of a trunk or chest (or perhaps framing them), these expectations created by glasspainting production were influential in shaping the direction followed by lithographers in their attempts to satisfy the popular market for reproductive art.[60] Because of this contribution to the mechanization of the graphic arts, the glasspainting workshops suffered from the decline into which they had sunk by the time the Blue Rider artists encountered Rambold in 1908.[61]

PART ONE

The Glasspainters and the Industrializing Process

1

The Rural Glasspainting Workshops: A Strategy for Survival and Advancement

A letter addressed to the Seehausen glasspainter Matthias Noder introduces us to the flourishing large-scale glasspainting enterprises established in the rural hinterlands of central Europe during the latter half of the eighteenth century.

Hofdorf, April 2, 1816

Dear Mr. Noder:

. . . I have . . . in my parish a very beautiful and widely known pilgrimage church [The Holy Trinity near Dingolfing] that was built a hundred years ago. In this church the cult image is the most sacred Holy Trinity in the form and manner depicted on this votive painting.—This year I wrote to Rome to get permission from the Holy Father for a Jubilee Celebration for this Church, and indeed I was in luck!—This high festival will therefore take place at the end of June, and lasts continuously for eight days. I can certainly hope that during this time at least 25–30,000 people will visit this House of God. Consequently, the thought came to me to order from you 4,000 glasspaintings of the same kind as the accompanying painting. . . . So, work night and day in your factory to meet my order by the middle of June at the latest, since I would still like to hold the Jubilee festival before harvest time. You don't need to worry atall about due payment and it could be that you will even come into some large-scale business, because there is not a glasspainter in this area. . . .

Father Heinrich Bäumer[1]

To fill the orders of customers like Father Bäumer, Noder and his fellow Lake Staffel producers issued forth the local glasspaintings that the Blue Rider artists so admired. Of the eleven glasspaintings chosen by the group for their *Almanac,* for example, no fewer than six were in the Upper Bavarian style.[2] However, the more primitive painting style of the Bavarian Forest glasspainters had caught the group's attention as well, and so four of the remaining five glasspaintings included in the *Almanac* are from that region. The discussion that follows centers upon glasspainting families from these two areas, since their experience typifies the dynamic interchange between the rural glasspainters and the transformative market processes underway in Europe during the Industrial Revolution. For, by contrast, there were individual families in Bavaria who filled for generations the role of *Dorfmaler* or village painter. They provided the local population with votive paintings, glasspaintings, and other artistic needs, but their activities were both circumscribed and diffuse. To be sure, a family like the Wittmanns of Neukirchen-Heiligenblut in the Palatinate could distribute its wares quite widely by serving the pilgrimage market associated with its home town. Yet the volume of work by these local painters was not sufficient to flood central Europe with the framed oil paintings that lithographers began to emulate; moreover, it was only through large-scale production efforts like the Noders' that glasspainters and their village communities became fully integrated into the industrializing process underway in the world beyond their rural enclaves. So our interest lies with the most active and streamlined producers who "wanted to paint more quickly, in larger quantities and more simply, to become even cheaper and to be able to trade in still wider markets than their competitors."[3]

Matthias Noder operated his business out of the Seehausen smallholding he had inherited from his father Johannes, and his marginal relationship to the land thus illustrates well the economic rationale from which Bavarian glasspainting developed. For, like so many other craftsmen in early modern Europe, the glasspainters were farmers who sought a means of forging their livelihood out of inadequate smallholdings. They were caught up in a general trend toward the fragmentation of larger farms that took place both locally in Bavaria and elsewhere during the early modern period. This process is well illustrated in table 1, which is based on the glasspainting village of Uffing's

Table 1 The Growth of Uffing Smallholdings, 1589–1808

Fraction of a Full Holding	Year				
	1589	1669	1752	ca. 1778	1808
1 (*Hof*)	7	0	0	0	0
½	15	10*	5	5	5
⅓	0	0	5	5	5
5/16	0	0	0	1	2
¼	3	14	13	12	10
⅛			1	5	5
1/12	32†	46	0	4	3
1/16			50	44	45
Other	0	0	0	0	4
Total holdings	57	70	74	76	79

Sources: BHA, Kurbayern Hofkammer Hofanlagsbuchhaltung 126, 265; BHA, Kurbayern Geheimes Landesarchiv 1229; SAM, Kataster 24987.

*In the records the designations "5" and "5" are given, which both seem to mean ½.

†Because the source does not specify whether the holdings were ⅛, 1/12, or 1/16, the numbers 32 and 46 are totals of ⅛, 1/12, and 1/16 holdings for the years 1589 and 1669.

landholding patterns from 1589 until 1808. In Noder's area of western Bavaria, in particular, a survey of seventeen administrative districts finds that by 1760 the holdings too small to support a family adequately had grown in number to over 50 percent to 91.8 percent of the total landholdings in each district. For the glasspainting districts of Weilheim and Ettal, the figures were 67 percent and 84.8 percent respectively.[4]

The Noder holding was classified at 1/32 of a full farm or "*Hof*" according to the "*Hoffuß*" system of taxation classification then used in Bavaria, although the family's glasspainting income does seem to have allowed them to enhance the basic holding with additional properties. Even so, they found themselves, as did other glasspainting families, at the low end of a range of possibilities that stretched from the substantial farmer's *Hof* through fractions of a full holding to the tiny 1/32 (at times some were as small as 1/64). These numbers were not rigidly related to the size of a holding's acreage but were based on the taxable potential of the land surveyed.[5] Of the lesser holdings, ⅛ holdings were by the beginning of the seventeenth century officially distinguished from even smaller holdings by having "something to farm." In contrast, 1/16 holdings were to include no more than a house with a garden

Table 2 Craftsmen in Glasspainting Districts

	1771–80	1792	1794
Rentamt München: Upper Bavaria			
Masters	12,634	17,428	
Journeymen	3,640	11,235	
Apprentices	1,171	3,223	
Total population			345,985
Masters and journeymen as percentage of population			8.3
Rentamt Straubing: Bavarian Forest			
Masters	9,617	9,388	
Journeymen	2,342	4,164	
Apprentices	811	1,482	
Total Population			219,369
Masters and journeymen as percentage of population			6.2

Source: Eckart Schremmer, *Die Wirtschaft Bayerns: Vom hohen Mittelalter bis zum Beginn der Industrialisierung: Bergbau, Gewerbe, Handel* (Munich: Beck, 1970), pp. 384–88, 434–37.

or a very small amount of land. In 1760 instructions for the classification of a 1⁄32 holding like Noder's ordered that it should consist of "a mere house, from which the inhabitant gains no other usufruct and income but to enjoy it as his dwelling and accommodation. He must in addition seek his livelihood and support through other craft or laboring work."[6]

Because of the general proliferation of these smallholdings in the Bavarian countryside, the glasspainters became part of a local efflorescence of craft activities that was concentrated particularly in the period 1750–1850.[7] Consequently, by the last decade of the eighteenth century, 7.2 percent of the population in Upper and Lower Bavaria were masters and journeymen.[8] The number of tradesmen found in tax districts covering or close to the Bavarian glasspainting centers is given in table 2. (Raimundsreuth was still administered by the archbishop of Passau in the eighteenth century.) By 1811–12 the new Bavarian kingdom counted 198,554 small businessmen and 74,924 helpers representing over 8 percent of the 3,330,000 inhabitants of the kingdom.[9] In addition, laborers living on smallholdings were available to work for the more substantial farmers, although farm chores were more often the responsibility of farm servants; a mere 34,500 laborers were recorded in 1771, compared with 146,300 servants.[10]

Many of the craft families lived in country areas of Bavaria, complemented by a rather low percentage of full-time craftsmen in most towns there before the nineteenth century. Indeed, the clear judicial differentiation between town and country established in the Middle Ages had largely broken down by the end of the eighteenth century, with so many country residents in crafts as well as many townsmen being either *Ackerbürger,* or farming burgers, or at the very least part-time farmers. (I am reminded here of the Kandinsky-Münter garden, a "peasant garden.") A 1616 law gave the children of farmers the right to learn a handicraft, and the activities of rural craftsmen were not restricted to the more clearly rural trades but included more specialized activities as well.[11] Sporadic attempts at the restriction of rural craft proliferation by the government met with very limited success, and a 1788 law reduced government pressure on country craftsmen still further.[12] As a result, in absolute numbers, the craftsmen of many professions were more numerous in the country than in the towns during the eighteenth century.[13]

This smallholding population has been characterized as "the 'dynamic' element" of an "otherwise thoroughly conservative settlement and agrarian structure."[14] And yet most rural craftsmen in Bavaria had developed their trade strictly within the confines of the local market, as the *Dorfmaler* did, so they could by no means be characterized as "dynamic." Many, typically shoemakers, tailors, and construction workers, worked on the *Stör* or as visiting workers, staying in the homes and using the materials of their customers. Others, such as some weavers of linen or wool and millers, often worked from their own homes but on their clients' materials. Others—bakers, farriers, tavern-keepers, and similar craftsmen—served local needs for a variety of goods and services.[15] And at least part of this marketing activity may still have depended on bartering.[16] To make the economic picture even worse, in the early nineteenth century Bavarian rural craftsmen faced overcrowding in their professions as too many localized tradesmen competed for a limited number of customers. The Wolfstein district, for example, in which Raimundsreuth was located, was reported to be overpopulated with shoemakers, tailors, and weavers, including rural inhabitants on the *Stör,* in the 1830s. Also Murnau's Weilheim district reported in 1819–20 "a lack of adequate markets and overcrowding in individual professions."[17]

Within such a context, the glasspainters represented one of the few groups of craftsmen in rural Bavaria that could truly be characterized as "dynamic" because they had managed to develop marketing skills far exceeding the norm for the country's rural workforce. Consequently, the story of the glasspainting villages that follows can best be compared with the development of industrial villages elsewhere in Europe. As with many other pockets of rural industry, the drive to develop their craft as an international business was largely provided by the inhospitable locations in which the glasspainters and their fellow artistic craftsmen lived, where the terrain was hilly and wooded or marshy.[18] Demographic growth in such places inevitably had to be supported by a large proportion of local inhabitants working to supplement the meager opportunities for farming. There were, therefore, too many jobseekers to allow all of them the hope of supplying services to local residents, and so outlets external to the immediate area had to be found for much of the village labor force. In the glasspainting villages, residents took advantage of their positioning on key trading routes to transform local resources like flax, wood, glass, wax, and feathers into exportable artifacts. Some of them, like the glasspainters, proved enormously successful in capturing an international market.[19]

Of all the Bavarian glasspainting villages, Oberammergau was the most committed to an economic life-style dependent on craft income. Consequently, the village's landholding profile came to resemble strongly that of other industrial villages in which virtually landless cottages proliferated.[20] In 1752, 98 percent of Oberammergau's population held properties considered smallholdings—holdings 1/6 or less of a full holding—and would almost certainly have been obliged to rely on craft or laboring income (table 3).[21] In particular, the 1/12, 1/16, and 1/32 holdings, which were most likely to house craft families, made up 87 percent of the total properties of the village in 1752 and 90 percent in 1810. For the villagers had taken advantage of an important trade route running through Oberammergau from Augsburg to Italy, which was also a key pilgrim route for German Catholics journeying to Rome. Until the decline of trade in the late eighteenth century, much activity connected with the wagons passing through Oberammergau was the

Table 3 Landholding Distribution in Upper Bavarian Glasspainting Villages

Fraction of a Full Holding	Oberammergau		Seehausen*		Uffing	
	1752/60	1810	1752/60	1808	1752/60	1808
1/64	0	5	0	0	0	0
1/32	43	64	8	15	0	0
1/16	28	64	10	12	50	45
1/12	74	61	17	20	0	3
1/8	14	9	2	4	1	5
1/6	3	3	3	2	0	0
1/4	3	5	1	9	13	10
5/16	0	0	0	0	0	2
1/3	0	0	1	7	5	5
1/2	0	0	0	2	5	5
Other	1	5	3	2	0	4
Total holdings	166	216	45	73	74	79
Percentage of smallholders†	98%	95%	90%	71%	68%	67%

Sources: BHA, Kurbayern Hofkammer Hofanlagsbuchhaltung 168, 265; SAM, Kataster 8791, 24906, 24987.

*Includes outlying hamlets.

†Having 1/6 or less of a full holding.

norm in summer months, and villagers appear to have provided, and so maintained, teams of horses.[22] These international connections also supported the village crafts, most particularly the woodcarving that gave practitioners the title of *Herrgottsschnitzer* or crucifix carver. Many villagers set out as peddlers to sell village products or became agents in far-off cities; others worked in the forest surrounding Oberammergau; and a substantial number were local craftsmen as well. Often they worked for the nearby monastery at Ettal until its secularization in 1803. The monastery owned a large number of the holdings in the village and also the *Gerechtigkeiten* or officially granted craft licenses for the basic trades, such as tavernkeeper, baker, and shoemaker, practiced there.[23]

Oberammergau also resembled other industrial villages in its dependence on outside suppliers for much of the food supply. For example, Father Joseph Daisenberger, priest in Oberammergau in the 1850s, calculated that no more than three months' supply of grain could be grown in the village itself. This would have encouraged the complementary development outside the village of areas specializing in agricultural produce, as was common in areas of rural industry. The villagers, however, never lost all contact with their farming roots because they combined their craft activities with polyculture to support the family economy. In this context, Daisenberger mentions potato cultivation on village plots, and he claims that almost every family owned a small garden in which to grow vegetables for home use, while many had orchards as well. Common rights to land around the village seem to have been available to smallholders as well, in particular to support the cattle still so common a feature of the local economy in both Alpine and Bavarian Forest regions. A smallholder might possess one or two cows, or perhaps no more than some goats; Alpine meadows were available for grazing in summer, and the combination of house and stall, still seen in the center of Oberammergau and in many other parts of rural Bavaria as well, served as shelter throughout the long winter.[24]

Into this village setting, glasspainting is thought to have been introduced in Oberammergau by Andreas Lang. Andreas and his brother Anton were two of five sons left fatherless when Joseph Lang died in 1753. They established an international business in the second half of the eighteenth century that included both glasspaintings and other village products.[25] By 1800 nine glasspainters were active in Oberammergau, although in 1815 the number was only four (the intervening Napoleonic Wars and the resultant slump in business may well account for this reduction).[26] In the apparent role of "putting-out" merchant, Anton Lang consistently ordered bundles of glass for the Oberammergau producers from the Aschau glass factory in the 1770s, 1780s, and early 1790s; he died in 1794.[27] The Langs are discussed in their capacity as entrepreneurs in Chapter 3. Suffice it to say here that firms owned by Anton's son Peter, Andreas's son Martin, and their younger brother Georg employed glasspainters as well as woodcarvers in the nineteenth century. Two full- or part-time glasspainters died in the village in 1834, one in 1839, one in 1845, one in 1850, and one in 1854.[28] Other craftsmen may have been involved on a part-time basis with glasspainting during the mid-nineteenth century, but they are hard to identify and by then the competition with lithographs seems to have been dictating the end of any large-scale production. It is not surprising to find that the glasspainters of Oberammergau were recruited from a range of property holders having 1/12 holdings (Alois Bauhofer or Alois Klaus), through 1/16 holdings (Dominikus Rutz), to 1/32 holdings (Josef Mangold). The merchant Georg Lang occupied a 1/16 holding in 1810 known as the *Kaufmannhof*.[29]

Of the three remaining Upper Bavarian glasspainting locations, Uffing most resembled the occupational structure of Oberammergau. In the eighteenth century, Uffing smallholders, like the Oberammergau villagers, became woodcarvers and *Kraxenträger*. In 1752 seventeen 1/16 holders were listed as peddlers, and four 1/16 holders and one 1/3 holder were listed specifically as woodworkers. Undoubtedly, the *Kraxenträger* would also have prepared "all kinds of small figures out of wood," as their counterparts in the village were reported to do in 1802, before setting out with their wares on their backs.[30] Their high numbers compare with only five weavers listed in Uffing for 1752, a figure that holds almost constant throughout the next century; there were six listed in 1825. Local craftsmen were well represented, constituting one-fourth to one-third of the households in the nineteenth century. Moreover, Uffing's five sawmills must have played an important part in the local economy.[31]

Uffing lies to the north of Lake Staffel, but not sufficiently close to the rim of the lake that its inhabitants became fishermen. Much of the land close to the lake is moorland, and in the more remote portions of the village holdings there is also substantial woodland. But Uffing enjoys considerably more farmable and pasture land than Oberammergau (table 4). Consequently, a substantial number of large-scale farming families balanced the 68 percent or so smallholders in the village. Table 3 notes the presence of over twenty larger properties in Uffing during the period after 1750. A village population smaller than Oberammergau's, under five hundred throughout the first half of the nineteenth century, could presumably have been fed from local produce. In this case, then, the commercial specialization between craft and agricultural production so essential to the development of rural industry would have taken place within the confines of the village itself.

The 1752 tax survey identified two merchants in Uffing and a *Handler* or dealer; all three men were members of the Landes and Schmid families who later were to provide glasspainters. As we have seen, Michael Kirchmayr's son Johann Paul brought the craft to the village in 1773. He married the widow of Nemesi Schmid's son Sebastian;

Table 4 Land Distribution in Upper Bavarian Glasspainting Locations in 1890s, in Hectares

	Meadows	Peat-fields, pasture, etc.	Fields and gardens	Forest	Other	Total	Population in 1890
Oberammergau	837	546	38	1,506	80	3,007	1,366
Uffing	1,143	136	117	355	201	1,952	656
Seehausen	426	0	358	83	786	1,653	403
Murnau	1,780	234	73	282	41	2,410	1,739

Sources: Wilhelm Götz, *Geographisches Historisches Handbuch von Bayern* (Munich, 1895), pp. 279, 448; *Beiträge zur Statistik Bayerns,* vol. 192 (Munich: Bayerisches Statistisches Landesamt, 1953); W. R. Lee, *Population Growth, Economic Development and Social Change in Bavaria, 1750–1850* (New York: Arno, 1977), p. 390.
Notes: 1 hectare = 10,000 square meters. Field and garden areas for the communities included in the two relevant administrative districts ranged from 7 to 567 hectares.

Nemesi was the merchant living on property number 711 in 1752, a 1/16 *Hausl* belonging to the village. His father Paul was listed as a tailor in 1686, and Nemesi was still listed in 1752 as both tailor and merchant.[32] Matthias, the son of Georg Landes, second of the two Uffing merchants in 1752, ordered glass for his paintings from Aschau for a time in the 1780s and 1790s, as did Johann Paul, while his brother Ignaz appears to have succeeded his father as a merchant. Johann Landes, the *Handler* listed in 1752 whose connection to the merchant Landes family is not clear, married Nemesi's daughter in 1740. Matthias stood as witness for the Kirchmayr-Schmid wedding in 1773. So a close relationship existed between the two families, perhaps because of their trading interests, and this seems to have facilitated the transmission of the glasspainting trade from one to the other.[33]

In the next generation, Matthias Landes's son, Gregor, became involved with glasspainting, and both Johann Paul's stepson Jakob Schmid and his two cousins Nemesi and Johann Baptist Schmid, sons of Sebastian's younger brother Antoni, adopted the trade as well. By 1808 Johann Baptist had married into the family of an artificial flower handler from Murnau and established his business there; Nemesi and Jakob were still occupying 1/16 holdings in Uffing. Jakob's property, however, was substantially larger than Nemesi's, as it had been augmented with extra land purchases. It was still known as *beim Schneidermesi* in reference to the family's origins as tailors.[34]

Three or four miles to the south of Uffing on the edge of Lake Staffel lies the village of Seehausen. It was small in the eighteenth and nineteenth centuries, with outlying farming hamlets; although the village itself, according to the 1752 tax survey, included at least 90 percent smallholders, 78 percent 1/12 holders or less, the presence of larger farms in the vicinity balanced the proliferation of craft families. Seehausen, like Uffing, must have been able to draw on food supplies from the immediate area. Moreover, substantial productive acreage was enjoyed by local farmers (table 4).

The most significant subsidiary occupation for the villagers in 1752 was undoubtedly fishing; there were nine fishermen in the village at that time, eight owning 1/12 holdings. But Seehausen supported fewer local craftsmen than Uffing: a baker, a tavernkeeper, a carpenter, and a tailor appear on the list in 1752; and two shoemakers, a smith, and two weavers (five in the immediate area) were listed in addition to the baker and tavernkeeper for 1805.[35] The 1826 request of a Seehausen man, Johann Georg Noder, for a concession as a shopkeeper throws interesting light on the plight of smallholders in this Alpine region of the country. He reports, "My holding does not occupy me sufficiently, and so . . . I cannot wrest the necessary livelihood from it." Retailing of agricultural produce would appear from his request to have taken place either through the nearby town of Murnau or through Uffing, since he suggests that homeowners had to run to either place when they needed to buy something.[36]

The two earliest Seehausen glasspainters were Johannes Noder and Michael Kirchmayr. Michael's 1/16 holding is recorded in the 1752 tax records, together with a six *Tagwerk* meadow, a small piece of acreage, and a cabbage patch. (A *Tagwerk* equals 3,407 square meters.)[37] The only Noder listed, Andreas, also occupied a 1/16 holding. He lived in that portion of the village strongly dominated by fishing households and, therefore, was undoubtedly nearer to the lake than Kirchmayr. The present Seehausen Number Six is known as the Gege home (Number Seven in the early nineteenth century), and this may well have been Kirchmayr's house as well, since his daughter Katarina married Paul Gege, a brewer's son from Munich, in 1785.[38] She is recorded living in Number Seven in 1808, after the death of her husband, on a 1/16 property. Today the house is vine-covered, with a large balcony facing the main street of the village, and sits away from the lake in the vicinity of the local church; it is divided in the usual way between accommodation for the family and the livestock. By 1808 three Noder brothers had inherited their father's trade and occupied landholdings in the village. Ignaz, son of the oldest brother, now held a 1/12 holding, while the youngest brother, Sebastian, owned a 1/16. Matthias, the direct heir to the business, we have already met in possession of his father's 1/32 holding, known as *Unterweiß*.[39] Of the next generation in this family, apart from Ignaz, only Matthias's son Michael and Katarina Gege's son Alois can be established to have continued practicing glasspainting. Alois's son Sebastian and grandson Josef carried on with the business despite its decline in the late nineteenth century, passing on the torch to Rambold and thus to the Blue Rider.

Within easy walking distance of Seehausen, the small town of Murnau clustered together a variety of tradesmen available to serve the needs of the surrounding countryside. A local historian, Simon Baumann, reported that in 1855 there were 132 businesses in this town of around 1,200 people, including several flourishing breweries and taverns. Four annual markets as well as weekly cattle and produce markets supplemented the town's economy; the cattlemarket on Saint Michael's Day was particularly well known in the area. And Murnau was clearly typical of the agricultural towns of rural Bavaria, for Baumann argues that "since almost every citizen combines both a business and a larger or a smaller farm, Murnau enjoys a firm foundation of material well-being that makes it possible to survive difficult times handily."[40]

Murnau owed its existence to the trade route from Munich to Innsbruck, although there were also substantial trading connections between Augsburg and Murnau as illustrated by the pattern of glasspainting purchases around 1780.[41] Local craftsmen served the needs of travelers as well as those of residents in the area. This connection with the larger world of commerce must account for the presence of artistic trades such as glasspainting in the Murnau area; there were certainly merchants in the town during the eighteenth century capable of sending local products to distant trading centers such as Holland.[42] Jakob März was such a man, and his eventual drowning in the Danube suggests his use of the river connections reaching to Vienna from Murnau that the three nineteenth-century raftsmen of the town still maintained.[43] Local merchants handled the artificial flowers that were manufactured in Murnau during this period as well as glasspaintings; pictures made of feathers were also a local specialty.

From its beginnings in the middle of the eighteenth century, when

Jakob März, Dominikus Gastl, and perhaps Simon Schwalb began glasspainting in Murnau, the craft grew in importance, and later at least five younger Gastls and several other families became painters.[44] The artificial flowerhandler Franz Xaver Eder, one of his sons, Michael, and Michael's son-in-law, Xaver Kistler, all began glasspainting. The public official Sebastian Seiz became involved when he married the sister of Paul Gege of Seehausen in 1786; Seiz's son-in-law Johann Chrysostomos Geiger and two of Geiger's sons were later drawn into the business. Both the painter Johann Michael Wittmer and his widow's second husband, Jakob Bergmeister, seem also to have been glasspainters.[45] In addition, of course, Johann Baptist Schmid was active after his marriage around 1800. A visiting historian was consequently able to count twelve families supported by glasspainting in 1802, that is, about 5 percent of the town's population. Two surveys from the first decade of the nineteenth century list six and five respectively but cover nine separate names. Sadly, by 1811 the five listed were reported extremely poor and surviving mostly by day labor; the Napoleonic disruptions had clearly reached Murnau.[46] Later, peace brought an improvement in trade for the Murnau businessmen, yet their former success never really returned; there were only six glasspainters listed for the Weilheim district as a whole in 1823.[47] Johann Baptist Schmid's son Ignaz did continue to incorporate glasspainting into his business in the mid-nineteenth century, but he had become a *Kunsthandler* selling a variety of artistic products by that time. His apprentice Johann Feyerabend helped the widow Rosalia after Ignaz's death in 1856 and then established his own business in 1866. By 1869, however, he is reported, perhaps apocryphally, to have thrown his stock into the local brook before leaving for Munich. There he appears briefly as a photographer.[48]

These similar stories of the origins of glasspainting in all the Upper Bavarian centers illustrate well the pressing need of smallholders in such mountainous or marshy and wooded areas to draw income into the community. By the 1750s, when substantial expansion had occurred in the number of smallholdings throughout Upper Bavaria, it is not surprising that craft expansion should be taking place in the countryside, particularly of the supraregional artistic crafts such as glasspainting. New smallholdings in glasspainting villages clearly depended for their continued existence on the possibility of bringing in the income pro-

Table 5 Glasspainters in Upper Bavarian Centers and Raimundsreuth, 1770s–1860s

	Upper Bavarian Centers					
	Murnau	Seehausen	Uffing	Oberam-mergau	Total	Raimunds-reuth
1770s	2–3	2	2	2	8–9	4
1800s	12	5	3	9	29	5
1830s	8	5	2	6	21	3
1860s	3	4	0	0	7	4

Sources: Friedrich Knaipp, *Hinterglas Bilder aus Bauern- und Bergmannsstuben des 18. und 19. Jahrhunderts,* 2d ed. (Linz: Wimmer, 1973), pp. 155–94; Heinrich Büchner, *Hinterglasmalerei in der Böhmerwaldlandschaft und in Südbayern: Beiträge zur Geschichte einer alten Hauskunst* (Munich: Filser, 1936), pp. 96–101; Raimund Schuster, *Das Raimundsreuter Hinterglasbild: Geschichte der Raimundsreuter Hinterglasmalerei und ihres Einflußgebietes* (Grafenau: Morsak, 1984), pp. 14–26; Murnau Marriage Registers, 1744ff, 1802–1879; Murnau Death Registers, 1743ff, 1802–34; Murnau Christening Registers, 1802ff; SAM, LRA 7332, Kataster 25181; Josef von Hazzi, *Statistische Aufschlüsse über das Herzogtum Bayern* (Nuremberg, 1802), 2:94–95; *Churpfalz-baïerisches Regierungs- und Intelligenzblatt* (1800), p. 431; SAL, Repertorium 164, Verz. 1, No. 4516.

vided by craft activities; without that income it seems likely that the villages would have contracted in size to previous population levels more suited to the inhospitable terrain. But instead the villages appear to have grown during the period between 1752 and 1808. The number of holdings rose, if only slightly in Uffing, and the villages continued to maintain a fluctuating but on the whole upward demographic pattern in the nineteenth century.[49] The glasspainters and their fellow artistic craftsmen contributed to the "thickening" of the countryside that typically accompanied the proliferation of rural crafts throughout Europe (table 5). They must also have encouraged the commercialization of agricultural production locally, either inside or outside the villages themselves. They thus partook of the dynamic transformation of European society that supported the Industrial Revolution.

We can see the pattern of "thickening" at work particularly by looking at the story of individual families whose income was derived from glasspainting. Some glasspainters initially came from families that had previously been involved in a poorly paid trade such as construction work or with an artistic craft such as flowermaking or woodcarving. So the extra income derived from glasspainting helped these struggling families already reliant on commercial activities to improve their economic situation. Other glasspainters came from families who, despite their humble situation as smallholders, were enjoying successful trading connections and had no doubt become comfortably off. For them, glasspainting must merely have supplemented the family business. So, despite the fact that glasspainters belonged to the poorer landholding strata of village or town society, they frequently came from families for whom the attempt to use business activities to solve the problem of survival was already a well-established pattern. Then, as a consequence of their successful adoption of the new craft, more than one child in the family was able to establish a household in the village or in the immediate area. For example, the three Noders, children of Johannes, all remained in Seehausen on separate landholdings. In Murnau as well the children of glasspainters could establish themselves locally and find a living within the craft, at least for one or two generations. The town was able to support a population at least 5–10 percent greater than local resources might otherwise have managed because of the opportunities offered by artistic crafts. For, as Joan Thirsk has pointed out in the context of late sixteenth- and seventeenth-century England, "a new project in a village could . . . transform a miserable collection of beggarly poor into a self-respecting community."[50]

It is clear that once a family became involved in glasspainting, the major source of recruitment for new workers was within the family circle. And the repeated adoption of the trade by glasspainters' sons was complemented by the frequent marriage of their daughters or widows to potential male recruits. Outsiders could even be drawn to the business in this way, as the marriage of Paul Gege into the Kirchmayr family reveals. His father was listed as a brewer in the Munich area, although he sold his business in 1765 and his whereabouts since that time are unknown.[51] Michael Kirchmayr's son could move to Uffing and become both merchant and glasspainter because of his marriage to the widow Maria Schmid. In fact, this role of women, either daughters or widows, as means to the end of participation in a successful business was strikingly significant for the overall development of the craft. It illustrates well Jack Goody's arguments about the high percentage of "uxorilocal" marriages in preindustrial Europe.[52]

Since recruitment into glasspainting depended mainly on business and family connections, the role of artistic talent in the selection process remains obscure. Some of the glasspainters were artistically gifted;

Nemesi Schmid's work, for example, has been singled out for its "elegance."[53] Yet Nemesi was recruited by his aunt's second husband, and chance rather than expertise seems to have played the greater role in his adoption of the trade. Perhaps Andreas Lang, chosen to undertake an apprenticeship in Augsburg with the painter Ignaz Baur, had shown artistic promise; the Hohenleitner apprenticed to Baur, on the other hand, seems likely to have profited from family connections. For the most part the new recruits were probably not chosen because of any special propensity to artistic excellence. This was, after all, a business venture from start to finish.

All these socio-economic patterns of recruitment to the craft of glasspainting hold true when we turn to examine the glasspainters of Raimundsreuth in the Bavarian Forest. This village center, where glasspainting emerged as a craft out of the context of glass decoration in local factories, provides an excellent counterpoise to the Upper Bavarian centers. In Raimundsreuth, five generations of glasspainters mass-produced religious images for central European Catholics with almost complete independence from urban influences. To be sure, other Lower Bavarian glasspainters, notably Andreas Lohberger in Deggendorf, also featured prominently in the production and distribution of glasspaintings for this popular market. The large scale and persistence of Raimundsreuth production, however, makes it a particularly good example of conditions in the European glasspainting centers located outside the Murnau area, often in even more remote rural areas of central Europe.

As in Upper Bavaria, the terrain of the Bavarian Forest is hilly, wooded, and unconducive to cultivation of any but the hardiest crops. At the Forest's southern rim sits the small town of Kreuzberg atop one of the steeper hills of the area. Its presence dominates the entire vicinity, drawing the wanderer's attention to its church and clustering buildings, as it must have done in the glasspainting days when pilgrims set out to visit the Saint Anna statue venerated there. To the north of Kreuzberg, clearings have been cut into the forest by the local Schönbrunn glassmakers seeking fuel for their operations. One such clearing is the site of the village of Raimundsreuth.

The village was founded in 1721 during the period in which a wave of settlements was underway in the Wolfstein district, encouraged by the local administration. Originally, eight houses were built, together with equal landholdings that were probably arranged in a three-field system of cultivation. These farms were not very large, being listed in 1788 as *Grosshausls* or roughly equivalent to the 1/16 holdings in Bavaria.[54] As a nineteenth-century map reveals, the houses were arranged in a straight row, unlike the larger, clustering villages of Upper Bavaria. The land belonging to each stretched out from the house in either direction, and outlying strips completed the allotted acreage. Forest lay to the north and the larger clearing of Schönbrunn further to the west. Strip cultivation remains to this day in that area of Lower Bavaria, modernized at least in one place by the addition of separate macadamized tractor runs to each strip. The land was used in the eighteenth and nineteenth centuries to plant flax and less desirable grains such as oats, although potatoes, cabbage, and similar foods became welcome supplements to a wretched dietary program in the period from 1760 to the twentieth century.[55] In 1804 an observer could write that "the poorer classes sustain themselves, especially in times of high prices, almost completely from the so beneficial potato."[56] But, as in Upper Bavaria, cattle grazing the local woodlands were the major source of livelihood apart from crafts in the Raimundsreuth area.[57]

By the late 1750s a new smallholding tinier than the original eight farms had been added to Raimundsreuth. There Tobias Peterhansl was finally able to settle down with his growing family after relatively brief sojourns in other area villages. He was a builder, but he also may have had connections with the local glass factory, and he founded the family most consistently connected with large-scale glasspainting production in the Bavarian Forest. Other families in Raimundsreuth also enjoyed connections with the glass factory; for example, the Dillingers, who appear in the early 1750s as godparents to the young Peterhansls, were referred to as glassmakers. Indeed, Raimundsreuth seems to have been founded to house Schönbrunn glassworkers. But there was also a surprising number of *Gerechtigkeiten* in this small village. In the first decade of the nineteenth century, there were three weaving concessions, one of which was combined with tavernkeeping, one shoemaker, and one wainwright.[58] Clearly, even the more substantial properties in the village required a supplementary source of income. So the Peterhansls and other families who later settled on small portions of the original Raimundsreuth landholdings were obliged to find outside employment as their major means of support, just as their Upper Bavarian counterparts were. And Peterhansl's versatility was not unusual for glasspainters; when one trade did not suffice, a mixture of two or three could provide the necessary support.

The Peterhansl family showed the same pattern of marital recruitment observed in Upper Bavarian glasspainting families, and table 6 illustrates the repeated efficacy of marriage as an entrée to glasspainting. Indeed, Tobias Peterhansl himself acquired his new profession by marrying the daughter of Simon Hölgarth, a glasspainter who lived in the hamlet of Vierkreuzberghäuser, near both Raimundsreuth and Kreuzberg. Hölgarth had been a glassworker, and it was his marriage to the daughter of Laurentius Neumaÿr that no doubt introduced him to his father-in-law's painting activities.[59] This marriage effected the convergence of circumstances that initiated glasspainting in the Raimundsreuth area. The presence of the Kreuzberg pilgrimage and Neumaÿr's work as *Dorfmaler* were undoubtedly connected, while the continuing demands of local pilgrims must certainly have maintained Hölgarth's interest in glasspainting as the needs of a pilgrimage center like Dingolfing were later to do for the Noders.[60] These preconditions, combined with the necessary presence of inexpensive, locally produced glass and workers already occupied with its decoration, created the opportunity seized by Hölgarth and his son-in-law. In this way the family joined the ranks of the glasspainters of Bavaria as the typical businessmen/farmers of this rural craft.

Production of glasspaintings was usually concentrated in the households of participating families once the craft had been established in both Upper and Lower Bavarian centers, although it could become quite a large-scale operation at times. This gave glasspainters an ambiguous relationship with local government, allowing some to work informally without registration or guild membership, while others met these normal requirements for practicing an officially recognized craft during the period. The degree of reward for individual glasspainters also varied. The craft provided a good living and even social advancement for some practitioners, but for others it must only have helped to stave off disaster for a time. Eventually, of course, all glasspainting families suffered from the competition of chromolithography, which forced them to earn a livelihood in other ways.

In the glasspainting workshops family members appear to have made up the majority of the work force. The sons must have been in effect apprenticed to their fathers, readying themselves to establish new house-

Table 6 Peterhansl Family Network

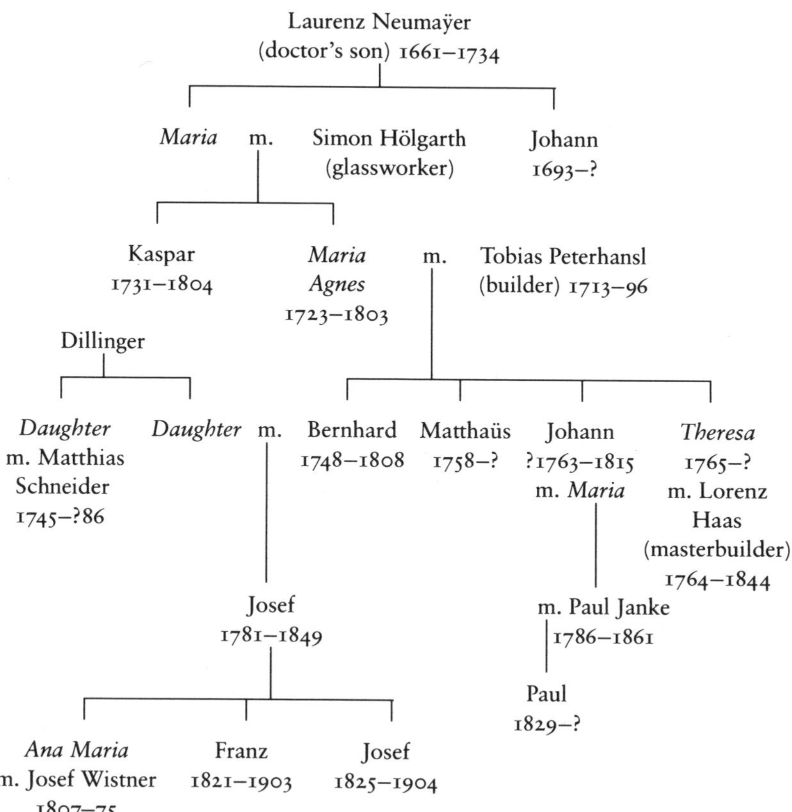

Sources: Freyung Christening Registers (1638–1768), Wedding Registers (1692–1847), and Death Registers (1785–1859); Hohenau Christening Registers (1731–97), Wedding Registers (1786ff), and Death Registers (1787–1883); Alfred Fuchs, *Die Raimundsreuter Hinterglasmalerie* (Passau: Gogeissl, 1965), pp. 6–9; Heinrich Büchner, *Hinterglasmalerei in der Böhmerwaldlandschaft und in Südbayern: Beiträge zur Geschichte einer alten Hauskunst* (Munich: Filser, 1936), pp. 38, 40, 51; Raimund Schuster, *Das Raimundsreuter Hinterglasbild: Geschichte der Raimundsreuter Hinterglasmalerei und ihres Einflußgebietes* (Grafenau: Morsak, 1984), pp. 14–26; SAL, Repertorium 164/22, No. 2407.
Notes: Other trades practiced by glasspainters are given in parentheses.

holds in their turn; the wives, daughters, and sisters of glasspainters could also support the family effort.[61] Indeed, both widows and daughters could themselves carry on business operations. Regina Noder, for example, ordered the glass supplies for her family's business after the death of her husband Johannes around 1788, and it was not until the marriage of her son Matthias in 1794 that he appears in the Aschau account book in her stead.[62] Theresa Peterhansl married Lorenz Haas at the age of fifty-five in 1820. Her previous residence in the Peterhansl household and the adoption of glasspainting by her new husband only after his marriage indicates that the glasspainting permit her new husband acquired at that time was primarily needed for Theresa.[63] Two unmarried sisters of Nemesi Schmid lived with him, probably throughout his career, and no doubt they too assisted their brother in his craft.[64]

Not only were women and children active as painters, but the elderly seem also to have lent an expert hand to the proceedings. Matthaüs Peterhansl, for example, who may well have been the son of Tobias born in 1758 and so would be over sixty years old in the mid 1820s, was the Peterhansl mentioned as the instructor of young Josef Wistner when he underwent several months of training at Raimundsreuth in 1825–26.[65] When the adult men of glasspainting families felt the need to seek work outside their homes to bring in extra income, the rest of the family could continue to produce glasspaintings. Or the productive potential of the household could become factory-like, as this kind of family business was sometimes described by contemporaries.[66] The father might then execute the more difficult steps in the preparation of each painting—filling in outlines, shading, and so on—and remaining family members filled in the colors or painted the frames.[67]

If mass production proved too challenging for a household, or perhaps for the extended network of a family, to manage on its own, the use of helpers and neighbors could extend the family's capacity to fill the demands of consumers.[68] This more extreme form of factory-like production was probably unusual for glasspainting in Upper Bavaria. We have no record of any but family-based enterprises for Murnau and Uffing; the description of Andreas Lang's operations in Oberammergau as "factory-sized" refers to the painting of wooden figures. The glasspaintings undoubtedly produced in this same environment were not of sufficient numbers, at least in the first decade of the nineteenth century, to justify the description. Lang sold only about 160 paintings in 1804 and over 200 in 1805; the numbers even decrease thereafter.

Such low numbers suggest quality work rather than mass production.[69] Yet Anton Lang made sizeable and regular orders for glass from the Aschau glass factory in the late eighteenth century, and we have noted the nine glasspainters reported in the village in 1800. There were also several framemakers in Oberammergau during the period, suggesting that household specialization between glasspainting and framemaking could have added to the productive potential of the villagers.[70] And later Georg Lang's firm sold over 1,000 paintings in 1832 and over 3,000 by 1834; other merchants in Oberammergau were also selling paintings in the mid-nineteenth century.[71] Nevertheless, these increased sales figures still do not compare with Seehausen production, which clearly did reach factory-like proportions at times. Both the Noders and the Kirchmayrs made repeated, substantial orders of glass from the Aschau glass factory in the late eighteenth century; moreover, we have noted the description of Matthias Noder's business as a "factory" by Father Bäumer in 1816. His order for 4,000 paintings clearly expected delivery in two to three months, that is, at a working rate of 1,000–2,000 paintings per month!

In Lower Bavaria, and in the glasspainting villages of southern Bohemia and Austria, glasspaintings were produced with little attention to painterly standards, which was why these glasspainters were able to mass-produce paintings. In 1798 the two sons of Tobias Peterhansl, with Simon Hölgarth's son Kaspar, were asked by officials of the Austro-Hungarian Empire to regularize their production activities in the village of Außergefild, just over the border from Wolfstein, because the glasspainters had been able to gross about 10,000 gulden in the ten-year period 1788–98.[72] Since by 1830 the 30,000–40,000 paintings produced annually by five Wolfstein glasspainting families were valued at around 5,000 gulden, the three Wolfsteiners in Außergefild must already have been producing 6,000–8,000 paintings a year during the 1790s, just from their base in Bohemia.[73]

Such high production figures no doubt required a streamlining of production under factory-like conditions similar to that adopted by a successor to the Bavarian painters in Außergefild during the mid-nineteenth century. Johann Verderber's factory had developed production procedures in which the specialization of labor became extreme:

> Mr. Verderber's picture factory is so constructed that, as a visitor enters the establishment by the door where the clear pieces of glass are unpacked and the painted and framed pictures are packed, he

> first encounters the framemakers. He can then follow the progress of the picture, going from one painter to the other, until he arrives without stopping at the door again together with the completed painting. . . . One or more [workers] are responsible for the green color of the knight's boots, some for that of the grass and the trees, some for that of the helmet feathers, others for the red on the cheeks, others on the cloaks, others on the bloody wounds, and so forth; some paint only eyes, some paint only nostrils, others fingers, others hair, several ears, several halos, and so on.

To do this, Verderber had to hire outside help, according to the account of the writer Josef Meßner quoted above.[74]

Meßner may have embellished his story for literary effect, but it is largely substantiated by an account of production techniques in the Bohemian glasspainting village of Buchers. The schoolteacher there, Franz Tomann, reported around 1918 that "in Buchers there worked a Master who had assistants, women as well, who either worked alongside him in the house or took the work home with them. The picture was painted onto the glass tablet according to a pattern (paper) laid under the glass, starting with the outlines; then the face was added, then the colors of the body were laid on, then the clothing with the shading. The work was passed from hand to hand. Some were responsible for the outlines, others for the face, etc., the Master usually for the shading. . . . They worked throughout the year, but mostly in Fall and Winter. Ten diligent workers could complete 100 paintings in a day."[75] A photograph taken around 1900 of three Thumayr family members from Sandl, Austria, over the border from Buchers, illustrates this division of labor. Each of the three workers, one a woman, completes a stage in the execution of a painting, from the outlining of the design to the application of color.[76] Earlier Thumayrs working all winter in the 1850s and 1860s had been able to paint up to fifty thousand paintings, according to one undoubtedly exaggerated report. The workers would sit on the two "window-sides" of the work-room, along the length of the walls on benches, while neighbors not already put to work as painters would help with packing or framemaking.[77]

We will never be able to calculate accurately the total number of glasspaintings manufactured in these central European workshops during the period of the craft's business success; however, the growth of production figures to annual levels in the many thousands can only suggest that the market was lively and sustained for several decades. Nevertheless, despite this substantial productive activity of the rural glasspainters, their profession only in some cases became officially recognized, either by the Bavarian government as needing registration or by a local guild as suitable for inclusion under their supervision. It was in Lower Bavaria, in fact, that a more official attitude to the profession seems to have prevailed, perhaps because so many glasspainters there were primarily *Dorfmaler* and, therefore, technically trained as painters. Thomas Aquinas Roth of Winklarn, for example, became the master for both Karl Ruff and Josef Wistner in the early nineteenth century; his apprentices completed both a training period with Roth and the requisite *Wanderzeit.* Ruff spent nine years on the road, although he was based mainly in Passau; Wistner was recorded as traveling to such glasspainting centers as Haibühl and Raimundsreuth during 1825–26, and he then acquired a permit to set up in business for himself in 1834. His training period with Roth lasted from 1820 until 1825, and he began working at around the age of thirteen.[78] No doubt these men would have been required to produce a *Meisterstück* or master work on completion of their training before obtaining a permit, as Johann Baptist Reisbacher was obliged to do.[79] Even the Raimundsreuth painters were operating with an official permit in 1810, and both Lorenz Haas and Johann Pomeisl of Oberanschiessing in Wolfstein also took out permits after they adopted glasspainting as a profession.[80]

In Upper Bavaria the Weilheim painters were recorded in 1823 as belonging to a guild centered not in Murnau but in Munich. Each master paid 9 kreuzer annually for membership, 32 gulden for the initial *Meisterstück,* which was to be a painting of Mary.[81] Perhaps this is why there are references in Upper Bavarian trade listings to "patents" belonging to individual glasspainters. Yet the general attitude of the local government was that glasspainting was not a trade requiring registration, and one finds reference to this decision either by means of clarification—tax-free—or by the crossing out of a glasspainter's name in a list drawn up of local tradesmen.[82] Ignaz Schmid ran into problems during the crisis of the late 1840s because of this earlier policy. He was by then involved in the sale of a variety of products, including the traditional artificial flowers and glasspaintings, but he needed a permit to continue his operations because he had come under attack from the other shopkeepers in Murnau. He was at one point reported to have taken over the "old glasspainter's property" without getting a permit, and this was now clearly not a mark in his favor. He had taken the precaution, however, of undergoing a test to qualify himself as a shopkeeper in 1843, which certified him as "fully diligent and masterly," so he was able to acquire the permission to continue as a tradesman.[83]

Glasspainting may not have been a *Gerechtigkeit* established as an official trade in many cases, but the glasspainting families were nonetheless often able to make a living from their trade comparable with that of successful local tradesmen. The seven master painters listed for the Murnau administrative district in 1792, for example, made about 35 gulden each, although six assistants had also to be accounted for out of the 245 gulden grossed. This compares favorably with the average of 20 gulden earned by four locksmiths in the area, although luxury craftsmen made much more, such as the two Murnau hatmakers who averaged 75 gulden each or the single lacemaker who grossed 80 gulden. Such trade occupations as construction worker or tailor, employment to which several glasspainting families had previously turned, were not always able to provide a comparable income. In the 1792 survey it was discovered that an average Bavarian builder grossed only 13 gulden, and a tailor made 24 gulden. Yet, in contrast to their Murnau counterparts, all three Uffing painters were reported as earning only 30 gulden in this period; their low income was, however, balanced by the substantial income of the two merchants there, who grossed a yearly total of 900 gulden.[84]

Figures for personal income in the nineteenth century were a great deal higher than the 1792 survey would lead one to expect. It is estimated that only 26 percent of the population in Bavaria earned under 200 gulden in 1825, while 54 percent enjoyed an income of 200–500 gulden per year. In 1816, moreover, it was reported that the woodcarvers of Oberammergau had formerly been able to earn 2 gulden daily, but that recent income had not reached half that amount. This suggests that an annual income of around 500 gulden had been a reasonable expectation for some craftsmen there. And, indeed, the villagers were earning 400–500 gulden a week, over 20,000 gulden annually, in 1800, although this sum had to be divided among the seventy or so craftsmen and their agents, hawkers, and suppliers. But many workers undoubtedly earned considerably less than the best craftsmen, and there were certainly "rich" and "poor" families within the village structure.[85]

Glasspainters in the nineteenth century may also at times have made equally substantial incomes. The high numbers of paintings produced in Wolfstein earned the local painters 5,000 gulden yearly and so averaged 1,000 gulden per family in 1830. Earlier, the three Wolfsteiners in Außergefild had earned an average of 1,000 gulden per year among them in the 1790s. No wonder the government order forbidding their foreign hawkers to operate within Bavaria after the end of the Napoleonic Wars was met with such strident opposition from the glasspainters. The condition of the Raimundsreuth painters at that time was described by the local glass factory owner as "tragic," and the Murnau painters became equally poor during the wars.[86] When conditions were right, nevertheless, the evidence shows that glasspainters were actually able to better both their social and their economic situation because of the income earned from their businesses; a few even became important and substantial residents of their home villages.

Improvement came particularly in the ability of some glasspainting families to buy land.[87] As early as 1767, Johannes Noder, whose father does not even appear in the 1752 tax survey as a landholder (his relationship to the Andreas Noder listed at that time is obscure), was able to buy a meadow worth 170 gulden from a weaver in Murnau.[88] His son Matthias, whose 1/32 landholding in 1808 was technically the smallest of the three sons' holdings, also enjoyed extra landholdings and a meadow listed in the Uffing tax records.[89] By the 1840s he was in a position to make a much larger purchase of land sold by the government than most of the other villagers of the area.[90] And his son Michael met the substantial marriage portion brought by his wife into their union in 1843 with a net worth of at least 3,000 gulden; the holding was made over to him by Matthias at that time.[91] The other Seehausener Alois Gege inherited the house with extra landholdings occupied by his mother in 1808, but there is less evidence than for the Noders of substantial improvement in the Gege family fortunes during the nineteenth century. Josef, Alois's grandson, did move to the still-imposing House Number 8 later in the century, but his grandfather died in 1864 leaving little but the Gege property, which he had already handed over to his son Sebastian in 1859.[92]

On December 14, 1814, Nemesi Schmid in Uffing won a local auction held in the tavern to sell off the tumbledown village tithehouse. He beat the mayor of the village in a square fight; Anton Streicher's initial bid was 50 gulden, which Nemesi topped with a counter-bid of 55 gulden. Further bids brought the price up to the 70 gulden finally put forward by Streicher, but he was again topped by Nemesi's winning bid of 70 gulden and 30 kreuzer. By contrast, Nemesi's cousin Jakob enjoyed the benefit of extra landholdings supplementing the basic Schmid landholding in 1808, as we have seen. But Jakob left the family home during his lifetime, and he died in 1849 as a day laborer on a newer holding numbered 85. In Oberammergau, Joseph Anton Lang is listed twice in the 1810 tax survey, suggesting the possibility that he enjoyed the benefit of a rental property. Several of the other village glasspainters owned some extra landholdings by 1810; around 1830 both Joseph Anton Lang and Joseph Mangold enjoyed more than one holding. In Murnau, Ignaz Schmid was able to exchange House Number 60 for a substantial property both agricultural and residential in 1841. He owned, it was later argued, sufficient acreage to support a family on his agricultural activities alone. Yet he may have been unusual among Murnau glasspainters in accumulating property so successfully. Other glasspainting families there occupied homes that were evaluated in the lower tax-brackets normal for town residents.[93]

In Raimundsreuth both the Peterhansls and later Paul Janke, who married a Peterhansl widow in 1816, were able to acquire additional landholdings that enabled them to narrow the gap between their precarious hold on the land and the more solid economic position of the original eight farmers there. Although in general little transfer of property took place within the village during the early nineteenth century, both glasspainters were able to profit from the splitting of Number 7 into Numbers 7 and 11; they may, indeed, even have initiated the split themselves in 1816, at the time of Janke's entry into the family. Josef Peterhansl owned both the smaller Number 7 and the original Peterhansl holding in the nineteenth century, and his purchase of Number 7 was in 1816 at a cost of around 1,215 gulden. Janke bought Number 11 in 1829 from his stepdaughter Maria Peterhansl for around 2,150 gulden. When Christian Wolf broke up the Number 3 holding in 1830, a smaller Number 3½ was created, but part of the remaining land was bought by Josef Peterhansl for around 410 gulden. He had previously bought a garden in 1812 for around 32 gulden from the owner of Number 2. Janke made several additional purchases of land in the 1830s, at a total cost of 1,545 gulden, so he spent 3,695 gulden in a period of under ten years. Only one purchase, meadowland costing 1,200 gulden, was of land lying outside the confines of the village itself. All other land acquisition, together with the creation of new smallholdings in the village, exchanged land between one household and another. The benefit accrued for the most part to the glasspainters, and the result was to increase their farming interests substantially at the cost of the integrity of some of the larger village holdings.[94]

This sometimes substantial accumulation of land by both Upper and Lower Bavarian glasspainters illustrates a general trend in nineteenth-century Bavaria toward redistribution of agricultural holdings in favor of medium-sized farming units. In the early nineteenth century, common pastures, woods, and moorland were often sold or subdivided by village authorities. Some smallholders thus gained the chance to acquire additional land during the process of division. Others bought church land when it was sold after the Secularization of 1803 or private land from individual owners. As a result the theoretical distinctions between themselves and the larger landowners became increasingly meaningless in this period.[95] This enhanced landholding position then encouraged craftsmen such as the Bavarian glasspainters to guard their holdings by careful marriage and inheritance strategies. For property transferral was clearly an important consideration for sons deciding to marry and continue with the trade, since they would frequently wait until the death or retirement of either the father or both parents. Matthias Noder, for example, who married young at around twenty-one in the 1790s, had already lost his father; he later retired in 1843 at the time of son Michael's marriage. His fellow Seehausener Alois Gege even waited to marry at twenty-four after the death of his mother in 1819. His father had long been dead, so he was then free to conduct the family business on his own behalf. He too became a retiree in 1859, probably in conjunction with his son Sebastian's marriage. In Raimundsreuth, Josef Peterhansl married in 1809 after the death of his father in 1808; he also bought the family holding from his mother at that time, which was normal practice in the village. These families seem to have followed what E. A. Wrigley calls the " 'peasant' variant of the European marriage system" as opposed to the " 'wage' variant" typical in rural industry that encouraged a lower age at marriage. They showed extreme caution in establishing new families, even when their businesses were flourishing, presumably because, like peasants, they had acquired a vested interest in a substantial inheritance.[96]

This ability to buy and transfer land was, however, the exact opposite of the continued proliferation of landless householders so typical of an industrialized village structure. Consequently, the opportunity for such alteration of the family's economic status appears to have been concentrated in the more agricultural glasspainting villages. In neither Murnau nor Oberammergau did so clear an improvement in the landholding fortunes of glasspainting families take place. Most of Murnau's artistic craftsmen were strongly affected by trade fluctuations and by the eventual decline of their craft's market, which became evident early in the nineteenth century after the negative impact of the Napoleonic Wars on international trade had disrupted their overseas business. Their enforced resort to day labor during the wars surely suggests a lack of resources sufficient to cushion them in times of disaster. Oberammergau craftsmen also suffered from this disruption, and it is made clear in the account book kept by Andreas Lang and later by his son Martin just how devastating the decline of the firm's overseas markets could become. But Oberammergau weathered that storm better than the Murnau glasspainters did. Glasspainters there adapted their product successfully to the growing mid-European market for popular religious art that Lower Bavarian painters had long been cultivating and that Seehausen painters had always primarily served. Nevertheless, the dependence of Oberammergau craftsmen on supplying the merchant Johann Evangelist Lang left them at the mercy of his charity during a severe crisis during the 1840s. There is little evidence to suggest that the village glasspainters would have fared any better in this crisis than other artistic craftsmen or been any less dependent on the entrepreneurs, such as Lang and Bierling, who handled glasspaintings. Oberammergau had clearly moved beyond the possibility of "reagrarianization."[97]

This variety and changeability of fortunes for individual glasspainting families is certainly striking. For example, just when in Murnau glasspainters were "as poor as beggars" during the Napoleonic Wars and in Oberammergau craft income had sunk to at least half its prewar level, Matthias Noder was considered worthy of the post of mayor in Seehausen, Nemesi Schmid could beat the mayor of Uffing's price on a land deal, and Josef Peterhansl could pay out more than 1,000 gulden for the purchase of a second landholding in Raimundsreuth. The success of Matthias Noder, in particular, is underscored by his son Michael's marriage to a woman from a well-endowed farming family. Yet all glasspainters must have hoped that their craft would improve the fortunes of their families, if only to provide a reliable subsistence for them. As the 1815–16 article on Oberammergau expressed it, "The workers [at that difficult time] are satisfied when they only earn enough to keep themselves and their families going honestly."[98] However, the Oberammergau craftsmen had earned more and no doubt hoped to earn more again, although their plight in the 1840s argues against their accumulation of substantial savings. The glasspainters who purchased land with their earnings must also have hoped in this way to improve their families' fortunes, although whether they saw beyond a chance to engage in subsistence-level farming through the acquisition of extra holdings is difficult to establish. They had certainly developed a strikingly commercial frame of mind, to which we will return in the Epilogue, and they must also have hoped to improve their social standing in the village by adding to the family's economic substance. For there were very distinctive social classes in Bavarian villages, and the possession of land could of course move the owner up the social as well as the economic scale.[99]

Thus, despite the fact that glasspainting as a rural craft was an ephemeral phenomenon lasting but a few generations, the century of glasspainting activities in Upper and Lower Bavaria did solve for several families the pressing problem of assuring a livelihood. A proliferation of smallholdings during the early eighteenth century and before had strained already meager village resources in mountainous parts of Bavaria. Outside markets for village products had to be found or expanded to support the population at its new level and to permit it to increase. This was a challenge that the glasspainters met in efficient and ample fashion. But their striking success in establishing a large mid-European market for their glasspaintings during the nineteenth century also led to the destruction of their business. For lithographers eagerly responded to the growing demand for framed replacements of oil paintings with a product increasingly similar to the glasspaintings that had created and shaped this popular market. It is, therefore, to the story of the development of glasspainting's competitor, chromolithography, that we turn in Chapter 2.

2

Industrial Competition from the Graphic Arts: The Development of Chromolithography

During the 1870s and 1880s, the production of popular art in Germany became fully mechanized on a grand scale. Producers of printed paintings felt increasing pressure to dismiss their colorists and replace them with the machinery that could transform a print into a believable replica of an oil painting. This victory of the chromolithographic process completed the industrialization in the graphic arts that had begun with the discovery of lithography by Alois Senefelder in the 1790s; it also sounded the death knell for glasspainting as a rural manufacturing business. But replacement of glasspaintings by lithographs had started much earlier, as handcolored prints produced in the decades before 1870 fueled an ever-increasing demand for printed paintings. So I will trace in this chapter not only the history of the printed chromolithograph but also that of the handpainted popular lithograph as well.

Senefelder and his colleagues soon realized that lithography was ideally suited to the reproduction of art works. Such reproduction in one or another graphic medium had already been well developed in Europe by the end of the sixteenth century, allowing original compositions by contemporary artists to be printed by the thousands, as well as copies of famous paintings. In particular, copper engravings were successful in rendering the detail required by an art-loving audience prepared to pay for a sophisticated product; later, etching too provided a quick and easy medium for reproductive work. During the late eighteenth century and throughout the nineteenth century, however, the popular demand for artistic products grew rapidly. In 1797

Wolfgang von Goethe could observe that "in the last twenty years the newly stimulated interest of the public in the visual arts has come out in conversation, letters and purchases." So it is hardly surprising that the inventor of a new technique better suited to the inexpensive and large-scale production of graphic art than engraving or etching should eagerly turn it to that purpose.[1]

Senefelder recognized the advantages of printing from stone for the cheap reproduction of art works even before he discovered the chemical planographic procedure unique to lithography in 1798. For using the stone as a surface for intaglio printing resulted in a substantial reduction in overheads as compared with printing from copper. One of his first clients, a certain Michael Steiner, school inspector for the Bavarian government, discussed the merits of the new technique in a letter to his superior in 1797. He reported that Senefelder was experimenting with the possibility of using his new discovery to etch works of art, adding that the inventor

> copied the picture "The Lost Son" drawn by Hauber. Both Hauber and other conoisseurs approve of this attempt, and they believe that seemly and saleable pictures could be produced by such means, particularly pictures for illumination. It is clear that these pictures could be sold easily because
>
> a) Senefelder can sell this kind of prepared stone plate for around five gulden, whereas the engraved copper plate costs 22 gulden.
>
> b) The printer from copper produces 200–300 copies daily, whereas 1,500 (and more) prints can be made daily from a stone plate.
>
> c) A stone plate renders 6,000–8,000 prints or more; the copper plate does not make half as many.
>
> d) Finally, it is easy to take four octavo-size pictures from one stone, printing them at the same time, with the result that 6,000 pictures can be produced in a day.

The press used to effect these gratifying results cost no more than 24 gulden, according to Steiner's calculations.[2]

With the discovery of the planographic procedure, lithography became not only cheap and prolific but also easily accessible to artists and extremely versatile. Free either to draw directly onto the stone or to cut into it, the lithographic artist was able to copy the stylistic effect of a woodcut, engraving, or any other desired graphic procedure, including drawing; this Senefelder was already in a position to demonstrate when he prepared his first text on lithography in 1808. The exciting opportunities offered by the new medium to contemporary artists were soon exploited in Munich, where an ambitious project known as the *Lithographische Kunstprodukte* (*Lithographic Artworks*) was already underway in 1805. Making available the work of six local artists in twenty-six monthly installments of six individual prints, the series explored the potentialities of lithography as a black and white medium and confirmed the possibility of producing beautiful handcolored lithographs. In addition, the artists twice used two colors of ink to print a two-colored reproduction of a flower, the head in red contrasting with the blackness of the stalk.[3]

Most of the prints in the *Lithographische Kunstprodukte* were original compositions. Both Joseph Hauber and Andreas Seidl, however, contributed reproductions of old masters to the project and thus anticipated the strong sympathy for reproductive work shown later by German lithographers. Soon Senefelder himself became involved with a company that set out in 1807 to reproduce the illustrations to Emperor Maximilian's prayer book by Albrecht Dürer. Later the reformed company, now without Senefelder's help, initiated a more ambitious project. Known as the *Oeuvres Lithographiques* (*Lithographic Masterworks*), this series of prints issued in monthly installments from 1810 to 1816 copied selected drawings from the Bavarian Royal Drawing Cabinet.[4]

Both the Dürer project and the *Oeuvres Lithographiques* reflected the growing interest of Senefelder and his colleagues in the color printing of art works. Almost immediately Senefelder attempted to apply his discovery to the commercial printing of colored patterns on cotton, but that attempt dovetailed into his early investigations into the possibility of printing in colors with several stone plates, apparently at the suggestion of Michael Steiner.[5] Yet the Dürer production used only one basic stone per print, merely changing the printing color several times in the complete edition of over forty prints.[6] It appears that "Senefelder's first thought to print a drawing with two stones" materialized in the form of a copy in red and black of a drawing by Joseph Cesari. All the red crayon strokes of the original were copied onto one stone, all the black onto another, and when both stones were applied to the same piece of paper, one after the other, "the most complete likeness of the original drawing was achieved."[7] In much the same way Senefelder was able to create the effect of illumination on maps of Bavaria by using separate stones to print the necessary colored borders. The inventor claimed that six presses could complete one thousand copies daily of this kind of print, illuminated in five colors; and indeed he had already furnished ten thousand illuminated maps in this way by the end of 1808.[8] Senefelder adapted yet a different form of this technique to illustrate J. von Stichauer's *Sammlung römischer Denkmäler von Bayern,* published in 1808. He cleverly highlighted the objects to be depicted by printing the background a solid black and leaving the white of the paper to become the color of the object itself. But he varied this technique in one or two cases by using a red tint stone to color the white. This early project closely approximated the "colored" manner of printing pictures that he discussed in his 1808 text. It soon proved possible to construct a far more complex image in this way, a realistic facsimile of a painting.[9]

But Senefelder's interest in color printing encompassed more than illumination. The idea that two or more stones could be used to print a drawing soon led both the inventor and his assistants to experiment with the creation of a tinted effect for their facsimiles of old drawings. The print of a Madonna drawn by Fra Bartolomeo is widely recognized as the first lithograph with a printed tint; it followed their earlier efforts to copy the look of an original drawing through the dangerous process of smoking the print over a flame.[10] During the course of production of the *Oeuvres Lithographiques,* the artists in charge of the color scheme experimented with the application of tints, creating in the process many different color mixtures. They often changed the color of the ink used to print the drawing itself as well as that of the tint, and they also tried changing the color of the paper on which the drawing was printed. Meanwhile, they worked on producing white highlights to accent the print as well, scraping away the areas to be left white from the stone before printing with it. As they became more proficient at the use of tints, they tried applying more than one at a time. The reproduction of a Salviati original, for example, approximated the effect of a chiaroscuro woodcut through the device of contrasting dark olive and ocher tones.[11]

The development of color and tinted lithography in the context of the artistic projects initiated by Senefelder and his associates was clearly a commercial venture. Senefelder himself certainly felt the pressing need for profit, because although many of his early patrons were rich men, he was a struggling actor and author when he first thought to experiment with the use of stone as a printing medium.[12] So too must have Senefelder's employees Johann Nepomuk Strixner and Ferdinand Pilotti felt a need for profit when they were lucky enough to be taken into Senefelder's business as partners in 1810 when the company was reconstituted to launch the *Oeuvres Lithographiques* project.[13] Color lithography offered a commercially promising field, although Senefelder's interest in color printing has been characterized as "rather naive," since at the time elite consumers would have rejected such "gaudy" artworks.[14] The targeted market must have been a more popular one, as is suggested by the fact that a series of prints such as the *Oeuvres Lithographiques,* which made original art accessible to the public, should have been the one in which experiments with tinted lithography played a central role. The project certainly set out to provide authentic reproductions of the drawings selected; this aim was firmly stated on the cover of one of the earliest issues: "Each issue will be of . . . a different size and color according to the originals." And yet there were "deviations, owing less to technical inabilities than to a concession to contemporary taste," some of which involved changes in the color of the ink or paper used for certain of the reproductions. Moreover, some of the later prints had to be completed with new tint plates. These were "mostly stronger and coarser in the color contrasts than the earlier ones" and so rendered the copy less true to the original drawing. These changes thus appear to represent submission to a public demand for colored prints.[15]

In this way, the *Oeuvres Lithographiques* and other schemes to reproduce inexpensively the collected works of famous artists compromise between the pure desire to teach and inform and the commercial need to succeed in reaching a large audience through the saleability of the product. I have already noted the juxtaposition of the concepts "suitable" and "saleable" in Steiner's 1797 report on the virtues of lithography. Steiner's aim at that time was "to circulate these pictures so generally that they could serve as gifts from the country preachers to their little Christian pupils" and "to ornament various school-books with pictures . . . [that would] replace the miserably drawn species of saints that generally fill the prayer-books of the pious households."[16] The same didactic enthusiasm was expressed by the promoters of the

Lithographische Kunstprodukte, coupled with clarification of the inexpensive nature of their folios. On September 1, 1805, a notice in the *Churpfalzbayerische Staatszeitung* announced the beginning of monthly installments at the "extremely affordable price of 1 gulden, 36 kreuzer" for six prints, a price, moreover, that it was suggested subscribers could reduce by sharing an issue with other art lovers. Further, the promoters argued that "this lithographic establishment has the charitable purpose of arousing the artistic industry of our country and setting it in operation. It also intends to promote good taste by means of affordable and at the same time beautiful sample drawings, and to provide instructional, natural-historical, and moralistic pictures of adequate size to display in public educational institutes and schools."[17]

The *Lithographische Kunstprodukte* certainly seems to have captured the interest of its public; 250 persons had subscribed by the beginning of 1807, and over 4,000 gulden had flowed into the publisher's coffers. Probably individual prints were also made available at that time, as they were later on in the 1810s. Many of these prints were illuminated, which made them relatively expensive, according to a price list issued later by the publisher. However, the "flower prints illuminated in natural colors" mentioned as inexpensive in 1805 were only 24 kreuzer in 1818, a price comparable even with Johann Evangelist Lang's glasspaintings. (In the 1830s his more expensive paintings did not top one gulden, whereas Andreas Lang's had sometimes cost as much as three or four gulden.)[18] This "popularizing" project thus showed the same emphasis on the production of colored pictures as the *Oeuvres Lithographiques,* a reflection, surely, of market pressures.[19]

In fact, the continued interest of German consumers in colorful art works encouraged local lithographers to continue printing tinted lithographs for art reproduction, in contrast to the concentration on monochrome for artists' lithography elsewhere in Europe. Even the early interest in tinted lithography of the two most important foreign lithographers to visit Munich in the days of experimentation with tints, the Frenchman Godefroy Engelmann and the Englishman Charles Hullmandel, dwindled in the 1820s and early 1830s. Probably this particular holdover in Germany owed its continued existence to the popularity of sixteenth-century chiaroscuro woodcuts.[20] German lithographers also drew inspiration from Senefelder's early efforts in illumination, both to color designs and to reproduce paintings. Wilhelm Zahn of Berlin commissioned color prints of ornamental designs for the first edition of his book on classical art issued in 1829.[21] Earlier, in Vienna, experiments in chromolithography took place at the Lithographic Institute that led to the production of sophisticated color reproductions. The most striking of these was Josef Lanzadelly's *Der Jahrmarkt in Hermannstadt* (*Market in Transylvania,* 1819), a complex, large print involving the use of nine stones.[22] (Figure 4 captures the portion of this print that depicts a glasspainting seller at the market.) In the early 1820s Senefelder's colleague Franz Weishaupt also completed a series of chromolithographs that served as illustrations for Johann Baptist von Spix and Carl von Martius's book about their travels in Brazil.[23]

Meanwhile, Senefelder was busy searching for a means to create successful printed reproductions of oil paintings. On January 1, 1809, he announced that among the many advantages offered by his discovery, his technique of printing with several stones "almost allows one to provide copies of complete oil paintings." By 1818 he could promise even more: "I have made such progress in color printing that, besides pictures illuminated with colors, I can also produce pictures quite similar to oil paintings, so that nobody can discover that they have been printed, because they possess all the distinguishing points of paintings."[24] Little visual documentation remains, however, to substantiate the inventor's claims. It is not even certain that a print in several colors of a girl with a dove attributed to Senefelder is actually his own work, although it does use his method and appears to stem from the 1808 period. This print lacks the heavy finish of an oil painting, but it provides a good example of clever chromolithographic printing. Its executor has even created shadow effects by varying the frequency of the dots of color.[25] Yet it was the Lanzadelly and Weishaupt efforts described above that best fulfilled Senefelder's persistent vision of successful chromolithography. Sadly, despite these experiments concluded during his lifetime, Senefelder decided to divert his own attention from multiple-stone printing to the *Mosaikdruck* or "mosaic print" project that occupied him from the mid-1820s until his death in 1834. This complicated procedure for printing oil paintings employed a porous medium such as cloth to which all the necessary colors could be applied at once. Many examples of the prints produced by Senefelder according to this method have been preserved, and their effect is certainly that of an oil painting. But the technique

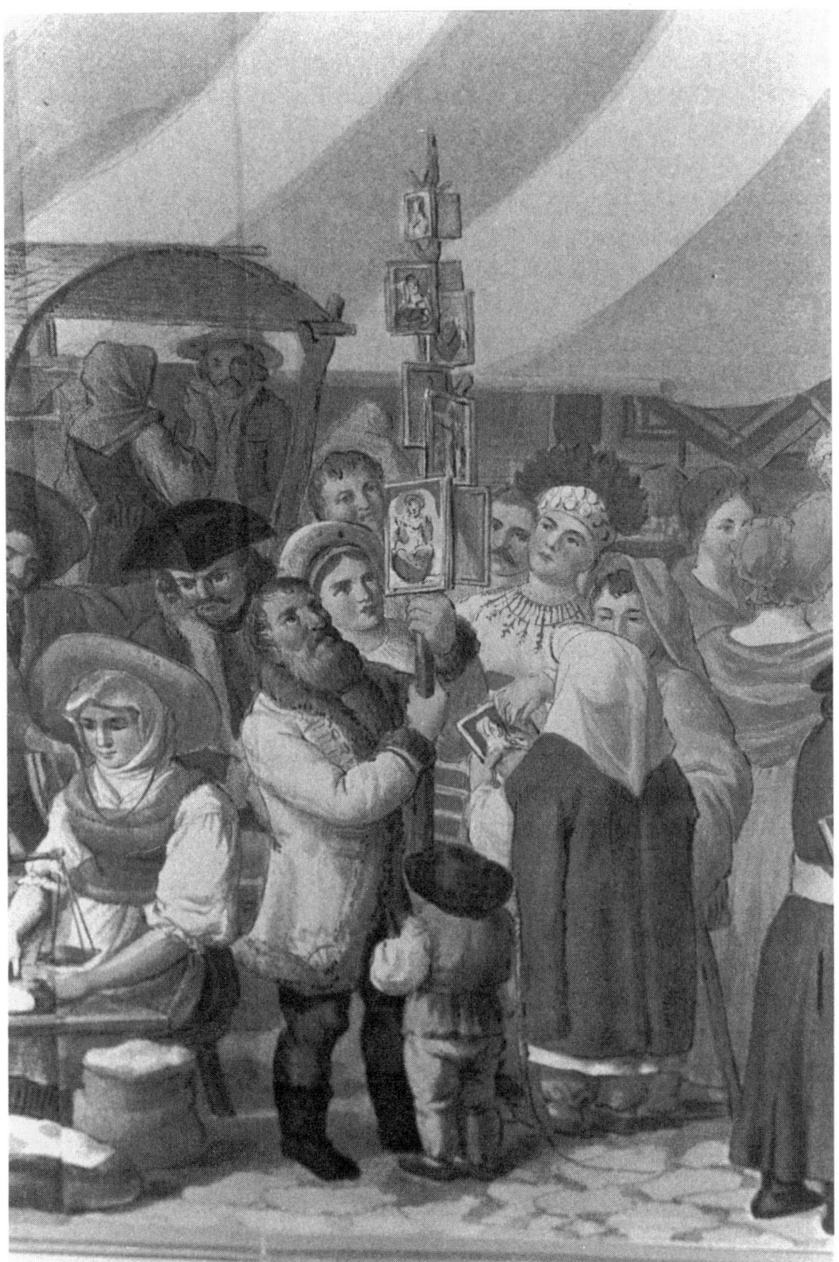

Figure 4. A hawker selling glasspaintings in Josef Lanzadelly's *Der Jahrmarkt in Hermannstadt,* 1819. (Germanisches Nationalmuseum, Nuremberg)

was not to contribute a workable method of producing inexpensive oil prints to the lithographic profession; rather, it provides yet one more example of Senefelder's constant commitment to the reproduction of oil paintings.[26]

How much this lifetime search of Senefelder owed to the example of the local glasspainting market will probably never be known. But it is certainly suggestive to note that it was Joseph von Utzschneider who eventually gave Senefelder employment at the Tax Commission Press in 1809, employment incidentally that provided him with both a laboratory in which to conduct his experiments and a salary sufficient to relieve him of the need to pursue commercial activities. For it was Utzschneider who later concerned himself with the declining fortunes of the glasspainters in the Lake Staffel area after the Napoleonic Wars. He even founded two schools for glasspainting at that time, one in Rieden on Lake Staffel and one in Munich.[27] According to an 1816 article reporting on Utzschneider's efforts on behalf of the glasspainters, he wanted glasspainting "to become again a more beautiful and cheaper object of commerce, and in still greater numbers."[28] His intention may have been to teach glasspainters to adapt to contemporary styles; the article certainly mentions his attempt "to correct the glasspainting in Seehausen and Rieden (his birthplace)."[29] This was the same kind of concern for the improvement of popular art shown by Steiner when he originally employed Senefelder to print lithographs for him, although it undoubtedly stemmed in Utzschneider's case from a desire to see glasspainting commercially successful again rather than from any purely didactic enthusiasm. It seems likely from the scanty evidence provided by his diary that Utzschneider had involved the artist Carl Selb in his glasspainting projects. He made an "agreement" with Selb in March 1816 and later in the year visited Rieden with him, apparently to set up the school there. He also consulted Senefelder's colleague Johann Mettenleitner when the two visited Seehausen on October 17, 1815, to observe local glasspainters at work. And he showed a continuing personal interest in lithography, founding a lithographic press of his own in 1815 along with the glasspainting school in Munich.[30] So both the artistic aspirations of lithographers in Munich and the expertise of a city artist seem to have been introduced to the Upper Bavarian glasspainters at a time when, ironically, their own market was increasingly centering on the popular Catholic market in central Europe.

This more popular market for glasspaintings later caught Sebastian

Haindl's attention in an 1843 article about a new method of producing inexpensive chromolithographs practiced at that time by Franz Weishaupt's son Heinrich. Haindl informs us that those numerous members of the middle class who "before the discovery of lithography were reduced to no more than badly-painted glasspaintings or woodcuts, especially devoted to the reproduction of religious subjects," now have "copies of good works by Masters" to enjoy instead. In this context, Haindl's designation "middle class" would certainly cover many of the country customers served by the glasspainters in the 1840s; for the bracketing of glasspaintings with woodcuts rather than with engravings designates the popular market.[31] So too does Heinrich Weishaupt's process, patented in 1837 and aimed at the rapid production of inexpensive color prints. For Weishaupt claimed to be able to use a base stone and three supplementary stones inked in the primary colors red, blue, and yellow to print the complete range of colors needed in a picture. To this kind of print it was possible to add accent shades that would give it "more of the character of an oil painting."[32] In this way, truly inexpensive printed pictures could become a reality.

Examples of Weishaupt's earliest experiments with his new procedure leave little doubt that his intention to make substitutes for oil paintings could be fulfilled. They depend, however, on large areas of flat, primary colors and are often touched up by hand.[33] The potential of the three-color process is perhaps better exemplified in his 1841 print of the Holy Trinity, which includes a good deal more nuancing in the colors. However, Weishaupt appears to have modified his process in this case, since he was clearly printing from more than the basic color stones.[34] (See figure 5.) The inventor continued to develop his process during the 1840s, until his lack of both capital and commercial expertise led him, by his own admission, into difficulties with the business. An attempt to raise 1,800 gulden from the government failed, obliging him to sell both his process and his patent to his fellow lithographers, Emil Roller and Roller's foreman Jakob Gramer. About 150 lithographic stones and over 2,000 finished prints changed hands as a consequence, although Gramer, who bought out Roller's interest immediately, seems to have resorted to the use of colorists in the business; he is reported using eighteen in 1852. Meanwhile, Weishaupt retained his interest in chromolithography and made public his invention in an instructional textbook on the subject published in 1848 by a Leipzig firm. This would have made the three-color process available to

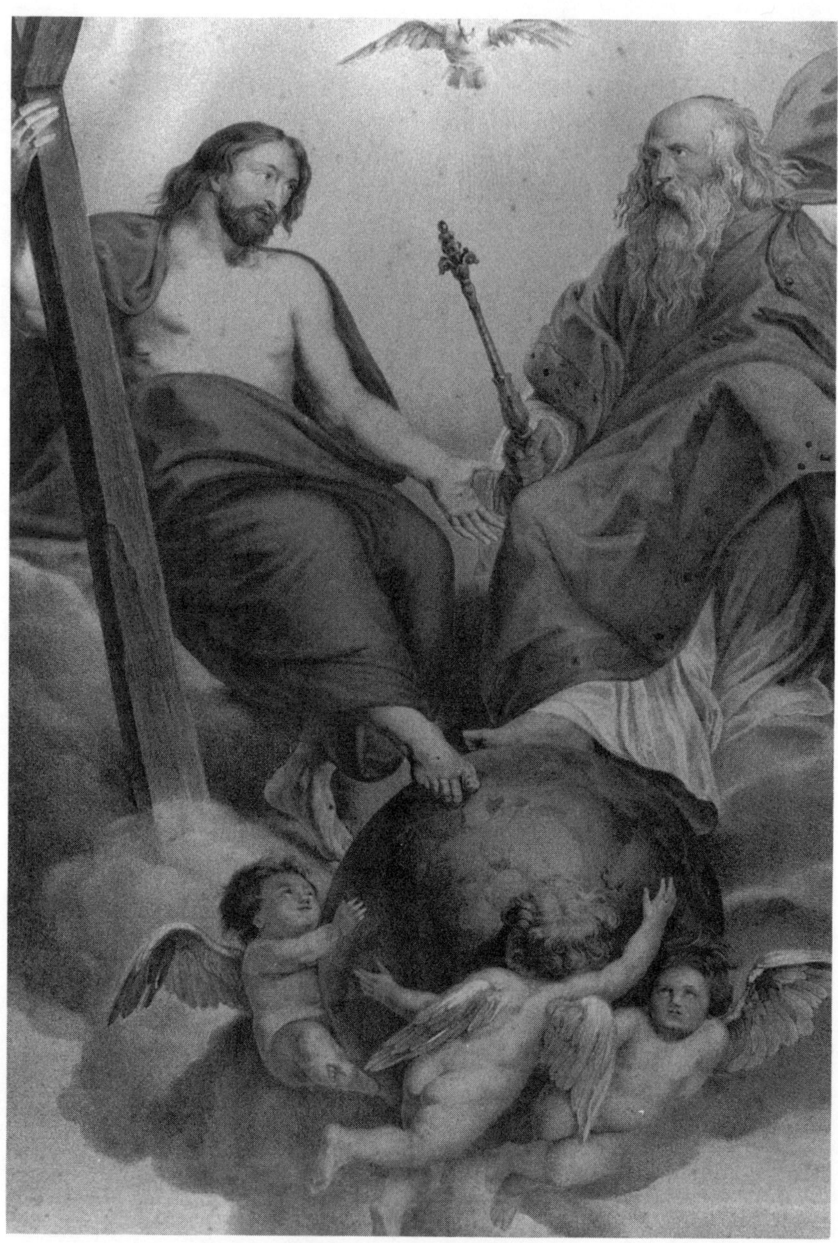

Figure 5. Heinrich Weishaupt's *Holy Trinity* of 1841. (Staatliche Graphische Sammlung, Munich)

lithographers who were not restricted in its use by the Bavarian patent, although the extent of the book's influence is impossible to gauge.[35]

Weishaupt was not alone in his experiments with inexpensive chromolithography even in Munich, since another patent for a three-color procedure was granted by the Bavarian government in 1837. The inventor Joseph Grosjean included a detailed description of his discovery in the sealed package he delivered to the authorities, together with a small example of his printing technique that resembled a colored woodcut. Religious in subject matter, this tiny print was clearly intended to imitate the devotional pictures so often placed by consumers inside their Bibles.[36] Two further discoveries were recorded in 1841, one by Franz Schleicher and the other by the painters August Schott and Heinrich Knauth. At much the same time Sebastian Haindl was collaborating with the Cotta literary and artistic institute in his production of chromolithographs, while Sebastian Minsinger was also developing a special technique for using primary colors in architectural reproduction.[37]

All these experiments suggest that Munich's lithographers were intrigued by the commercial possibilities offered by chromolithographic printing during the late 1830s and 1840s. Yet Weishaupt himself admitted that it was the announcement in 1837 of a discovery similar to his own made by the Frenchman Godefroy Engelmann that spurred him to reevaluate the worth of his own experiments and protect his invention with the fifteen-year patent.[38] Engelmann was but one of several Frenchmen to investigate chromolithography in the 1830s, and he was not even the first to try out the three-color process. The trade journal *Le Lithographe*, which was edited by Jules Desportes, who was himself proficient in color printing as early as 1830, reported that already in 1834 a certain Monsieur Garson had printed an image of the Virgin with several stones. While imperfect, this print apparently demonstrated the possibility of a three-color system, and the journal added that M. Garson was currently (1839) printing with four plates, inked in black, yellow, red, and blue.[39] It was Engelmann, however, whose work was considered sufficiently promising commercially to win a 2,000 franc prize offered in 1828 by the Society of Encouragement for National Industry for a means of producing one thousand or more color prints. He patented his discovery in January of 1837 and received the prize in 1838.[40]

When the Fine Arts Committee of the Industrial Society at Mühlhausen, Engelmann's home town, observed Engelmann at work on his new technique in 1837, they were led to exclaim: "How desirable it was . . . that so useful, so well-developed, and so popular an art as lithography should become still more helpful and see itself incorporating, at least in part, the very power that gives painting so great a predominance." They later noted that "the whole procedure was less expensive than any other," since one hundred prints daily could be prepared according to its principles.[41] Unfortunately, Engelmann did not live long enough to exploit the distinct commercial advantages inherent in his procedure that the Mühlhausen Committee so astutely perceived. Instead, his son, in partnership with Auguste Graf from 1842, was able to enjoy the benefit of the ten-year patent, and the firm was certainly selling chromolithographs in the 1840s.[42] However, the evidence provided by a lithographer trained by the firm and later transplanted to America suggests that the firm may have adopted a modified version of the three-color process. Christian Schluessele, an Alsatian like both Engelmann and Graf, printed chromolithographs in imitation of oil paintings during the early 1850s. But when he produced his portraits of Washington and Lafayette in 1852, he used as many as thirteen stones, despite the fact that he "overlapped the tones in each portrait, creating the range of subtle color variations found in oil paintings." Nevertheless, the Philadelphia *Public Ledger* complimented the thirteen-stone projects for "the cheapness of their production." And two years earlier Schluessele's expertise induced *The Bulletin of the American Art-Union* to predict that "in a few years the most accurate copies in color of pictures will be printed, and the great work of popularizing Art . . . carried nearly to perfection."[43]

The firm of Engelmann and Graf was not to be alone in its continued pursuit of chromolithographic printing in France. There were already four other Parisian workshops capable of displaying color prints at the Industrial Exposition of 1839, as well as the Simon firm from Strasbourg and the Barbat firm from Châlons-sur-Marne. By 1845 eighty presses were printing chromolithographs in Paris alone, according to the author of an article in *Le Lithographe* who felt justified in suggesting optimistically that in ten years' time there would be five hundred. By 1846 Lemercier's, "the leading lithographic house in France in the middle of the nineteenth century both in size and reputation," was reported to be printing in colors. The Minister of Commerce paid a visit to the establishment at that time, where he observed the application of "up to three or four colors."[44] Clearly, chromolithography attracted in France the same kind of interest in its commercial possibilities shown by the lithographers of Munich.

But Munich and Paris were not the only important European centers for the production of chromolithographs in the 1830s and 1840s; Berlin's lithographic community was also expanding rapidly into this branch of the business during the same period. As I mentioned earlier, Wilhelm Zahn had initiated a project in Berlin that included chromolithographic plates. The three editions of this work that appeared in the period between 1829 and 1859 provide a unique overview of the capacity of lithographers in Berlin to print in colors, because the contributions of several different workshops were included in each edition. The most famous of these workshops at the time seems to have been the one headed by C. Hildebrand; Engelmann even mentioned it in his account of the background to his own discovery. He distinguished the procedure followed by the Berlin printers from his own, however, because they still needed as many as ten to fifteen stones to provide all the shades required in the production of a single print. This, he felt, made their products expensive and limited in their uses. Nevertheless, *Le Lithographe* claimed in the same period that German chromolithographs had long been favored by commerce "both because of the delicacy of their execution and because of the vivacity of their colors."[45]

The chromolithographs clearly labeled as such provided by Hildebrand, Storch, and C. G. Herwig for the 1829 edition of Zahn's book were essentially decorative, and thus they lent themselves admirably to the printing techniques typical of ornamental illumination.[46] So it is hardly surprising that Zahn became involved with a further printing project in the 1830s and 1840s that required the provision of one hundred chromolithographed plates to illustrate ornaments from all classical periods. Possibly Hildebrand cooperated in this work also, since he reportedly worked on "a collection of the coats-of-arms of different states" and on "illustrations of ornaments" for use in trade schools by the Prussian government. Certainly, by 1842 he was one of the very active contributors to the second edition of Zahn's first book, for which he printed sophisticated and complex ornamental plates.[47] By the time this 1840s edition was underway, however, experimentation in Berlin with the printing of plates resembling paintings could also be reflected in the contributions made by both H. Delius and Feller, while even Hildebrand attempted one print in this style. Most of these printed pictures were dominated by large flat areas of colored background, yet two of the Feller prints do anticipate the more sophisticated printed paintings of an 1850s edition.[48] Similarly, surviving prints by the Storch associated with these Zahn productions show that he was also printing attractive chromolithographic paintings in midcentury; his company of Storch and Kramer was still prominent in the world of chromolithography when the Munich Exposition was held in 1876.[49] All these efforts suggest that Berlin, like Paris and Munich, had become a major center of chromolithographic printing by the mid-nineteenth century.

Finally, significant developments in the techniques of chromolithography were also taking place across the Channel in England. Like most of the chromolithographic printing commissioned by Zahn in Berlin, English chromolithographers concentrated on illumination. The leading figure in this development was Owen Jones, whose book on the decorations of the Alhambra was produced lithographically in the 1830s and 1840s and whose subsequent career in the production of colored illustrations of decorative subjects depended on chromolithography. As Charles Hullmandel pointed out in 1839, "in mere decorative subjects the colours are positive and opaque, the tints flat, and the several hues of equal intensity throughout." Nevertheless, the technical perfection of Jones's printing in the Alhambra project was particularly noted by the Frenchman H. Bouchot when he summarized the history of chromolithography later in the century. And the popularity of medieval manuscripts and other antiquarian objects as subjects for reproduction in the mid-nineteenth century assured success to the Jones style of printing both in England and elsewhere in Europe. Jones himself capped his career as a chromolithographer with the production in 1856 of *The Grammar of Ornament.* His statement that "form without colour is like a body without a soul" certainly informed his contribution to chromolithography in England.[50]

Hullmandel was eager to pinpoint the difference between his own experiments with "chromalithography" and the illuminative printing technique epitomized by Jones's recent efforts when he commented on the lack of tonal quality in that kind of chromolithography. The veteran lithographer had become committed to resurrecting tinted lithography by that time, since the use of tint stones had largely been abandoned outside Germany in the 1820s and early 1830s. Instead, Hullmandel and others had concentrated on the perfection of tonal lithography by "building up tints on the stone that carried the drawing." They aimed to reproduce the tonal quality of watercolors and thus to compete with the very successful aquatint procedure that still dominated the market for the reproduction of watercolor paintings in the 1820s. In the 1830s, however, Hullmandel returned to the use of a tint stone that would contribute tonal nuances to the finished print. So successful was this technique that during the next twenty-five years or so, the tinted lithograph "became almost the accepted idiom for lithography."[51]

But Hullmandel pressed on further in his experimentation with tint stones, and he perfected a form of "chromalithography" that made use of as many as four or more tints. He explains that in the prints he provided for Thomas Shotter Boys's *Picturesque Architecture in Paris, Ghent, Antwerp, Rouen, etc.* (1839), "the various effects of light and shade, of local colour and general tone, result from transparent and graduated tints."[52] Hullmandel himself did not pursue this avenue of research; nevertheless, lithographers using the tinting technique were able to draw successfully on his example of printing with more than two stones.[53]

Because of these continuing efforts by chromolithographers in the great European centers of artistic production, by the time of the Great Exhibition in 1851 chromolithography had become an established branch of the lithographic profession. In 1856 H. E. Peschek could argue that until recently that kind of lithography had been considered a merely "playful occupation." "However," he continued, "since people in Germany of taste and education like Asmus, Hildebrand and Storch in Berlin, Förster and Leykum in Vienna, and also Engelmann in Paris and many other similar people have paid it greater attention, the chromolithograph . . . has become an independent art, and truly admirable works have appeared out of the workshops of the abovementioned masters." Peschek proceeded to survey the various methods available to the chromolithographer, discussing the printing of both flat and graduated tints, overprinting, and the printing of many colors from one stone, a procedure that had earlier been pursued by at least one lithographer in Berlin, Gustav Ballerstedt, whose textbook on the subject appeared in 1839. It was similar in intent, of course, to Senefelder's *Mosaikdruck*.[54] Chromolithography was sufficiently well established by the late 1850s that an advertisement could appear in the 1859 Munich Address Book for "*Ölfarbendruckbilder*" or "printed pictures in oil colors." These pictures were for sale in the artistic establishment of Ernst Bayer, 43 Singstrasse, whose copies "after the most famous masters" were available "at the cheapest *en gros* and export prices." Meanwhile, the enterprising chromolithographer Thomas Driendl was producing *Ölfarbendruckbilder* in Munich and then distributing them in both Bavaria and Austria, which is discussed in Chapter 3. So, while a cautious assessment of the rate of growth in German chromolithography seems justified for the 1850s, there was by then a solid base of mostly luxury printing from which a more spectacular increase in production could spring.[55] This was clearly true of the other major centers for chromolithographic production surveyed above as well.[56]

There remained the question of how the techniques of chromolithography might most successfully be directed toward continued commercial success, for much of the early interest in color and tinted lithography had centered on the ability to provide illustrations for books or folio collections of art works. Yet other graphic procedures, and later photography as well, were also available for this purpose. In particular, the use of wood engravings permitted the printer to offer a less expensive product to the growing public for illustrated books, leaving chromolithographers to find a different avenue for their own products if they were to corner a popular market. In this context the lithographers of Munich complained in the late 1840s about the threatening competition of other graphic procedures, ironically, given the huge success of chromolithography later in the century. But the versatility of lithography led to its application in so many different directions that its practitioners were bound to encounter the competition of similar procedures better suited to specific printing tasks.[57]

So chromolithographers began to concentrate on the particular suitability of their medium for the large-scale reproduction of art works. They worked hard to provide convincing and inexpensive replicas of oil paintings, often complete with frame, for customers long prepared, at least in Germany, for their ready consumption. This was a path already followed from the early 1840s by the English wood engraver George Baxter, who soon chose to concentrate his newly patented procedure for printing with oil colors largely on the production of single prints. Baxter's market was later captured, as the glasspainters' market was, by chromolithographers. Thus, these men could benefit not only from the example of the popularity of glasspaintings but also from the wood engraver's clear perception that, as Lord Brougham expressed it, "whatever makes good prints, that is, coloured prints almost with the merit of pictures of easy access to the common people, to the cottagers and labourers, is of great use to them in every respect."[58]

But the decision to develop chromolithography for the satisfaction of the popular demand for printed pictures was further mediated by changes effected in the production of cheap colored broadsheets during the nineteenth century. Lithography had soon been recognized as a boon to the manufacturers of these popular products; it provided a vast number of inexpensive black and white prints that were easily transformed into brightly colored pictures by the numerous colorists employed in lithographic factories. With the help of stencils to control the rapid application of colors, such workers could illuminate enormous numbers of the same print in a short space of time. Consequently, most German factories for popular broadsheets appear to have converted to lithography by around 1830–40; others were founded as lithographic establishments. Many French manufacturers, on the other hand, appear to have remained faithful to traditional techniques rather longer than the Germans; the famous Pellerin firm in Epinal did not adopt lithography in a big way until around 1850.[59] Gustav Kühn's Neurippin firm provides an excellent example of the success enjoyed by these German firms in the decades before the victory of chromolithography. Originally founded in 1790, the firm converted to lithography in 1825; production there sky-rocketed in the next decade from eight thousand to one million prints per year. Yet this scale of operation grew still further, so that in 1870–71 Kühn's firm was able to produce three million broadsheets. These inexpensive prints were known for their "rakish reds, garish blues, thunder greens—printed and for sale at Gustav Kühn's."[60]

The big Neurippin firms, Kühn and Oemigke and Riemschneider, found export markets primarily in eastern Europe and Scandinavia, but they also expanded into the Catholic market for religious prints. Kühn's firm added at least ninety-one pictures of saints to its repertoire, mostly between 1842 and 1863.[61] Even earlier, though, Pellerin had begun to supply southern German Catholics with religious picture sheets. Writing before the advent of World War II, Adolf Spamer recounted that by 1830 Pellerin's brightly colored woodcuts "hung (and still today often hang), accompanied by German texts, in many peasant houses of the Southern German Highlands." In addition, during the 1830s Frédéric-Charles Wentzel founded a bookbinding establishment in Weißenburg, Alsace, to which he added the production of religious broadsheets and *Gebetszettel* or "prayer sheets," used by country customers for protective purposes. Wentzel used woodcutting techniques to print these old-fashioned items, but he appended a lithographic branch to his business, hiring draftsmen and workers from Munich and Frankfurt and purchasing lithographic equipment from Paris. He soon entered successfully into competition with Pellerin for the southern German market, in particular for the Bavarian and Austrian Alpine regions.[62]

Ludwig Steub, wandering through the Bavarian Alps in the early 1860s, encountered with dismay the results of Wentzel's prolific output of prints. In the taverns and in two Alpine cottages that he visited, he found "the most varied pictures stuck up, religious and secular, all from L. Wenzel in Wissembourg." He was told that these pictures of saints, or of hunting and fishing scenes and the like, were brought round in their hundreds by hawkers. Steub does not mention whether these prints were lithographs, but he does suggest that they were colored, which would have been quite normal for the firm's products at that time.[63] Its better prints, destined for use as framed *Wandschmuck* or "decorative wall-paintings," would definitely have been lithographs since Wentzel judged lithography the most suitable medium for the purpose. As early as the 1850s his prints seem to have taken on the form of the *Feine Bilder zum Einrahmen* or "high-grade pictures for framing" later identified in the firm's price lists. They were frequently given the appearance of a *Sofabild* (picture over the sofa) by the provision of multiple borders, while they could be made to look and last more like oil paintings by the judicious use of varnish. Wentzel did, however, put out more traditional pictures of saints in three languages that the firm had adapted to the popular taste for attractive colors and varnishing.[64] (See figures 6 and 7 for similar prints by Thomas Driendl. The lace-edged one is varnished, although it in no way resembles a full-fledged printed oilpainting of the sort described in his sales operations of the 1850s.)

Despite Wentzel's attempt to broaden the appeal of his products, the colorful nature of his lithographs still hints at a popular audience.[65] And the transformation taking place in these prints is fascinating because of the connections the firm enjoyed with the Catholic consumers of central Europe. They were, of course, the key consumers of glass-paintings as well, and Wentzel prints had made substantial inroads into

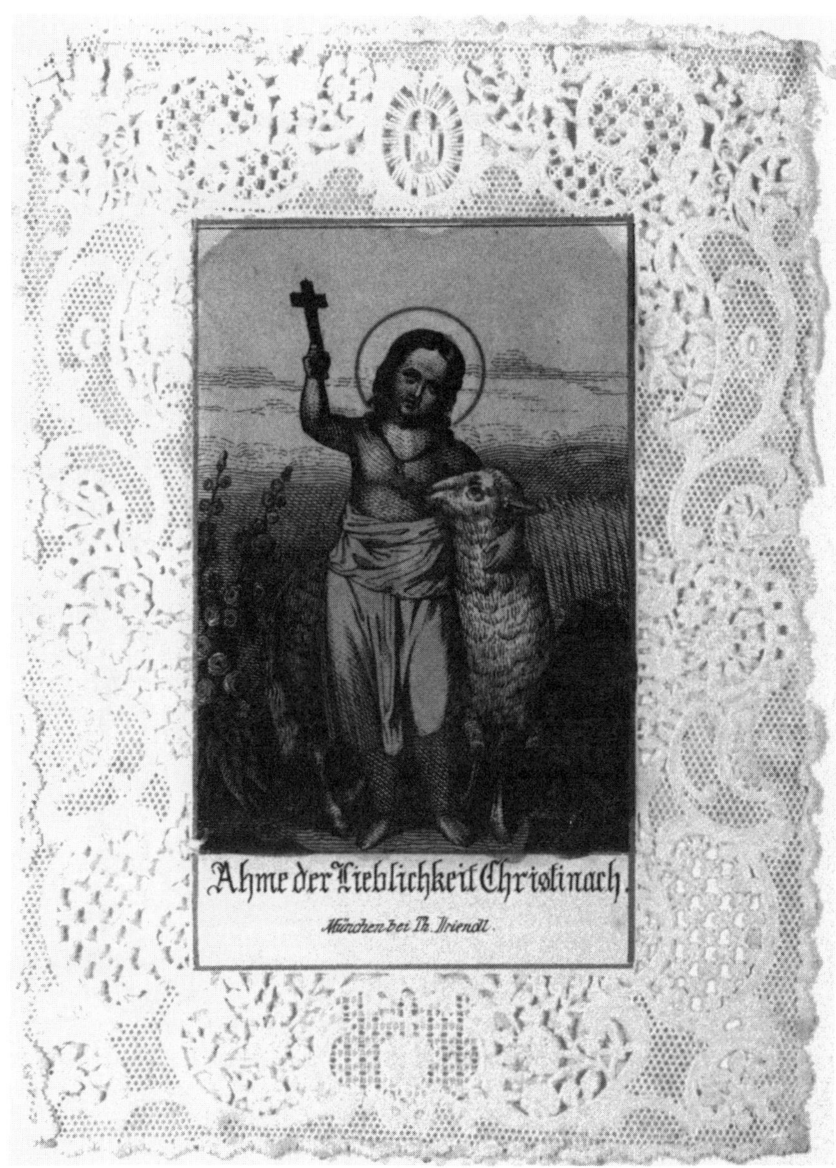

Figure 6. Thomas Driendl, devotional print.
(Bayerische Staatsbibliothek, Munich)

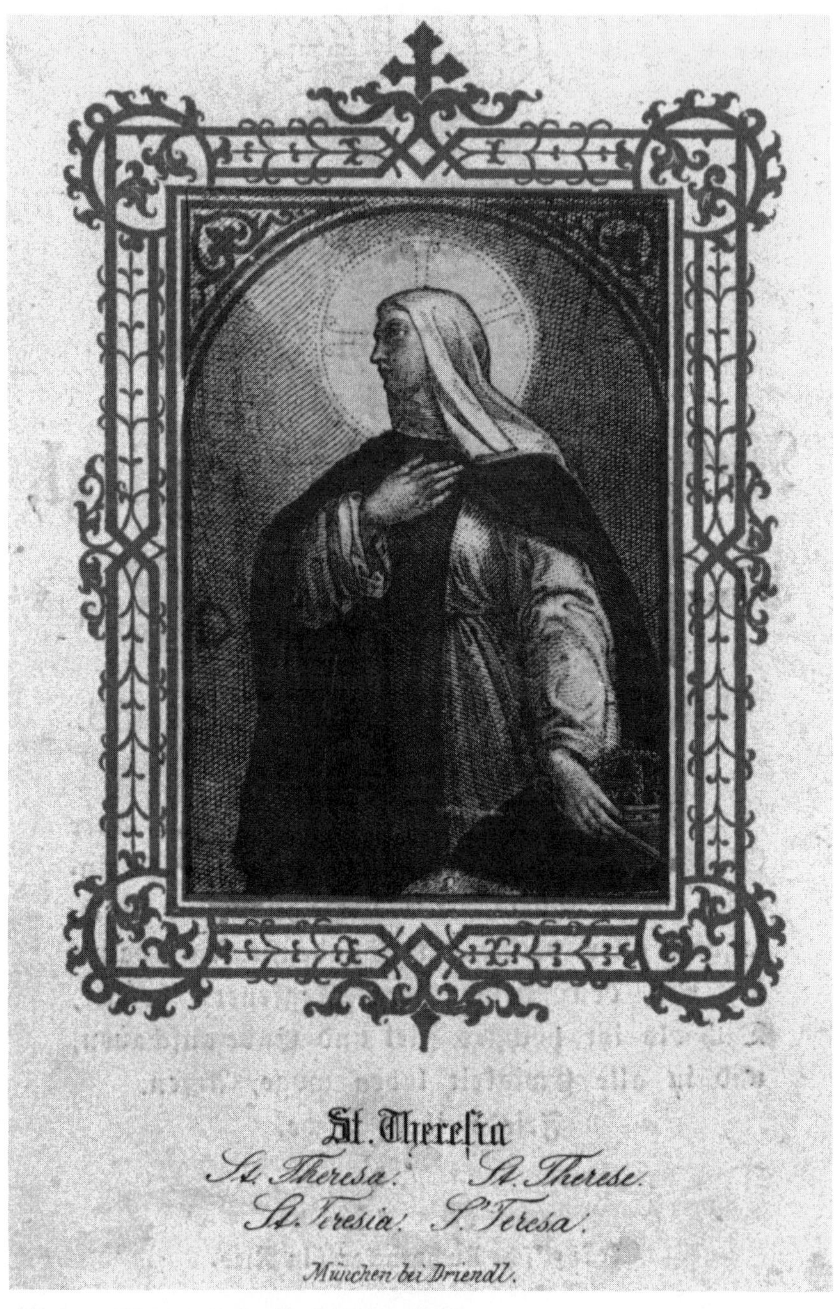

Figure 7. Thomas Driendl, devotional print.
(Bayerische Staatsbibliothek, Munich)

this market by the time the popular chromolithograph was available in sufficient quantities to offer any competition. It is certainly reasonable to argue that the success of glasspaintings helped to direct the course of the firm's development into the production of colorful and varnished *Wandschmuck*.[66]

Wentzel's lithographs must, nevertheless, be seen against a general background of interest shown by the manufacturers of graphic art during the nineteenth century in producing framable prints for the middle classes. Important centers for the production of these large prints emerged in Europe, notably in Paris, Berlin, and London, the same centers most significant for chromolithographic printing in the middle of the century. For Berlin alone, one author was able to count around thirty businesses handling *Wandschmuck*. Lithography made possible its increased availability, although older, more expensive techniques remained in use for exclusive products. In the period after 1840, the influential French producers were laying greater emphasis on copying contemporary artists' works in the less colorful tinted style of lithography—unlike oil painting—used at the time. Meanwhile, in Germany and the Anglo-Saxon countries commercialized lithography rapidly became popular. Little wonder that producers of broadsheets such as Wentzel who aspired to emulate the success of this market should attempt to translate fashionable styles into an idiom acceptable to their own more humble clientele.[67]

Outside Berlin, other centers for the production of *Wandschmuck* began to emerge in central Europe. In particular, the May factory in Frankfurt has attracted the attention of researchers into popular art, who have made it "paradigmatic" for the growth of a full-fledged chromolithographic factory out of a coloring establishment. E. G. May began his business in 1845 with the intention of making it an outlet for artistic prints, but he soon began producing colored pictures for the popular market, copying Wentzel and entering his markets among others. Later he also copied the products issuing from the major centers discussed above; by the mid-1850s he was even exporting "carefully colored genre prints" to England in addition to supplying his Continental markets. For successful businessmen like May, the 1860s and 1870s became a watershed between an intensified use of hand-applied colors and devices such as printed frames to provide satisfactory *Wandschmuck*, and the adoption of chromolithography for the same purpose. But to make this transition to full chromolithographic production possible, technological improvements were necessary that would make truly inexpensive printing a reality.[68]

The major breakthrough came with the manufacture of large numbers of mechanical presses beginning late in the 1860s. These high-powered machines were made necessary by lithographers' continued practice of printing even popular chromolithographs with many stones, and it was certainly no coincidence that such a burst of activity should take place in the technological side of the business at a time when the pressure of an expanding popular market for colored prints was becoming so strong. For only chromolithography could adequately satisfy this demand for inexpensive and colorful oil painting substitutes. By 1867, when a fifteen-year patent on the successful press invented by G. Sigl of Vienna and Berlin had expired, French manufacturers were displaying mechanical presses at the World's Fair. Soon German manufacturing plants were busily selling presses as well, and from that time on mechanization became more and more dominant in lithographic establishments, which took on to a still greater extent than before the characteristics of the modern factory. By 1882, for example, there were no less than 119 *Farbendruckerei* or "chromolithographic factories" in Berlin, according to official statistics, although this figure had apparently shrunk to 71 by 1895. Even in the city where lithography had been discovered less than a century earlier, now operating under the shadow of the German capital, the four *Farbendruckerei* identified in 1875 had only seven years later dramatically risen to 23.[69]

Although we must certainly bear in mind that other colorful products such as greeting cards, postcards, and calendars were likely to be manufactured in these factories alongside chromolithographs, the popular print was clearly responsible for a great part of this remarkable development. Pouring off mechanical presses by the thousands en route for popular markets were indeed the oil painting substitutes that Senefelder and his successors had dreamed of. It is interesting to note that the German chromolithographers singled out by one author for their "superiority" particularly favored "heavy strong colors" rather than the "fine, delicately modelled tints" of the French or the "soft effects and broad contrasts" of the English, according to an article in *Art Interchange* written in 1881. This was true as early as 1859 of the chromolithographs printed by Driendl, which could be admired by the anonymous author of an article in the *Bamberger Zeitung* because of their "brightness . . . and splendid color" that, together with their "durability," approximated the qualities of real oil paintings. Such qualities were also to prove of great importance for the popular chromolithograph; they were enhanced in these prints by the fashionable practice of including the varnished finish anticipated in Wentzel's colored lithographs. Manufacturers who wished to stress still further the role of their products as *Wandschmuck* could imprint them with the look of canvas as well.[70] Of course, much the same role had been filled by glasspaintings for at least a century before lithography became the primary means by which the popular taste for wall-paintings was met. So it is not surprising that one can trace the way in which colored prints were shaped into pictures that resembled not only the oil paintings hung in art galleries or in the homes of wealthy families but also the glasspaintings that decorated the humbler *Herrgottswinkel* as well. With the advent of these chromolithographs, urban factory workers had triumphed over the rural producers of glasspaintings, and the process of replacement begun with the lithographs issuing forth from Weißenburg, Frankfurt, and other city centers was complete. That replacement depended, however, on lithographers' use of distribution networks linking them to the consumers of their products, just as they had linked the glasspainters before them. So the story of these networks of agents and hawkers developed by glasspainters and lithographers provides the focus of the next chapter.

3

A Market Shared: The Distribution of Glasspaintings and Lithographs

The manufacturers of glasspaintings, and later lithographers as well, inherited long-established methods of distribution for artistic products. They could rely on a network of European trading centers, linked by road or river, that in turn connected with overseas routes reaching as far as the Americas, Africa, and India. And both postal and freight facilities combined with the ready service of a large number of hawkers to enable them to distribute their wares efficiently over long distances. The Upper Bavarian glasspainting centers were fortuitously situated on major trading routes (see map). The ancient *Römerstrasse* or Roman road running from Italy through the Brenner Pass to Augsburg had passed through Murnau. Later, the emergence of Munich as a royal center led to the establishment of a link between that city and the flourishing traffic still passing through the Brenner along a major trade route known as the *Rottstrasse*. Since Murnau lay on this route, the town became a *Rottniederlage* or halting station. Oberammergau too was situated on another of the main stretches of *Rottstrasse* that linked Augsburg to Venice, passing through Innsbruck, Mittenwald, and Garmisch before it reached Oberammergau, and continuing on via Schongau to the city itself. These direct links with Augsburg and Munich enabled glasspainters to take advantage of extensive trading connections lying beyond the major southern German centers. Water routes, long established as the primary means of transporting merchandise from southern Germany to international ports such as Amsterdam and Hamburg or to the central European heartland around Vienna,

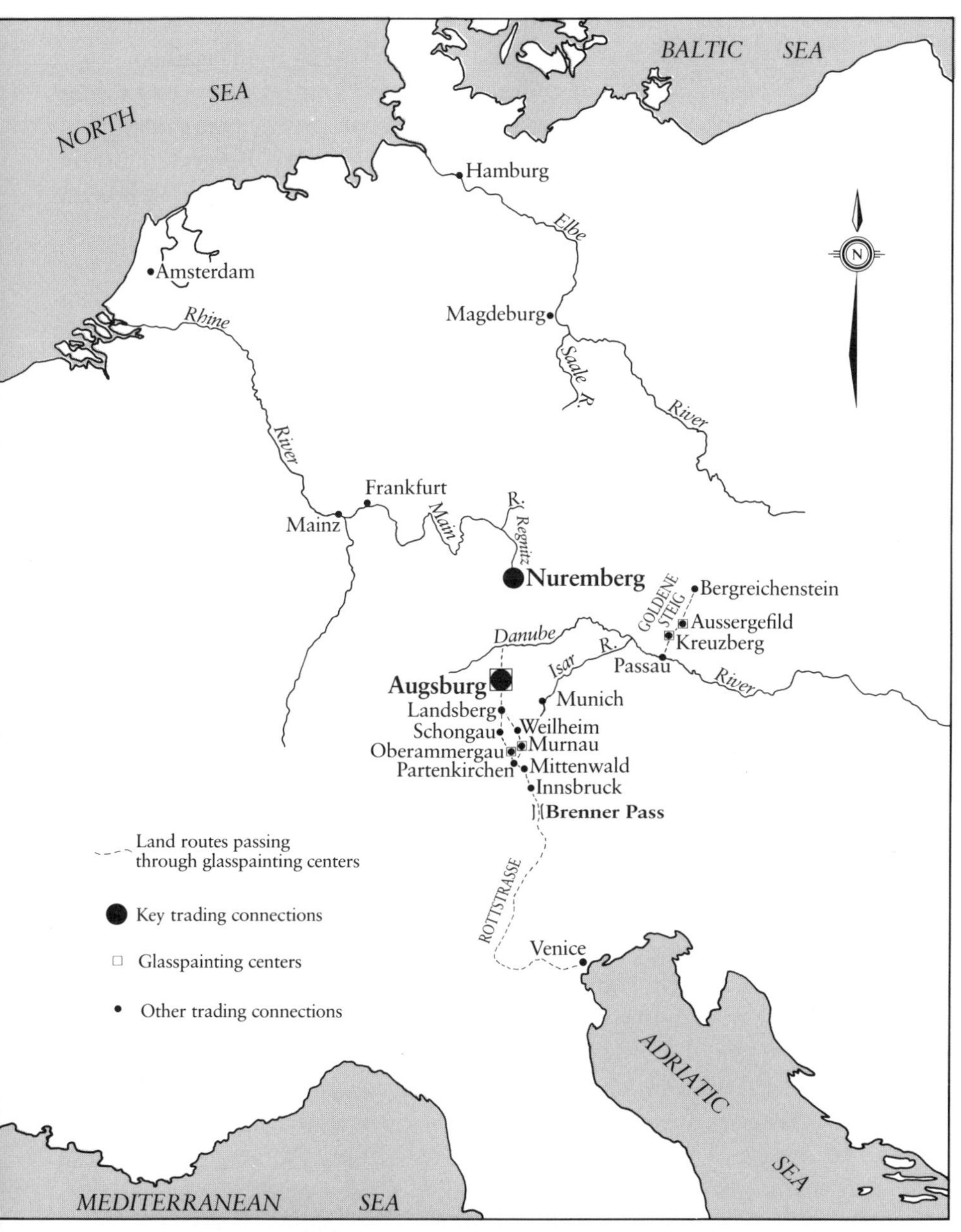

Central European Land and Water Trading Routes Open to Glasspainting Centers

were within easy reach of both cities and of Nuremberg as well. Even Murnau was linked by the Loisach and the Isar to the Danube.[1]

The Bavarian Forest glasspainters were also located on trading routes long established in the area. One branch of the *Goldene Steig* ran from Passau through Kreuzberg and Außergefild to Bergreichenstein in Bohemia. Here the *Säumer* or muleteers would pass through with their loads of salt or grain, setting the pattern for subsequent trading links between the two countries. We have observed the presence of Raimundsreuth and Kreuzberg glasspainters in Außergefild late in the eighteenth century, and their activities serve to emphasize the large Austro-Hungarian market for glasspaintings that lay beyond the Bavarian border. Colonies of glasspainters in Buchers, Bohemia, and Sandl, Austria, also developed the potential of this area; they made use both of the Danube flowing east from nearby Linz to transport their wares into eastern Europe and of routes running south through the Alps, probably to reach the Italian markets also served by Upper Bavarian painters.[2]

Thus, village entrepreneurs such as the Langs could call on wagon and postal services, together with the transportation available on river routes and the larger cargo ships setting out from the ports of western Europe, to connect them with the many trading centers mentioned in their account books. Sometimes their shipping methods are referred to specifically in these records, giving the reader a glimpse into the mechanics of this very complicated operation. At other times the implication of a network of wagons, shipping, and agents lies behind a simple notation that an order has been delivered. Only at the very end of our period could railway communications have made any substantial inroads into the shipping of freight; even in the mid-nineteenth century branch lines linking small places like Murnau and Oberammergau to the major rail system were still lacking. The Murnau line, for example, opened in 1879.[3]

Over land routes such as the *Rottstrasse,* wagoners drove their horse-drawn wagons bearing *Kisten* (crates) packed with goods entrusted to their care. An excellent source for envisaging the activities of these wagons is provided by the numerous accounts of their accidents recorded in votive paintings. Not only do these paintings reproduce for us the physical appearance of the different styles of transportation vehicles employed for freight haulage, but they also remind us of the hardships and dangers involved in such travel during this period before good roads became available.[4] And freight services continued to play an important role into the 1830s. Several of the towns in the Oberammergau area offered this convenience, for much of Johann Evangelist Lang's shipping made use of them rather than of the Royal postal service. By the mid-nineteenth century the Bavarian post was in full operation as the successor to the *Reichspost* or Imperial post run by the Thurn and Taxis family throughout the old Empire; so Lang used it as well, to ship goods to Nuremberg in particular. Yet the records suggest that a customary recourse to freight carriers was still proving extremely advantageous to businessmen as a supplement to the regular postal system.[5]

Goods like glasspaintings traveling beyond the range of local haulers must usually have been shipped along the river routes outlined in map 1. Both the Rhine and the Elbe provided obvious links between the southern German trading centers and the coast, with the consequence that the routes followed by merchants from those centers clung to the rivers. To Hamburg the route from Munich passed through Nuremberg, Leipzig, and Magdeburg, and to Amsterdam the route followed the Rhine valley through Mainz and Cologne. The Rhine could be reached by way of towns either on the Danube and the Main or on the Danube and the Neckar. Fernand Braudel has revived the Werner Sombart thesis that "overland transport carried more goods than inland waterways," and in recapitulating how these "inland waterways . . . carried big boats and little boats, barges, rafts, tree-trunks roped together," Braudel does suggest that the handiness of river transport has been overestimated. But he also refers specifically to the "substantial river traffic" of the Rhine and the Elbe (without mentioning the Danube), and all manner of boats and rafts were certainly available as resources to the tradesman, although there is little direct evidence to prove that the glasspainters took advantage of them. Georg Lang does mention the use of lake shipping, and Vinzenz Köck of Sandl could ship goods via the steamboat service available on the Danube by the 1860s. Closer to home, the three raftsmen of Murnau must have offered their services to local craftsmen. Jakob März's drowning in the Danube may well have been due to the open arrangements of these rudimentary means of transport.[6]

When goods sent out from village centers reached the sea, they were entrusted to overseas vessels headed for England; Russia, Poland, and Scandinavia; Spain and Portugal; or the New World, Africa, and India.

Again, direct glimpses are rare, although a ship carrying goods for the Oberammergau merchant family Buchwieser stationed in Amsterdam was reported sunk. A member of another Oberammergau family, Joachim Steinbacher, was drowned at sea in 1762, apparently off Rotterdam. In 1785, Sebastian Hohenleutner returned to Oberammergau from Cadiz, where he had established a business with connections in Lima. He traveled home via Genoa, a port that may have been used by the merchants in Augsburg who handled glasspaintings, despite the fact that the most obvious trading route leading into Italy from Augsburg and Oberammergau was the one through the Brenner Pass to Venice discussed above. Hohenleutner's route indicates the possibility that goods destined for Cadiz were shipped from Genoa as well as from Amsterdam. From Cadiz "whole shiploads" of Oberammergau merchandise are reported leaving for Africa.[7]

The flow of goods over these extended trading routes was facilitated by the establishment of family agencies or businesses such as Hohenleutner's in important ports and outlets. According to an article written in 1800 to describe the village's trading activities, "all shipments result from the orders of local tradesmen settled in all parts of the world," a claim not unreasonably made at that time on the basis of a current list of the many locations in which villagers were to be found:

Denmark

Copenhagen:
Jakob Lindner.
Veit Blankensteiner.

Norway

Christiania:
Sebastian Widder.
David Lindner.
Anton Seiler.

Drontheim:
Hohenleutner.

Sweden

Göteborg:
Georg Echtler.
Martin Echtler, d. 1785.

Russia

St. Petersburg:
Andreas Seiler.
Georg Stickl's widow, now in Augsburg.

Spain

Madrid:
Saam now in Augsburg.

Cadiz:
Sebastian Hohenleutner, together with others from Eschenlohe and Huglfing.

Holland

Amsterdam:
Steinbacher, Faistenmantel and others.
Steinbacher, whose brother has an outstanding business.

Poland

Warsaw:
Stephan and Bauchofer are active there.

Danzig:
Vogel.

Wiltau:
Stephan the younger.

Germany

Vienna:
Hohenleutner, active.

Bremen:
Buchwiser, together with others from Farchant.[8]

Similar lists of family names connected with a variety of European trading centers were compiled around 1815 and in the mid-nineteenth century by Daisenberger. They vary to some extent from this one, suggesting the possibility that some families were less permanently involved abroad than others. In general, however, the claim of all three sources that Oberammergauers were settled in many European cities during the eighteenth century is substantiated by information on the locations of villagers' deaths away from home during that period. While some took place in areas relatively close to the village, indicating perhaps that the victims had set off on foot to hawk village goods, others occurred in more distant countries: Sardinia, Denmark, Poland, Italy, Hungary, Sweden, Norway, and Russia.[9] It was not at all unusual for villagers specializing in goods for export to enjoy these kinds of extended trading connections. For example, Daisenberger reports that Grödner craftsmen from the Tyrol, who were competitors for Oberammergau's markets, had established around 150 firms in Germany, the Netherlands, Italy, Spain, Portugal, and America by the end of the eighteenth century, a time by which, he claims, the number of Oberammergau's foreign outlets had substantially declined. But despite these farflung interests, ties to home remained strong for the men residing abroad; Oberammergauers at least would retain a holding in the village and leave behind both wife and children to whom they would return for visits. When possible, they would also retire there, handing on business responsibilities to their children.[10]

These local agents continued to play a key role in maintaining the village's business connections into the period of the Napoleonic Wars. Andreas Lang, however, also developed a pattern of business that his nephew Johann Evangelist Lang was to pursue very successfully in the mid-nineteenth century by establishing business relationships with firms unconnected with the village and located in cities all over Europe.

Andreas commonly shipped goods to customers located in many different parts of Europe, including Cadiz and London, during the first few years covered by the account book he started in 1804; the firm's trade then declined substantially during the extremely delicate period after about 1808 and only temporarily picked up again around 1815. At times, Andreas even used an intermediary company or business associate to whom the goods were dispatched for forwarding to their final destinations. For example, he used Joseph Carmine from Augsburg to send on a shipment of goods destined for Bruges in 1804; in the same year he entrusted Georg Hartman in Venice with the "disposition" of an order for the Italian city of Modena. Yet Andreas's business methods still represented a compromise between dealings with local personnel on the one hand and less community-based modes of operation on the other. He sent goods to Copenhagen for a local man, Jacob Hois, and to Luzern for his brother-in-law, a Deisenberger from Unterammergau. Both he and his brother Georg employed another brother, Joseph, to convey goods to Hamburg. Moreover, when the firm's business became greatly circumscribed after 1820, his son Martin dealt a good deal with members of his own family, while his best customers in the 1830s and 1840s were first Johann Baptist and later Ignaz Schmid from Murnau.[11]

In these ways, village merchants made use of the major international trading routes and facilities described above to distribute a wide variety of products that must often have included glasspaintings. As a caution, Georg Lang's records from the period from 1797 to 1811 show no sign of any orders that included glasspaintings at all. So it is unwise to assume, without the direct evidence provided by a detailed accounting of his shipments of goods, that a merchant would necessarily have handled glasspaintings. Nevertheless, it does seem reasonable to argue for the strong possibility that these ornamental or devotional objects would have found their way to at least some of the locations with which the glasspainting centers had established connections during the eighteenth century. There is no doubt, in particular, that paintings from Upper Bavarian centers were being exported to Spain before the Napoleonic Wars, and they may even have traveled on from there to the colonial customers cultivated by village agents. For we do know from contemporary sources that the Augsburg merchants who handled glasspaintings had already developed markets in Spain, Portugal, America, and India, while the article describing Utzschneider's efforts on behalf of the Lake Staffel glasspainters confirms that the glasspainting business in general had reached as far as Spain, Holland, and America before the war. And when Franz Schrank visited Oberammergau in 1786, he was able to observe the contents of a shipment of goods prepared by the Lang brothers for dispatch to Cadiz. Apparently, Andreas Lang was including glasspaintings of birds for such shipments, and Schrank felt impelled to give him the name of Edward's *Naturgeschichte der Vögel* as a future source of reference for this enterprise. He was sure that by the time he was writing down his memories of this encounter, Lang was already "lecturing in Spain on natural history by means of his paintings."[12]

When the detailed records of Andreas's business affairs begin in the early nineteenth century, however, he was no longer including glasspaintings in the crates of goods ordered by a company from Cadiz. Nor were his paintings included in many of the other shipments that he made during these last few years before his company's decline. Nevertheless, he did send paintings to firms in both southern and western Europe at that time by the standard international routes to destinations in Austria, Belgium, France, Italy, and Switzerland. His connections with foreign trading centers were thus influential in establishing outlets for this branch of his business as well. It is unfortunate that we cannot augment the evidence for a widespread market in glasspaintings provided by Andreas's accounts with any surviving records for the Peter Lang business reported to be the most important in Oberammergau by 1815. For since Peter's father Anton was the merchant who had ordered glass for the village painters from the Aschau factory before his death in 1794, the likelihood is strong that his son's operations would have encompassed glasspaintings too. Certainly the presence of nine glasspainters in Oberammergau, twelve in Murnau, and several more in Seehausen and Uffing around 1800 suggests a more substantial trading potential than Andreas's rather limited orders for glasspaintings and the local market could have accounted for. Even after the war, two of the Weilheim district's painters registered in 1823 were listed as trading "abroad."[13]

As supraregional businessmen, those villagers whose trade depended on these far-reaching foreign connections were exposed to the disruptive effects of war and other international crises. Naturally, the agencies located in other countries could be of most benefit to their home firms when peace reigned both at home and abroad. Such peaceful conditions prevailed throughout large parts of the eighteenth century, but the Napoleonic Wars upset both Oberammergau and Murnau's trade drastically, although the Grödner agencies mentioned above do not appear to have been similarly affected. Daisenberger notes that together with the conditions created by the wars, competition from the Grödner craftsmen was damaging Oberammergau's trade, and, moreover, Utzschneider's concern to reeducate Lake Staffel glasspainters to contemporary styles finds an echo in the priest's comment about changing tastes as well. All these problems resulted from engaging in a business that far overreached local boundaries and local standards.[14] Despite their apparent recovery of some international outlets in the 1810s, the Upper Bavarian painters clearly suffered from a permanent alteration in the shape of their market. All surviving records of the mid-nineteenth century trade in glasspaintings suggest that their radius of operations had contracted to encompass primarily the central European Catholic heartland supplied by Lower Bavarian painters. Not even within the context of the growing international connections enjoyed by Johann Evangelist Lang in the 1830s did glasspaintings find their way to the more important European centers with which he was doing business. Certainly, he sent shipments to places as far away as Fulda, Offenbach, Coblenz, and Cologne, and to the pilgrimage center of Kevelaer on the Dutch border.[15] But the majority of the orders for glasspaintings that he filled traveled no further than to southern German locations, in response to the traditional demand for religious paintings so well-developed there.

Because Lang's paintings were destined for the central European market, it is not surprising to find that several of his customers were almost certainly traveling salesmen. The producers who concentrated on local markets had always relied on the services of such men to distribute their paintings. However, the peregrinations of *Kraxenträger* such as the seventeen recorded in Uffing in 1752 or the many who operated under the aegis of Oberammergau's hawking concession also accounted for a good deal of the international trade conducted from glasspainting villages. For foreign trade was easily handled on foot, and both men and goods could make use of the traveling facilities available on both road and river routes. For example, the *Kraxenträger* employed by Andreas Lohberger of Deggendorf in Lower Bavaria during the late eighteenth century were able to peddle their wares as far as

France and Switzerland. By the nineteenth century the most enterprising forays were those being conducted by the Tyrolean *Kraxenträger* who sold paintings produced by Buchers and Sandl glasspainters in the farther reaches of the Austro-Hungarian Empire. The glasspainting seller in figure 4, who is portrayed in the early chromolithograph *Market in Transylvania,* must have been one of these men. In any case, the ability of *Kraxenträger* to cover enormous distances meant that their employment could complement the more sophisticated entrepreneurial practices developed by village merchants. At the same time, however, they also remained at the heart of the local trade in glasspaintings, and their ready service goes far to explain the strength and persistence of this traditional market.[16]

Whatever the actual range of an individual *Kraxenträger*'s journey, the profession was becoming an international one during this period. Initially, local men and women would set out on foot to sell the products of their own villages. Indeed, Lohberger himself and other members of his household actually both produced and distributed their own paintings. However, this combination of productive and marketing activities within a single village or within the same family gave way to the establishment of manufacturing centers on the one hand and villages specializing in the sale of specific products on the other. Because of this development, villages particularly significant for the distribution of glasspaintings emerged in the Fersental valley of Southern Tyrol and in the Gottschee district of Carniola, both areas in which the inhabitants had been obliged to seek additional incomes for their families because of the general poverty of their agricultural holdings. Meanwhile, the streamlining of productive efforts in places like Raimundsreuth led to the increased dependence of workers there on the services of these salesmen from outside the village. Government interference with the free passage of foreign *Kraxenträger* could consequently result in the kind of hardship that Raimundsreuth experienced in 1819.[17]

The typical *Kraxenträger* would have been male, although women were not excluded from participating in this arduous employment. Anna Maria Hansbäurin, a retiree, sold paintings for Lohberger in 1780, as did Barbara Schmidin in 1784, his own daughter Katharina in 1785–86, Johannes Steinbeißer's sister Theresia in 1803, and the wife and daughter of Lorenz Simbeck in 1804. Many of these salesmen were young, such as seventeen-year-old Andreas Schuster who worked for Johann Pomeisl of Oberanschießing in Lower Bavaria in

1823–24 or eighteen-year-old Johann Stephandl employed by Joseph Peterhansl. Andreas Meditz was twenty-seven and Andreas Schuster's brother Peter twenty-one when they too obtained passes in 1823 to sell paintings for Johann Pomeisl. Josef Deutschmann, who worked for Johann Verderber out of Außergefild, was twenty-three in 1826 when he entered the profession. According to a report sent in 1807, the Fersental hawkers were also twenty to twenty-five years old. Since both the Gottschee region and the Fersental valley were areas with German-speaking populations, there was no language barrier to overcome. Most of the Fersental men apparently even spoke Hungarian as well.[18]

Because of the part-time nature of the profession, most *Kraxenträger* traveled during the winter while their holdings did not require their attention, which must have made their work particularly challenging and even dangerous at times. The death of two Oberammergau men found frozen by the roadside near Kassel in Hesse on January 17, 1770, says as much. There was also the chance that an accident such as the one that overtook an informant of Josef Blau's might bring sudden ruin to the entire enterprise. As this man was carrying not paintings but glass panes in his pack, he slipped on the icy road and "fell so heavily on his back that the whole load splintered into thousands of pieces." Only the kindness of the supplier in replenishing his stock saved him from losing the last of his financial resources in this way. Quite apart from the rigors of winter travel, the heavy wooden pack in which the *Kraxenträger* customarily carried his goods from place to place must have demanded considerable strength and endurance of its bearer. One such *Kraxe* laden with crucifixes, toys, and other village products shows visitors to the Oberammergau museum just how cumbersome a burden this form of portable, at times even lockable, shop could be. The charming statue that stands in the center of the village outside the Lang establishment pays tribute to the fortitude of these enterprising travelers.[19]

The *Kraxenträger* from Carniola and the Tyrol would, of course, have to make arrangements to pick up the paintings prepared in the village centers in order to convey them to their customers. Usually this entailed a journey to the center itself, unless the individual had established himself in the village as some hawkers were able to do. In the case of the Fersentalers, as many as twenty to thirty would travel together in a group to Buchers, where they arranged for the paintings to be shipped down the Danube to the southeastern areas in which they had established their markets. There they parted, after agreeing to rendezvous later at a prearranged location in Styria or Austria in order to settle accounts and travel home together. By contrast, it is touching to find that the two Schuster brothers traveled close to each other throughout the duration of their tour around Bavaria in 1823–24. The official stamps affixed to their passes show them repeatedly meeting at intervals after separate forays into the Bavarian countryside. And for the final leg of their journey, they joined forces all the way from Wolfstein to Parsberg. Some of these hawkers were even able to settle (at least temporarily) in the glasspainting centers out of which they worked. The glasspainter Paul Janke was one of these, comfortably integrated after his marriage into the Peterhansl family in 1816; so were Michael Verderber, founder of the Außergefild family, and the hawker Josef Deutschmann. Janke underlined the connection when he stood as witness at Deutschmann's wedding in 1841.[20]

These traveling salesmen appear to have established friendly depots in key areas where paintings might be sent to await their arrival. It is likely that the extended nature of Stephandl's journey, for example, depended on shipments of paintings sent to him at the points along the way that he visited repeatedly. In addition, a visit to Murnau later in his journey makes it possible that he was selling Upper Bavarian paintings on the last leg of his long trip. This is even more likely to have been the case for Andreas Meditz, since he passed through Murnau several times during the few months he was on the road. By contrast, both the Schusters returned twice to Wolfstein during their travels, once in late December 1823 and again in March 1824. In the 1830s we find Johann Evangelist Lang shipping paintings to Carniolan salesmen; he even required cash on delivery for this service on occasion. He also supplied paintings to several local men from the Thaining area, who may well have been traveling salesmen, gathering up their wares at various locations. Quite often an innkeeper would store the shipment of goods for Lang's customers in anticipation of the salesman's arrival. In 1844 a letter written by Josef Braker of Carniola requested Wistner in Schönstein to send his paintings either to Vilsbiburg or fourteen days later to Landshut. A similar letter written in 1853 to Alois Gege by a traveling salesman ordered paintings to be delivered by the next Ingolstadt freight at the Post in Reichertshofen. The Fersentalers would also have their paintings shipped to eastern locations, as we have seen, and they even ordered paintings for their own district, where they had developed a good local market.[21]

These records illustrate the kind of detailed coverage of a sales district that only the *Kraxenträger* could achieve, because they were so mobile and flexible. They were able to take advantage of all the opportunities offered both by the local fairs and markets and by church festivities and pilgrimages. Moreover, it seems likely that they would also have visited individual houses, as the word *Hausierhandel,* often applied to their occupation as hawkers, implies. Nevertheless, markets and similar gatherings seem to have been their major source of custom. An official letter dated 1825 suggests as much when it states that the hawkers "primarily gad about in small towns and markets . . . [and] treat parish fêtes and fairs as if they belonged there." This letter clearly exemplifies the hostility that existed between the salesmen and Bavarian officialdom, as may be observed in the Raimundsreuth painters' loss of hawking support in 1819. There are also reports of hostilities expressed between the visiting salesmen and local tradesmen. For, of course, established shopkeepers could certainly be expected to exploit the market for paintings that lay at their doorsteps. Often special events in localities could draw substantial crowds and, therefore, potential customers. We have noted, for example, Matthias Noder's order from Father Bäumer in Dingolfing for four thousand paintings; the priest expected no less than twenty-five to thirty thousand visitors for the jubilee festival that he was planning. Regular pilgrimage attendance often drew even larger crowds, such as the sixty thousand counted during the three "Golden Saturdays" in October 1777 at Kreuzberg. When local glasspainters were not on hand to take advantage of these visiting pilgrims, local businessmen, priests, and monasteries must often have seized the opportunity to profit from their ready custom along with the hawkers.[22]

Edward Shorter has drawn attention to the way in which the hawkers, as distributors of industrial products, were instrumental in forwarding the transition from traditional to modern forms of production. In this context, the role of the *Kraxenträger* in the dissemination of glasspaintings was matched by that of the hawkers who sold lithographs for firms like Wentzel and May during the mid-nineteenth century. For lithographic producers had inherited this traditional means of reaching rural customers from the engraving and woodcutting workshops of the past. An article written in 1807, for example, discusses the printsellers from the Tesino area of the Tyrol, neighbors of the Fersental glasspainting salesmen. The author claims that after about 1750 "the engravings from London, Paris, Rome, Venice, Florence, Vienna, and Augsburg were now sold primarily by Tesiners throughout Germany and in many other countries as well." The success of these "Tyrolean peasants," however, had permitted some of them to set up *Niederlagen,* or permanent agencies, in many key European cities in addition to the hawking activities of their fellow villagers. And big firms in Augsburg and the other urban printing centers must have enjoyed the benefit of the more sophisticated kind of trading connections that entrepreneurs such as the Langs later developed. Shorter correctly stresses the importance of this kind of resource for the industrial producer as well.[23]

When Wentzel began to print popular broadsheets in the mid-nineteenth century, he started humbly enough, employing hawkers both from the mountainous regions of Gascony in southern France and from his local town of Weißenburg and the surrounding areas. In particular, a small group of professional salesmen from the Bavarian Palatinate made up the core of a more permanent sales force working for Wentzel on the French side of the border. Other Bavarians must have covered the German market, such as the thirty-nine-year-old "'print seller' Heinrich Schmidt in company with his daughter Margaretha Schmidt, 18 years old, domiciled in Pirmasens, who travels the Zollverein states and Switzerland to sell pictures." These men seem often to have been older than the hawkers we have identified as working out of glasspainting centers. Frédéric Hartmann of Pirmasens, for example, was thirty-five years old when he obtained a colportage permit. Léonard Kassner of Saarunion was older still, fifty-eight in 1850 and over seventy when he last took out a permit in 1865. Several were women, such as Margarete Türk (the widow Kuntz). Their coverage was as successful as their Carniolan counterparts; in the Department of the Lower Rhine alone Wentzel's hawkers sold an average of around one hundred thousand prints a year between 1858 and 1869, roughly one for every six inhabitants.[24]

Wentzel's competitor May soon saw the advantage of employing hawkers from the Palatinate as well, using them to introduce his products to the same markets that Wentzel was supplying. Both firms also worked with the Tesiner hawkers, now back to working with central European customers. Possibly they used the Fersental hawkers as well, since some of these men were selling printed pictures of saints in the late nineteenth century, according to a description of them written in 1884. May's first contact with the Tesiners may have been as late as 1879, although it is possible that the firm had used their services to compete with Wentzel much earlier. Just when Wentzel himself began to enlarge his markets in this way is not certain, but the presence of his prints in Alpine houses already noted by Ludwig Steub in 1862 suggests that he had made use of the Tesiners by that time. In 1869 Karl Stieler observed these traveling printsellers as they journeyed through the Tyrolean and Bavarian heartland, laboring mightily, "for the chest that they carry on their backs sometimes weighs a hundredweight. Since they are frequently on the road for a long time, they often bring with them the trappings of a household as well as their art treasures: pans, linen, sewing-kit, and other things. A minor son of more or less mysterious origin and a shaggy dog make up the retinue. . . . Thus they proceed over hill and dale, from cabin to Alp." Thus, by visiting markets and church festivities as well as individual houses, Bavarian and Tyrolean hawkers put the lithographs produced by city workers into the hands of the rural Catholic customers of central Europe.[25]

Meanwhile, when Jakob Gramer took over Weishaupt's chromolithographic factory in Munich, he began working with a group of *Geschäftsreisenden*, or traveling salesmen, made up of a mixture of local and out-of-town men, some from as far away as Baden. In 1847 at least ten men set out on his behalf, some entrusted with the task of securing orders for prints from Bavarian customers. This may have meant that the stock-in-hand of the *Kraxenträger* was becoming a case of samples from which consumers could select the prints best suited to their needs. However, even in 1860, Gramer was still using his personnel to sell prints in the fairs and markets of both Bavaria and the other Zollverein states.[26]

Similarly, Thomas Driendl found the services of a *Geschäftsreisende* indispensable when he began to organize ways of promoting his new *Ölfarbendruckbilder* in the 1850s. In Kaufbeuren he made contact with a certain Ludwig Gerzabeck whom he supplied with samples of the large prints that were his specialty. Gerzabeck then set out to visit the larger towns in Bavaria and Austria, including centers like Bamberg, Nuremberg, and Innsbruck. In such places he would rent a room in order to arrange an exhibition of his prints to which art lovers and both secular and religious officials were invited. This gave them the chance to view Driendl's products and make their orders. Gerzabeck claimed that his method helped Driendl to avoid having to deal with the inadequacies of artistic retail stores and to send out samples to a great many different places at once. Moreover, the prints were mostly too big to make colportage an option for him.[27]

Perhaps the services of *Geschäftsreisenden* taking orders for prints helped Wentzel and May establish the customer networks that first must have complemented the sales activities of their hawkers and later far outstripped them, if Wentzel's records are any guide.[28] In any event, both firms were soon able to expand their business horizons well beyond local limits by entering the international export market in prints. May found customers in England, Austria, and Poland during the 1850s, and the Danish market also established at this time remained a lucrative one for the firm until the early twentieth century. An attempt to create a sales network for chromolithographs in southern Germany apparently failed, leaving May with the alternative of calling on the Tesiners instead. In France, on the other hand, May was able to find a helpful representative in the Lyon firm of Gadola and Company, at least until the imposition of prohibitive tariffs after 1890. Late in the century the May firm was exporting all over Europe, "from Sweden to Malta, from Spain to Poland," and beyond.[29]

Surviving records of Wentzel shipments give us a clear picture of the very similar export business conducted by that firm around 1870. By this time the railway had become an important means for exporting prints, and the firm could also rely on the agency of intermediate firms as the Langs had done. The assistance of Philippe Edouard Scherer, located near the Weißenburg station, was particularly significant for Wentzel in this respect. Like other provincial exporters of prints, the firm formed a special relationship with a distributor in Paris, Nicolas Humbert of 65 Rue Saint Jacques and later his widow. In the mid-1860s one of Wentzel's sons took over this important outlet for the huge number of his family's prints destined for French customers; in 1869–70 French markets accounted for 50 percent of the firm's income, and Alsace for a further 11 percent. Yet they had also made contact with a network of retail outlets extending over the better part of central and eastern Europe that, with France, became "Wentzel territory." This area reached Dublin and London to the west, Saint-Gaudens in southern France, Milan, Brixen, Graz, and Warsaw to the south and east, and Amsterdam and Kiel to the north. Eight percent of the income derived from the non-French part of this huge market resulted from sales to the Polish national pilgrimage center in Czenstochau, while ten other strategically located cities, among them Cologne, Nuremberg, Milan, and Vienna, accounted for a further 42 percent. Curiously, Munich and Innsbruck each provided less than 1 percent, but the retailers of other Bavarian and Tyrolean towns were also customers, thus augmenting the total flow of prints to that important center for the diffusion of Catholic imagery.[30]

The petition for a loan submitted by Karl Heindel of Munich to the Bavarian government in 1859 provides another glimpse of the pattern of distribution adopted by lithographic producers. Heindel's business had been seriously disrupted by the Franco-Italian war, but he was expecting payments totaling over 16,000 gulden from his customers, and he listed these outstanding debts for the government's information. The significant number of priests and monasteries included in this list, over one-quarter of the total entries, is particularly interesting because it confirms the continued importance even in the mid-nineteenth century of this traditional sales outlet for popular prints. Like Wentzel, Heindel also sent prints to the Czenstochau pilgrimage center, while he supplied several retailers in the pilgrimage centers of Andechs and Mariazell closer to home as well. He claimed to have established agencies in key cities like Vienna, Breslau, and Bucharest, and to be shipping his lithographs to "Austria, Hungary, Italy, Greece, . . . Turkey, and Poland." But the general picture of his operations as they were revealed by the list of his debtors does not fully substantiate his own estimate of the situation. What his list does reveal, however, is the convergence between this market for religious lithographs and that of the glasspainting merchant Vinzenz Köck. Added to the evidence given above on the eastern extent of Wentzel's markets, the Heindel documents and Köck's accounts of his Austrian-based customer network both provide confirmation of the persistent significance of the central European Catholic consumers of religious pictures.[31]

At the heart of the marketing operations we have been considering stood the entrepreneur. Often he would distribute no more than the products of his own household's labor, but he also might act as a mediator between producer and retailer; at times he could even be responsible for organizing both the manufacture of the final product and its diffusion. Of course, this diversity of methods adopted by individual contributors to the industrialization of popular art is only to be expected, since the process encompassed both rural and urban producers, both household workshops and factories.

At the simplest level of business operations, the *Dorfmaler* was no more enterprising than any other village artisan whose direct working relationship with the consumer may be classified as *Handwerk* or *Preiswerk*.[32] On the one hand, he bought his raw materials from the glass factory and from artistic suppliers, and on the other he made personal transactions with his customers, sometimes, like Johann Baptist Reisbacher of Kollnburg bei Viechtach, recording them in an account book. Typical entries in his records read:

> 27 December (1832): In the Brackenbach parsonage one small votive tablet: St. Erasmus painted on glass—paid – gulden 9 kreuzer.
>
> 1 January, 1833: For Barbara Link, smallholder from Viechtach Mary the Helper painted on glass—paid – gulden 24 kreuzer.
>
> 22 January, 1844: To Bocksberg a St. Aloisius painted on glass, along with procurement of the glass without frame—paid – gulden 16 kreuzer.[33]

This direct system of consumer-producer relationships was effective even at some distance, given both the agency of hawkers and the ordering of goods from the producer by mail; we have observed both visiting salesmen and customers like Father Bäumer at this practice that would permit the customer to communicate particular iconographical requests directly back to the producer. Often, however, the system became more complicated when local merchants took charge of distributing local products. Ignaz Schmid, for example, was described as a distributor of artificial flowers for local workers, an activity from which he derived a percentage of the proceeds. It is very likely that his family were also distributors for the local glasspainters and that earlier Murnau merchants like Jakob März had also handled the town's paintings. To be sure, these men or members of their families were sometimes themselves glasspainters; Schmid for one must have painted, since he suffered from painter's colic. Yet the agency of these merchants also fits the classification *Kaufsystem* provided by theorists to characterize the distributive system of middlemen who sold the products of local workers as their agents. The simple relationship between customer and producer thus disappeared into the more complex network of trade that the industrializing process depended upon.[34]

The clearest example of this kind of mercantile mediation between petty village producers and the international market emerges from the records of Oberammergau's merchant family, the Langs, and its dealings with the glasspainters and other craftsmen of the village. Particularly under the leadership of Johann Evangelist Lang in the mid-nineteenth century, the Georg Lang sel Erben firm took such a commanding position in village commercial affairs that it could be argued to have usurped the independent distributive role of the craftsmen employed to fill its many orders for goods. The crisis of the late 1840s made the dependence of more than one hundred workers on Lang's ability to find customers for their products painfully clear, while his apparent sense of commitment to these craftsmen only serves to underscore their loss of self-sufficiency. Yet the description of their agreement with Lang states that they were under no obligation to deal with him; there were other merchants in Oberammergau at the time, and, indeed, some of these men may have supplied several distributors at once. Nevertheless, Lang's status as a distributor and the obvious dependence on his agency of the large workforce from which he gathered his merchandise qualify his operations as a *Kaufsystem*.[35]

There is even some evidence to suggest that the Langs had once run a *Verlagsystem*, or putting-out operation, in which raw materials were supplied to the producers by the merchant. As I mentioned in Chapter 1, Anton Lang was the only Oberammergau glasspainter recorded purchasing glass from the Aschau glass factory in the late eighteenth century, although there were apparently several glasspainters active in the village at that time. He may well have distributed the glass tablets to individual painters and received back their completed work; we know that Augsburg merchants were operating like this during the same period. If so, by the mid-nineteenth century, this intensely dependent relationship had diminished. For Johann Evangelist Lang's relationship to his workforce was no more than a *Kaufsystem*, in possible defiance of the teleology normally associated with rural manufacture.[36]

In contrast with the rural glasspainting workshops, the production of lithographs was clearly based in factories as a system of *Manufaktur*. It is true that this classification might also apply to the Verderber glasspainting setup, but for Wentzel and May, for instance, there is no mistaking the fact that they were the owners of lithographic factories.

On the other hand, the smaller establishments of men like Gramer and Driendl might have borne a closer resemblance to the preindustrial artisanal workshop. Quite when the designation factory becomes applicable is rather ambiguous. Nevertheless, under the direction of both Wentzel and May we find concentrated many workers earning wages for their labor in a single workplace. Stages in the completion of each print were coordinated under the same roof, and the development of a marketing network was the responsibility of an entrepreneur who at the same time remained in charge of organizing its manufacture. The gradual accumulation of ever more complex machinery completed this picture of a truly industrial workplace, marking the culmination of the industrializing process.[37]

Theorists of industrialization have linked the simpler *Kaufsystem* with this complex *Manufaktur* in their explanations of the transition to factory industry; they identify the transferral of "entrepreneurial skills" and "capital accumulation" as important reasons for this connection. It is certainly true that the smooth operation of both glasspainting and lithographic businesses relied on competent producers or merchants who could procure customers and identify their changing needs and tastes. Sufficient capital was also needed for the replenishment of stock, and in lithography for the upkeep and improvement of machinery and workspace together with the payment of the workforce as well. This necessity sometimes sent lithographic producers and even Johann Evangelist Lang searching for partners or for government support when their own private resources were insufficient. Neither the skills nor the capital to be found in the rural glasspainting centers, however, contributed to the founding of lithographic factories. There are simply no incidents of a glasspainting merchant moving into chromolithographic production. Rather, it was "market connections" that linked the rural glasspainters with the urban chromolithographers.[38] The next section of the book, therefore, examines the consumer networks shared by the two groups of producers and reconstructs the cultural rationale that lay behind the purchasing of religious images.

PART TWO

The

Glasspaintings

and the

Cultural

Context

4

Paintings for the Herrgottswinkel: *The Popular Market in Religious Art*

This chapter examines the products manufactured by glasspainters and lithographers; it also follows them as they travel home with their new owners to hang on the walls of living or sleeping quarters. These inexpensive glasspaintings and lithographs proved remarkably popular, as we have seen, in part because they represented the transformation of reproducible graphic artworks into bright and gleaming substitutes for oil paintings. Their appearance and style thus hearkened back to an older, more prestigious form of art, while making that form readily available to a much wider range of customers than the original paintings could ever reach. The key to the popularity of both glasspaintings and lithographs, however, was undoubtedly their iconographical content, which was usually religious in the case of popular glasspaintings and often religious even in nineteenth-century popular lithographs. When the story begins in the eighteenth century, the middle-class and colonial consumers of these framed paintings were buying a variety of both secular and religious themes; the customers of lithographers and chromolithographers also selected from a broad range of iconographical offerings. But it was the popular consumption of religious images for use in the home setting, more than any other consumer impulse, that stimulated the industrializing process by which the mass production of oil paintings became possible during the late nineteenth century. Both the attractive appearance of these products and their reiteration of traditional religious motifs therefore deserve our attention as motivating factors for the consumers who supported this redirection of the graphic arts industry.

The glasspaintings hanging from hawkers' poles or resting in the framework of their packs were carefully designed to appeal to a wide range of customers with varying degrees of ability to pay for these popular purchases. In this way the glasspainters reached a market that emphasized wealthier farmers and craftsmen but also reached those in the lower levels of the rural social scale. Not surprisingly, therefore, the size, the style and degree of schematization, and the decorative quality of these paintings varied enormously. For all price ranges, however, glasspainters could borrow from the graphic arts an array of decorative features that would enhance the attractiveness of the final product. Framing added the finishing touch to this charming furnishing of a family's home.

Surviving records confirm that the glasspainters made sure to provide many different sizes of glasspaintings for their customers. For example, when Father Bäumer placed his large order with Matthias Noder in 1816, he was careful to request that it include three or four sizes of paintings, "that is, smaller and somewhat larger ones, so that everyone can buy something." The Oberammergau account books give an excellent picture both of the possible variations in size and of the consequent variations in price that the priest was concerned about. A typical order registered in the Georg Lang sel Erben account book for the mid-1830s lists paintings in pairs:

Number of pairs:	10	3	6	6	6	5	3	2
Price in kreuzer:	6	8	10	12	15	22	30	38

for a total of 41 pairs at 9 gulden, 42 kreuzer. Lang's prices in the 1830s do not exceed a gulden for the most expensive pairs of paintings, whereas three decades earlier Andreas Lang's prices for single paintings could reach as high as 3 or 4 gulden for large ones and averaged around 45 kreuzer or 22½ kreuzer for smaller ones. A mixture of secular and religious themes offered at these substantial prices suggests the middle-class market for Andreas's firm; the prices offered by Georg's firm, on the other hand, were clearly intended to appeal to the much wider market of less wealthy customers. A letter to Josef Wistner written in 1844 links content to price at this lower end of the spectrum:

2 Last Supper	18 kreuzer each
2 Holy Trinity and four House Patrons	18 kreuzer
4 Holy Trinity and four House Patrons	12 kreuzer

4 Joseph and Mary	8 kreuzer
12 assorted Saints	8 kreuzer each
12 ditto	6 kreuzer
20 Souls in Purgatory	3 kreuzer
100 Souls in Purgatory	2 kreuzer

By the 1850s Alois Gege was able to offer pairs of these souls in purgatory at only 3 kreuzer as well, while his prices ranged overall by pairs from 40 kreuzer through 30, 15, 12, to 3 kreuzer. The cheapest of these nineteenth-century paintings were of necessity very small, only a few inches wide and tall, as extant examples of the souls in purgatory and the stylized Oberammergau paintings bear witness. Inexpensive glasspaintings enjoyed the additional advantage that they cost less than some contemporary graphic prints. Even the Wentzel prints peddled to Alpine consumers cost around 3 kreuzer.[1]

These substantial differences in the size and pricing of popular glasspaintings reflected the craftsmen's efforts to market their products to all but the least well-paid members of their society. Indeed, comparison with food prices in Bavaria during the early nineteenth century suggests that a pair of Wistner's saints would represent little more than the sacrifice of a Bavarian pound, or .56 kilograms, of meat for the Sunday meal, while a pair of Gege's souls in purgatory would cost no more than a large glass of beer.[2] (Table 7 provides a survey of early nineteenth-century prices for the staples lard, potatoes, and rye flour, and for such dietary supplements as meat, eggs, dairy products, and fruit as a contextual framework for the glasspainters' price scale.) And with the considerable commercialization of country life in Bavaria and in other parts of central Europe during the eighteenth century came potential customers with cash incomes sufficient for the purchase of inexpensive glasspaintings. These customers must to some extent have been drawn from the substantial network of part- and full-time craftsmen and laborers to which the glasspainters themselves belonged, although many such craftsmen would have been extremely poor. Owners of the larger landholdings, by contrast, were paying resident farm servants yearly wages of up to 50 gulden or more by the nineteenth century. This considerable cash orientation suggests that both master and servant must have been in a better position than the poorer craftsmen to make the "luxury" purchases noted by contemporaries.[3] Indeed, the importance of these landed farmers as consumers of glasspaintings, along with the wealthier craftsmen, particularly inn-

Table 7 Early Nineteenth-Century Bavarian Food Prices, in Kreuzer

	Munich 1805	Iller Dct. 1815–16	Regen Dct. 1819	Schongau 1844
Staples				
Lard, .56 kg.	3?	28	20–22	20
Potatoes, ca. 25 kg.	—	48	18–20	—
Rye flour, ca. 25 kg.	—	—	78	—
Extras				
Beef, .56 kg.	11	8–11	8–10	10–11
Veal, .56 kg.	—	9	9	11–12
Pork, .56 kg.	15	12	12–13	—
Hen (each)	—	15	16–20	—
Eggs (each)	—	8–9 eggs @ 8	4 eggs @ 4	7 eggs @ 4
Butter, .56 kg.	—	23	20–22	15
Cheese, .56 kg.	22 (Swiss)	16	—	—
Apples, ca. 6 kg.	—	40	—	—
One large *Weißbier* (beer)	—	—	3	—

Sources: R. Arnim Winkler, *Die Frühzeit der deutschen Lithographie* (Munich: Prestel, 1975), p. 436; *Königlich-Baierisches Intelligenz-Blatt des Iller-Kreises,* Beylage zum XLVI. Kreisblatte, (1815/1816); *Königlich Baierisches Intelligenzblatt für den Regenkreis* 5 (1819): 127–28; SAM, LRA 724; *Wochen-blatt für das Königlich bayerisches Landgericht Schongau* 36 (1844): 144; W. R. Lee, *Population Growth, Economic Development and Social Change in Bavaria, 1750–1850* (New York: Arno, 1977), p. 390.

keepers, millers, and shopkeepers, shows up clearly in a study of inventories from the Bodenmais area of Lower Bavaria. The ½ farmer Jakob Seiler, for instance, owned fourteen glasspaintings in 1772. Unmarried persons, servants, and retirees, however, owned fewer paintings than married couples, if they had any at all. So poorer households, it seems, must have had their share of paintings but on a smaller scale than that of their wealthier neighbors.[4]

Glasspaintings from the craft centers differed markedly not only in size and price appeal for this varied clientele but also in style. For this reason, it is usually possible to attribute a painting to a particular center, if not to an individual artist. Stylistic idiosyncrasies in the treatment of figures combine with an intensely schematic approach to distinguish the Raimundsreuth paintings, for example. Features are hastily sketched, and bodies lack proportion and modeling. One such painting portrays the figure of Saint Notburga (see figure 8) and conveys its simple iconographical message with a minimum of fuss about realistic depiction of Notburga's female form and identifying attributes, the sickle and jug she carries. Upper Bavarian painters tried more diligently to portray a realistic image, although they still varied a good deal in the degree of their modeling and intricacy of detail. Comparison of the Tyrolean version of Saint Notburga (figure 9) with its Raimundsreuth counterpart (figure 8) illustrates this different approach. Eighteenth-century paintings executed in Upper Bavaria in the standardized Augsburg style are often indistinguishable from those produced by Augsburg craftsmen for middle-class consumers. With the pressures of mass production, however, Upper Bavarian painters adopted a simpler, more graphic technique for their country customers and schematized their subjects still further.

The use of a graphic style in popular glasspainting was facilitated by the glasspainters' normal reliance on devotional prints to create their *Vorlagen* or patterns; many such prints were produced in nearby Augsburg.[5] As discussed in the Introduction, Augsburg was a great center for the production both of graphic art and of glasspaintings in the eighteenth century, and glasspainters there had relied heavily on prints as patterns for their work. The two fields indeed could be united in one artist, within the tradition of those graphic artists who had contributed designs for the small stained glass roundels and heraldic panels so popular as decoration in the windows of city and guild buildings and even of private homes in the sixteenth and seventeenth centuries.[6] The sophistication of these miniatures depends in large part on the wealth of their graphic detail, which often copies the style of engravings very closely and eventually came to dominate the medium; grisaille on white glass became the fashion in the seventeenth century.[7] It is not surprising that country glasspainters would perpetuate the linear style of both stained glass and devotional prints, particularly when rapid execution of an inexpensive painting was their prime consideration. Yet when Lower Bavarian painters tried to compete with lithographers in the mid-nineteenth century by returning to the grisaille style, they failed completely. For it was of course the infusion of luminous color into graphic reproduction that gave glasspainting its special appeal on the popular market.[8]

Much of that color derived from the elaborate bordering of many

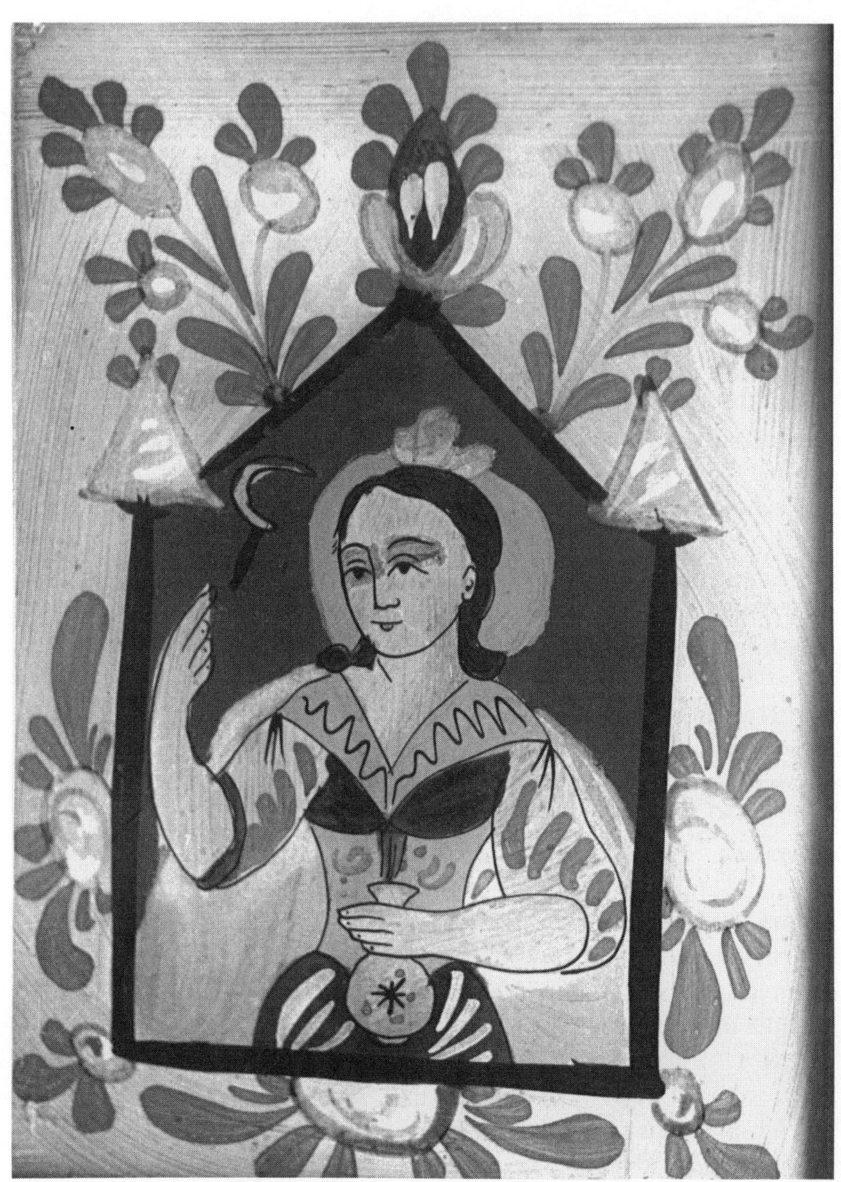

Figure 8. Saint Notburga, Raimundsreuth.
(Herr Herbert Fastner, Zwiesel)

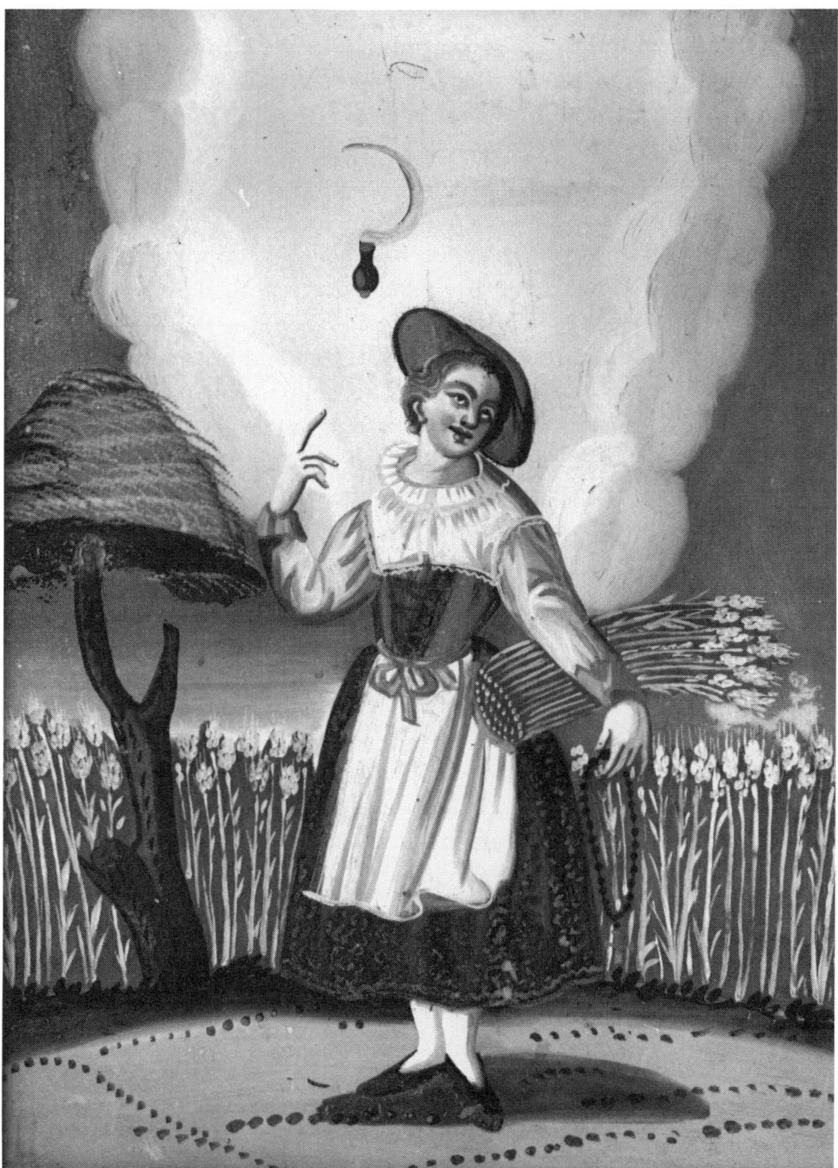

Figure 9. Saint Notburga, probably Tyrol.
(Bayerisches Nationalmuseum, Munich)

glasspaintings, which was also carried over from devotional graphic art. The glasspaintings thus belonged to a long tradition of decorative work in religious products that reached back to the medieval illumination of missals and bibles. (See figures 10 and 11 for a comparison of the intricacy of bordering possible in both glasspaintings and devotional prints.)[9] Choices could range from the stark presentation of a painting's subject matter, augmented only by a thin bottom strip bearing the title of the subject at hand, to a black-contoured oval lavishly surrounded with flowers above and below, as is typical of the standardized Oberammergau paintings. The colors used in these borders are often intense, like the startlingly beautiful blue in the sprig of flowers suspended over the oval in some Lake Staffel paintings. Consequently, a great deal of the beauty of glasspaintings emerges from the pleasing design and coloring of their purely decorative features. But bright colors are also characteristic of the treatment of subject matter in glasspaintings, such as the beautiful deep blue used for Mary's cloak in many depictions of her. Juxtapositions of strong colors, often avoided in elite art, give the paintings a brilliance and power that clearly attracted the eye of local consumers. Father Bäumer appreciated this fact when he placed his order with Matthias Noder in 1816. "The crown over Mary's head and the stars, also God the Father's hat and the halo around Jesus's head, also the Holy Ghost must be made with gold rays and the background must be completely white, so that the painting shines more brightly to the eye." To this brilliance of colors must also be added the inevitable gleam of the glass itself as an enriching factor that emphasized the desired close relationship between the humble glasspainting and the elite oil painting. Iconographically, both subject and bordering might still resemble the prints used in the preparation of glasspaintings, but the final product was dramatically transformed by its medium.

Framing was also an important selling point, as Father Bäumer's letter confirms; he specifies not only the color and design of the paintings but also that they must be framed. Such frames could be simply constructed of plain or colored wood, or decorated with floral designs; the Georg Lang records distinguish among black, lacquered, and colored frames. Some of these frames became extremely elaborate, although they do not seem to have reached the decorative heights of the rococo framing provided for prints in the eighteenth century. Often identical framing emphasized the pairing of paintings so common in the dis-

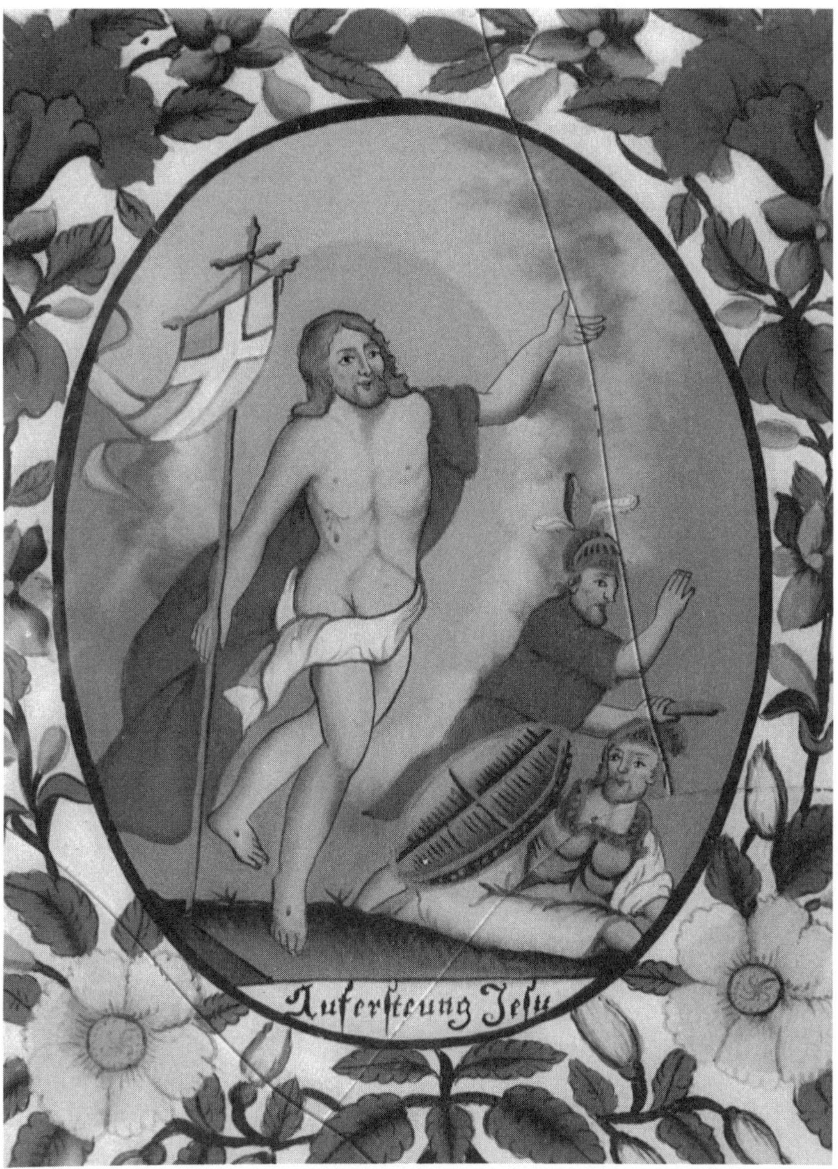

Figure 10. The legacy of manuscript illumination in glasspaintings. (Heimatmuseum, Oberammergau)

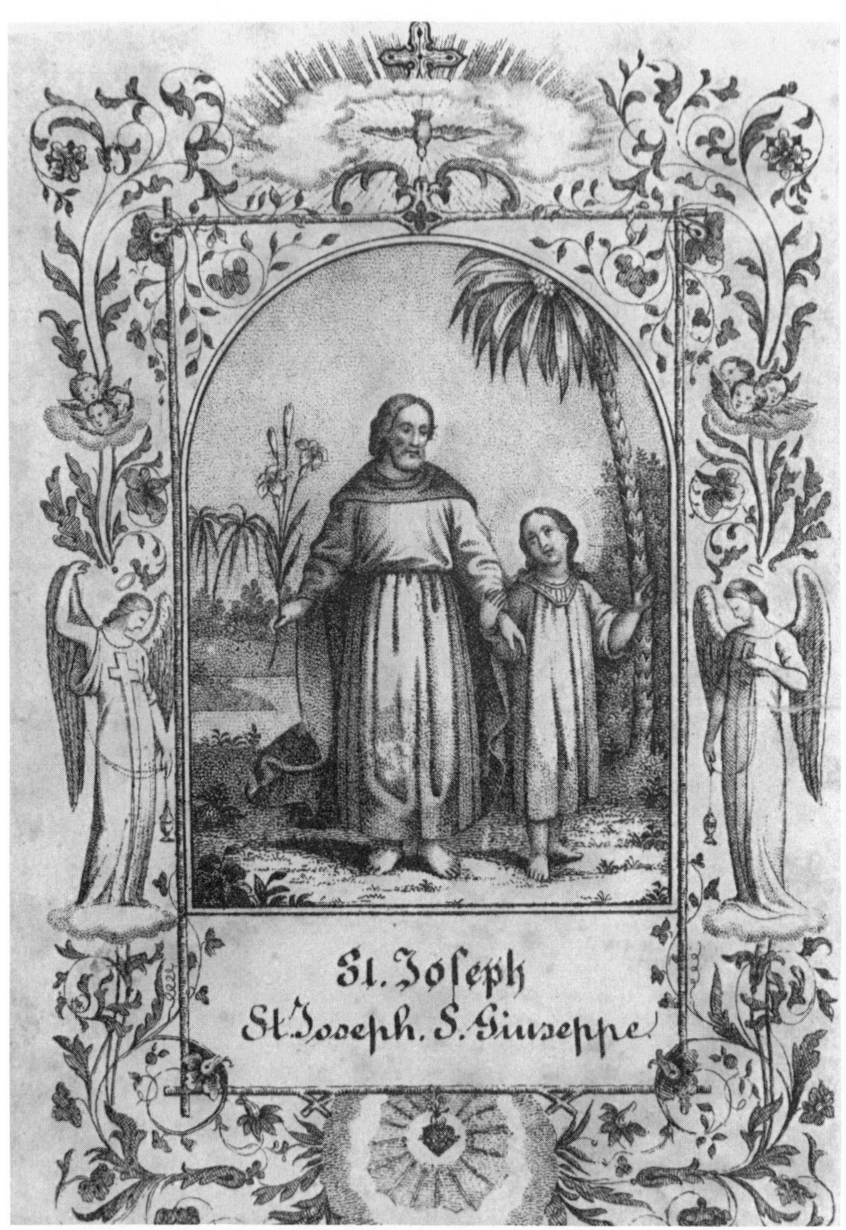

Figure 11. The legacy of manuscript illumination in devotional prints. (Bayerische Staatsbibliothek, Munich)

play of images in the *Herrgottswinkel.*[10] Framing thus added to the attractiveness of glasspaintings as furnishings for the Baroque living rooms in which other elaborately painted pieces such as chests and dressers would also be displayed. Unlike prints, they could, of course, only be fixed to the wall in a frame, but the untidy practice of pinning up unframed prints must have been receding as well, if the business in frames enjoyed by the Langs is any guide.[11] The late eighteenth-century votive painting reproduced in figure 12 captures this old habit still in operation, albeit combined with the display of a crucifix and framed paintings. But by then the framing of prints had become popular, because "ordinary glass, whirled from a lump, . . . [and] cut into small, green, bubbly pieces" had been replaced by "clear" glass during the eighteenth century.[12] It was a highly desirable finishing touch to products so clearly intended to mimic the oil paintings owned by the upper classes.

Whatever the size, price, and style of paintings selected by glasspainting consumers, they were most likely to contain a religious motif. The consumers of baroque and rococo Augsburg glasspaintings had of course encouraged producers to paint such secular themes as the Four Seasons and Continents, or shepherd and hunting scenes; however, only echoes of these themes remained in the rural painters' repertoire, at least in that of the Upper Bavarian painters. The Four Seasons was a theme frequently mentioned in the Andreas Lang account books during the early nineteenth century, but it may well have been aimed at middle-class rather than popular markets. The Lake Staffel painters, however, also reproduced these rural scenes. Moreover, shepherds and shepherdesses have traditionally translated easily into religious terms as Jesus and Mary, the Good Shepherd and Shepherdess. Patriotic portraits and military figures also attracted the attention of village painters, for example, the exported portraits of George Washington and other American heroes to North America. Religious imagery nevertheless clearly predominated in the production of popular glasspaintings.[13]

Both biblical and doctrinal themes provided subject matter for glasspaintings. New Testament scenes were frequently painted, drawing from stories of Jesus's life and passion. The Annunciation, the Nativity, the Flight into Egypt, the Holy Family at work, the Last Supper, Jesus on the Mount of Olives, the Scourged Christ, the Stations of the Cross, the Crucifixion itself, and the Holy Grave were all popular subjects. In addition, portrayal of the many saints augmenting Catholic religious beliefs was extremely popular. They appear singly or in combination,

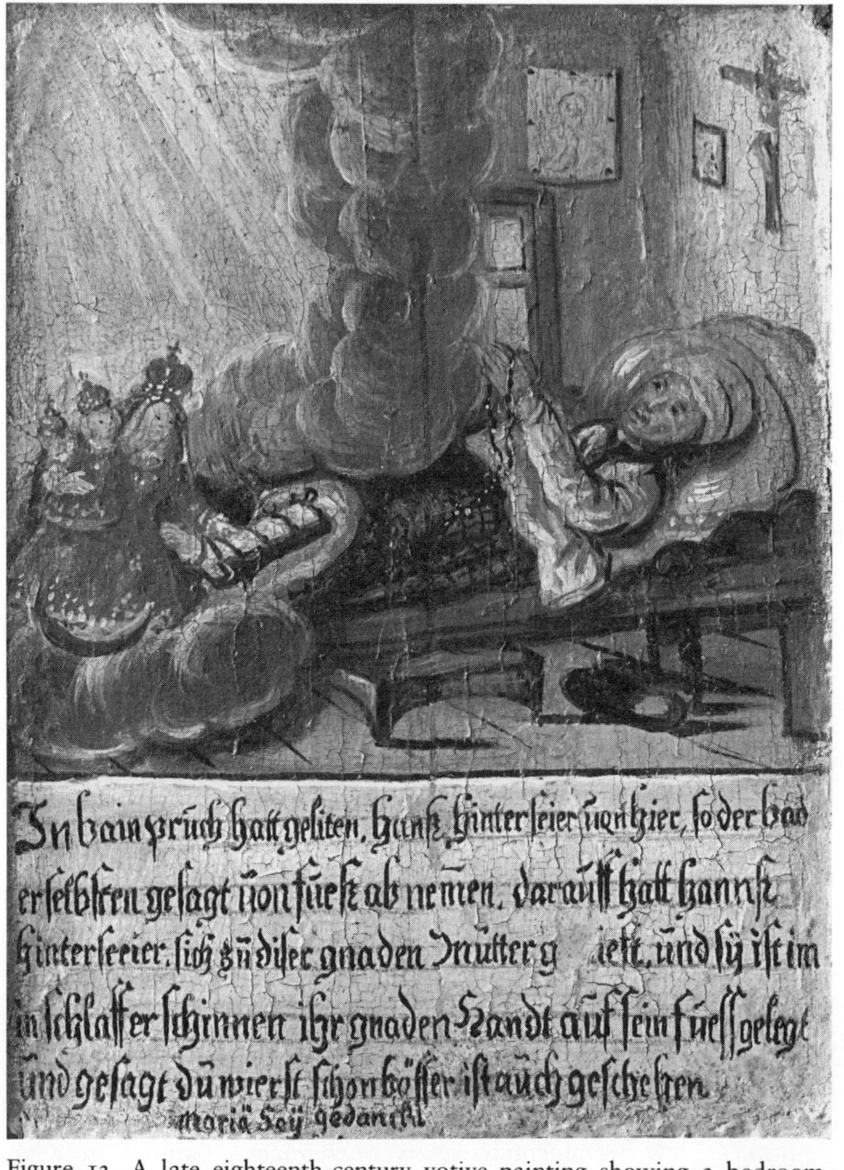

Figure 12. A late eighteenth-century votive painting showing a bedroom. (Bayerisches Nationalmuseum, Munich)

bearing attributes that draw attention to their life stories and the nature of their intervention on behalf of the supplicant. The similar efficacy of the Souls in Purgatory as mediators with God on behalf of the living assured their continued popularity as an iconographical theme also, as we have seen.[14] But the central doctrinal figures of Jesus, Mary, and the Holy Trinity were even more popular, and they too appear, as the saints do, singly or in combination, subject to many different interpretations.

Within these major thematic groupings, the opportunity for iconographical variety was immense. During the period after the Council of Trent when a pattern of pilgrimage to local shrines had developed, the central figures of Catholic belief were fragmented into a myriad of local renditions. Glasspainters could thus draw from two centuries of iconographical development since the Council, in addition to the legacies of the Middle Ages and the Renaissance, particularly since they used popular devotional prints to create patterns for their work. But they would often reproduce motifs from pilgrimages located no further from home than the surrounding countryside; the collection of patterns found in the Gege home, for example, included the "Seehausen Mary, the suffering Mother Mary from Murnau, the scourged Lord Jesus from the Wies bei Steingaden, the 'Bountiful Lady' from Ettal, the patron of cattle Saint Leonhard from Tölz and Froschhausen, the suffering Mary from Gaisach, the miraculous Cross from Polling, and . . . the black Mary from Absam in Tyrol."[15] Similarly, Raimundsreuth painters took advantage of the popularity of the local Kreuzberg pilgrimage to reproduce images of the Saint Anna statue venerated there. Nevertheless, because of their multiple heritage from medieval, Renaissance, and Baroque iconographical traditions, these localized motifs reproduced by glasspainters could emphasize widely varying degrees of humanistic or hieratic qualities in their central figures. The multiplication of locally venerated images thus created a wealth of iconographical material, with the result that the consumers of glasspaintings could be offered as wide a range of choice in the subject matter of their purchases as in their decor, size, framing, and price.[16]

Lithographers were quick to assess the market in popular art for which both older graphic procedures and the new technique of glasspainting were being used to produce the immense variety of images we have discussed above. Moreover, when Senefelder invented his planographic printing method at the end of the eighteenth century, he made possible an explosive growth in the distribution of paintings that changed the shape of the popular consumption of graphic art during the course of the nineteenth century. Already in the 1830s the demand for glasspaintings was so great that the Wolfstein painters were producing thirty thousand to forty thousand paintings yearly, and Verderber had streamlined his workshop along the lines of a factory assembly line by 1850 in an attempt to keep up with the market. But the demand required the level of manpower and equipment that were assembled in the city workshops of lithographic printers to satisfy the public's growing appetite for decorative art. So it is not surprising that the second half of the nineteenth century should mark the decline of glasspainting and the victory of chromolithography.

In Chapter 2 I outlined the way in which the original black and white lithograph was transformed into a satisfactory substitute for both oil paintings and glasspaintings. The brilliant color, gleaming finish, and sturdy appearance of the resultant chromolithographs seem to have recommended them to late nineteenth century customers who might earlier have purchased a glasspainting for much the same reasons. Moreover, the framing of lithographs was as strong a selling point as it had been for glasspaintings. In the early 1860s advertisements placed in the Munich Address Book by the local Kitzinger firm were already stressing gold framing. And by the mid-1870s even country residents were gaining access to chromolithographs encased in "gold baroque frames," at least in the small town of Viechtach where Josef Hetzenecker began selling them in 1876. In order to make these frames available to their customers, some firms producing prints began to make agreements with framing companies. Even when expensive frames were beyond the means of less wealthy consumers, cardboard frames or clever bordering of the print could be provided instead.[17]

In comparison with popular glasspaintings, however, both the early unframed chromolithographs and the later framed prints tended to be expensive. Indeed, the price list quoted by Haindl in his 1843 article discussing Heinrich Weishaupt's chromolithographic procedure can only be compared to early Andreas Lang price levels for fancy glasspaintings. Weishaupt's list included:

Our Father in subscription price here in Munich	4 gulden
Our Father in subscription price outside the city	4 gulden, 30 kreuzer
Ecce Homo after Hemling	3 gulden

Mater dolorosa after Kling	3 gulden
Madonna di Sisto after Raphael	3 gulden
Christ on the Cross after Kling	3 gulden
Christ as a child after Carl Dolce	3 gulden
Martin Luther	2 gulden, 30 kreuzer
Melanchthon	2 gulden, 30 kreuzer[18]

These prices were somewhat higher than those quoted by the Munich Sunday School Press in 1818 for their hand-colored prints, although a good many of the press's better reproductions did cost upward of 2 gulden at that time. Other prints, however, were priced at only 1 gulden, 48 kreuzer, and illuminated pictures of flowers, plants, and the like could be purchased for a mere 24 kreuzer. The popular stencil-colored lithographs produced by firms such as Wentzel's or May's could be much cheaper still. But the combination of frames with popular chromolithographs later in the century clearly caused a dramatic rise in the price of these prints. The twenty-one prints with gold baroque frames bought by Hetzenecker from the Straubing firm of Heinrich Fischer in 1876 cost him about 93 gulden, while four unframed prints cost only 35 kreuzer each.[19]

Popular lithographic prints also differed from popular glasspaintings because the close connection between lithography and other graphic procedures, including the printing of books, music, and maps, meant that a much smaller proportion were religious in theme. Indeed, classification of German single-leaf woodcuts produced in the sixteenth and seventeenth centuries has shown that religious subjects accounted for only 34 percent of all titles produced during that earlier period, and nineteenth-century printers certainly included the variety of secular themes that they had inherited from their predecessors in their thematic selections.[20] Kühn's firm, for example, included all manner of entertaining and instructive subjects together with their devotional pictures; among the motifs that the firm distributed to their vast public were illustrations of soldiers, fairy tales, battles, and animals; games; puppets; children's theaters; and even targets for shooting practice. Traditional themes such as the Four Seasons and hunting scenes also appeared frequently in popular graphic pictures and were later transformed into "genre oil prints" for the "lower-middle-class drawing room and bedroom" during the nineteenth century.[21]

Nevertheless, despite the obvious popularity of secular motifs, many of the lithographic firms serving popular markets in the early days before the victory of the chromolithograph did find religious imagery to be a very substantial sales item. Based on an 1860 catalog of French graphic sheets registered with the Ministry of the Interior during the 1850s, we can conclude that the demand for religious prints still outstripped that for prints covering all secular subjects combined. In 1858 Wentzel's firm, for example, registered for colportage 72,000 religious images out of a total of 103,000, roughly 7/10 of the total produced. May's production in the 1850s aimed mostly at providing religious prints for the *Herrgottswinkel*.[22]

Similar themes appear in the products of both French and German firms. In the 1860 catalog Mary was listed in 172 separate forms under the title "Notre Dame," while other versions of her portrait were listed under a variety of different titles. Christ appeared 200 times as "Jesus" or "Christ," and the usual scenes from his life, like the Nativity (8), the Flight into Egypt (10), and the Last Supper (10), were also repeatedly produced. About 1,500 different portraits of saints rounded out the picture, and many of these prints must have been lithographs. When Christa Pieske cataloged surviving prints from the May factory, she found familiar motifs as well, such as Mary as "Helper," paired with Saint Joseph (as in many glasspainting pendants), the Holy Family, the *Ecce Homo,* as usual paired with the Sorrowing Mary, the Crowning of Mary, the Hearts of Jesus and Mary, and assorted saints, among May's religious themes. Thomas Driendl's small devotional pictures, moreover, remind us that many of the religious motifs printed lithographically must have drawn from the iconography of local shrines, for Gustav Gugitz found examples of Maria Dreieichen, Maria-Kumitz, Maria-Lanzendorf, Maria-Luschari, Maria-Neustift, Maria-Plain, Maria-Taferl, Maria-Trost bei Graz, and Mariazell, a very popular shrine, among surviving devotional prints produced by his firm.[23] Clearly, the profitable market for religious glasspaintings and small devotional pictures had provided manufacturers of lithographs with a stimulating field for their own productive potential.

From Senefelder onward, the developers of chromolithographs were interested in both religious and secular subjects for their experiments. They operated within a general context of graphic production for middle-class consumers that included a strong bias toward secular themes. Yet Senefelder himself was almost immediately involved in a project that brought him in touch with the popular taste for religious art. One of his first artistic prints was the picture of Jesus as a child entitled *Der Liebenswürdigste* (the one most worthy of love) that School Inspector Steiner ordered in large numbers for local school children; for at least seven years after he created the original in 1798, Senefelder printed a couple of thousand copies yearly of the print and accompanying text.[24] The majority of his work in color, however, did involve secular subjects, and of course it was the procedure by which oil paintings could be successfully copied lithographically that preoccupied him most during these experiments.

Senefelder's two disciples whose work in chromolithography led to the discovery of the three-color process shared his interest in reproductive art. But though Engelmann's products revealed his preponderant interest in the secular themes popular with Parisian and middle-class customers, Heinrich Weishaupt's experiments in the Bavarian context reflected those more traditional motifs that belonged in the *Herrgottswinkel.* His first chromolithograph was an *Ecce Homo,* and it met with such success that he had reportedly printed and sold over 1,500 copies by 1843. He followed this effort with one that was logically the pendant to the first, the Sorrowing Mary. And we have seen from his price list that the boy Jesus theme already reproduced by Senefelder, and a very popular theme with the glasspainter Verderber as well, was also one of his early motifs in chromolithography, together with Raphael's Sistine Madonna and other religious subjects. Even his early attempts at secular chromolithography were reminiscent of the popular Four Seasons theme; Spring and The Reaper appear, possibly intended as a pair.[25]

Weishaupt made explicit his appreciation of the importance for the popular market of religious motifs when he requested permission in 1842 to reproduce three paintings from the Pinakothek. He wrote that he had used his discovery "particularly for religious reproductions" with the "public taste" in mind. Rubens's *Holy Trinity,* Van Dyck's *Rest in Egypt,* and Reni's *Ascension of Mary* were the three paintings that he considered would be suitable as chromolithographs; two of these works still hang in the Alte Pinakothek, and their simple color schemes appear easily adaptable to color printing. But Weishaupt was not the only printer whose understanding of the importance of religious art for popular consumers influenced his search for an inexpensive color process. A Dr. Netto's description of the procedure developed in

Berlin by one Liepmann for printing oil pictures includes the remark that such paintings "mean more than decoration" to their owners.[26]

Although their products grew ever closer to resembling the glasspaintings so beloved by country consumers, chromolithographers did not ignore the secular themes popular with middle-class customers earlier in the century. In an 1870 advertisement placed by the Artistic Institute for Chromolithographs in the Munich Address Book, for example, the firm announced the availability of "portraits, landscapes, genre and animal pieces," as well as religious prints. Yet chromolithographers continued to produce religious subjects, including the popular local images, as extant examples such as the cult figure of Mary with the Rosary owned by Wistner and Souls in Purgatory chromolithographs distributed in the Bavarian Forest attest.[27]

Glasspaintings and lithographs sold on the popular market carried into the homes of their customers an enormously wide range of images, many of which were attractively packaged for prominent display. Once these art works arrived in their new locations, the evidence suggests that, at least in southern Germany, they were placed in the family shrine or *Herrgottswinkel* located in the dining corner of the living room. Because of variations in local customs, there were many ways in which these shrines could be arranged. One common configuration centered around a crucifix hanging in the corner with glasspaintings or paper prints flanking it on either side; this schema might even include built-in benches running along the two walls of the assigned corner as well as the dining table and chairs.[28] Lorenz Quaglio captured a slightly different arrangement in his *Das Tischgebet* (*Grace*), included as figure 13. Whatever the arrangement, however, it is clear that Catholic families, as Dr. Netto suggested in 1840, wished to adorn "their house altar with a Raphael Madonna or with protective saints in a copy which radiates the brilliant color of an original."[29] Consequently, in the Bodenmais survey of inventories dating from 1730 to 1818, which identified 542 glasspaintings listed from about 1750 onward, 98 percent of the paintings cataloged were found in the living room of the house.[30] Of course the hanging of such paintings was never exclusively restricted to the *Herrgottswinkel;* souls in purgatory, for example, were hung beside doorways so that a passerby could sprinkle them with water to cool them down in their fiery torments. Farmers also liked to hang religious images, such as the cattle patron Saint

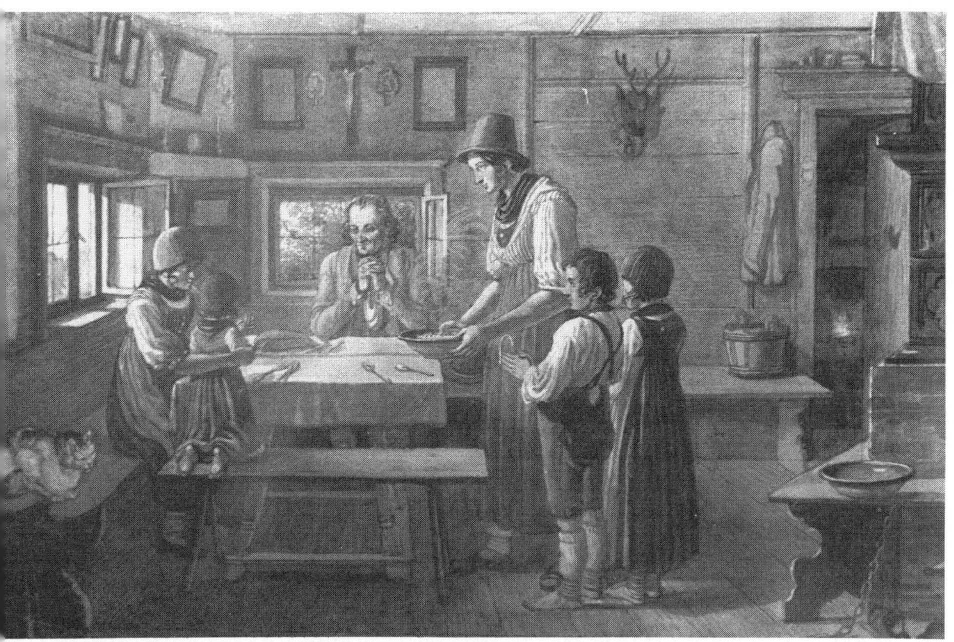

Figure 13. Lorenz Quaglio, *Das Tischgebet*. (Staatliche Graphische Sammlung, Munich)

Henry, on stall doors. There is in addition some evidence of the hanging of religious paintings in bedrooms before the nineteenth century (as in the votive painting in figure 12), and similar religious imagery could also be introduced in the form of decorations on beds.[31]

As emphasis on the possession of exclusively religious imagery lessened during the nineteenth century, however, the practice of hanging paintings throughout the home appears to have become common at the popular level. Religious paintings could still be used to decorate and sanctify the living area, of course, but secular themes suitable to the individual character of each room in the home could also serve to embellish them in a way acceptable to the social aspirations of the family —"hunting scenes and still-lifes for the dining room, and wine- and tavern-scenes and patriotic motifs for the smoking room." Landscapes suited the living room, for which the sofa arrangement suggested a wide format. We find, for example, this type of *Sofabild* included in an Italian votive painting dated 1889. There it hangs over the sofa, together with an impressive collection of elegant living-room furnishings and a second landscape vertically oriented to hang beyond the edge of the sofa itself. Yet, in the adjoining bedroom also depicted in this votive painting hang a crucifix flanked by two framed pictures of religious figures, along with another framed landscape. Other nineteenth-century votive paintings attest to this use of religious paintings in the bedroom as well.[32]

It is intriguing that evidence of nineteenth-century consumers displaying secular paintings in their homes should appear in votive art. For this seemingly anomalous juxtaposition of sacred art and secular living habits suggests a lack of perceived conflict between the modernizing influences reshaping the social environment of all Europeans and more traditional religious beliefs and behaviors. Certainly, the specialization of function that underlay the deployment of secular as well as religious paintings in carefully delineated areas of the home paralleled other forms of secularization occurring during the last half of the nineteenth century. But, as the ready acceptance of secular changes in votive art reveals, the strict conceptual division between sacred and secular belief systems posited by theorists is an artificial construct. For the dynamic interchange between these two systems can survive even dramatic shifts in the relative strengths of either one, and the negotiation process between them is still ongoing.[33] For example, even contemporary studies in the United States suggest "that individuals have a remarkable propensity actually to *mix* religious and scientific world views."[34] "Religion" thus is undergoing "not a precipitous decline, but merely a gradual transformation" by which shifts in the popular usage of art works can be contextualized.[35]

Before this particular transformation was underway, however, first glasspaintings and then lithographs had served Catholic customers well as inexpensive, colorful, and aesthetically pleasing objects of religious art. A skeptic might argue that even this type of painting's appeal was no more than a conventionalized form of household arrangement and decor. Its function represented little more than a social "keeping up with the Joneses," or an echo of familial custom, mixed with personal aesthetic preference. This case could even be strengthened by discussion of the general boom enjoyed by the furnishing crafts during the eighteenth and nineteenth centuries. Not only paintings but all kinds of decorative furnishings became desirable consumer items for those who could afford them. And just as the paintings became elaborately finished with richly painted frames and borders, so too did other furnishings become ever more sumptuously decorated. Furniture and paintings could thus be integrated into a costly and pleasing statement of affluence and taste by the homeowner.[36]

The function of these religious paintings was, however, far more fundamental to the operation of their owners' households than our skeptic gives them credit for. There is a great deal of evidence to show that their significance for the members of the household included a frame of reference that extended far beyond these limited social and economic implications. For these devotional objects were not "luxury" purchases but necessary household items; Dr. Netto's remark that such paintings "mean more than decoration" to their owners correctly emphasizes that deeper level of meaning.[37] In Bavaria, this is because delimitation of the *Herrgottswinkel* "is connected to the importance and early development of the living room in upper German farm houses. It is the scene of common meals and of all the communal activities of the household."[38] Before the secularizing trends of the nineteenth century the dining area provided a focus for both the religious and the secular orientations of the family.

A picture of this fundamental role played by the *Herrgottswinkel* in Bavarian households emerges clearly from surviving inventories like those of the Bodenmais study. They illustrate the fact that not only the dining table but also the crucifix even became part of the fixtures belonging to the house itself. Perhaps the *Herrgottswinkel* paintings too remained as fixtures with the house when it was sold. Retirees usually took few or no paintings with them to their rooms; and even when the widow of Mathias Bergmann was permitted by testament to enjoy the use of the couple's paintings and other devotional objects during her lifetime, they were to revert to the holding after her death. When inventory takers entered the home of a deceased Bodenmais villager, their orientation in listing the household's possessions reflected the customary prominence afforded the *Herrgottswinkel*. Crucifix and paintings always appear first on the list, followed immediately by the dining-room table. For example, the list of possessions cataloged in 1754 for the Wendlberger household in Upper Lohwisen begins with a crucifix and two glasspaintings, one of Mary the Helper and one of the Holy Trinity. Clearly, the central role of the family shrine shaped the understanding of their task by inventory takers as well.[39]

Because the *Herrgottswinkel* was constructed as a religious image that focused the activities of the household, it took on the ambiguities inherent in any fusion of religious and practical frames of reference.[40] Its location in the secular context of a home rather than in the explicitly sacred enclosure of a church emphasized its range of significance for practical as well as spiritual concerns. It was by drawing on the suggestive combination of physical nourishment and spiritual communion symbolized in church by the altar/table that the dining table became both the focal center and the shrine of the home. The obvious emotive and physiological resonances of the locus of food consumption in a household for which, as we have seen, survival might well be a major concern thus merged with the normative and didactic functions of spiritual "nourishment" suggested by the communion of believers.[41] This seems to be the message of Quaglio's watercolor *Das Tischgebet*, which captures both the emotive force of the *Herrgottswinkel* and its multiple reference to both spiritual and practical considerations. It is no wonder that so strong an identification of household with household shrine influenced the purchase of glasspaintings by homemakers rather than single persons, while the importance of this symbol for household unity begins to explain the width of the popular market in religious paintings.[42]

Thus, glasspaintings and lithographs served both as decorative furnishings and as religious images located in the secular context of a household's living room. To understand the relationship between these two functions filled by the paintings, we can turn to anthropologist Robert Redfield's distinction between the "immanent" and "transcendent" functions of artworks.[43] Redfield associates immanence with the aesthetic impact of form, and certainly the decorative nature of glass-paintings did fill an aesthetic need for the consumer. Yet each glass-painting primarily presents a subject that extends the implications of the image beyond form to substance, beyond immanent or aesthetic enjoyment to transcendent meanings, "to knowledge and experience that is somewhere else—in custom and society, in personal life."[44] Redfield also reminds us that primitive artists use "a highly formalized, intensely local and very long established style."[45] We have the apparent advantage that the glasspainters' and lithographers' formalized style is familiar to us as part of our own historical tradition, although particular local variations may not be. But interpretation of the transcendent references to which the imagery in religious paintings led their central European Catholic customers involves taking careful account of the specific cultural context in connection with which they were used. The next chapter, therefore, examines the ways in which the consumers' culture infused meaning into the religious imagery of both glasspaintings and lithographs alike.

5

Spiritual Insurance: The Meaning of Glasspaintings and Lithographs

In 1837 Anna Nimerfall, daughter of a farmer in the parish of Aukirchen, Bavaria, carelessly stuck a needle into her neck. The local doctor labored mightily for two hours to remove this foreign object embedded in his patient's flesh, but he was unsuccessful. As such objects are wont to do, however, the needle worked itself out in good time (three weeks). Anna explained her "miracle" as the work of "the merciful Mother at Altötting," who had "requested" that the needle dilemma be solved.[1] Her approach to this medical emergency thus typified the practical and trusting relationship enjoyed by her fellow Catholics with the saints and doctrinal figures of their cultural environment. For their spiritual world was peopled with willing helpers like the Altötting Madonna who would petition God's help for a believer in need. Indeed, in the case of the popular Fourteen Helpers in Need, the skies became thick with saints working to support any supplicant who might turn to them for assistance (see figure 14).[2] The power base of these saints was an impressive array of shrines sprinkled throughout the Catholic landscape.[3] For while many medieval pilgrims journeyed to faroff places where the relics of their preferred saints were located, early modern pilgrims most often set off to visit local shrines. This localization of cults was made possible when the veneration of statues and paintings of beloved saints (as opposed to relics) encouraged fragmentation of the Catholic church's central doctrinal figures into a myriad of local variants.[4] The result was to integrate well-established local saints into their followers' identification with family and community.[5] There were, however, also

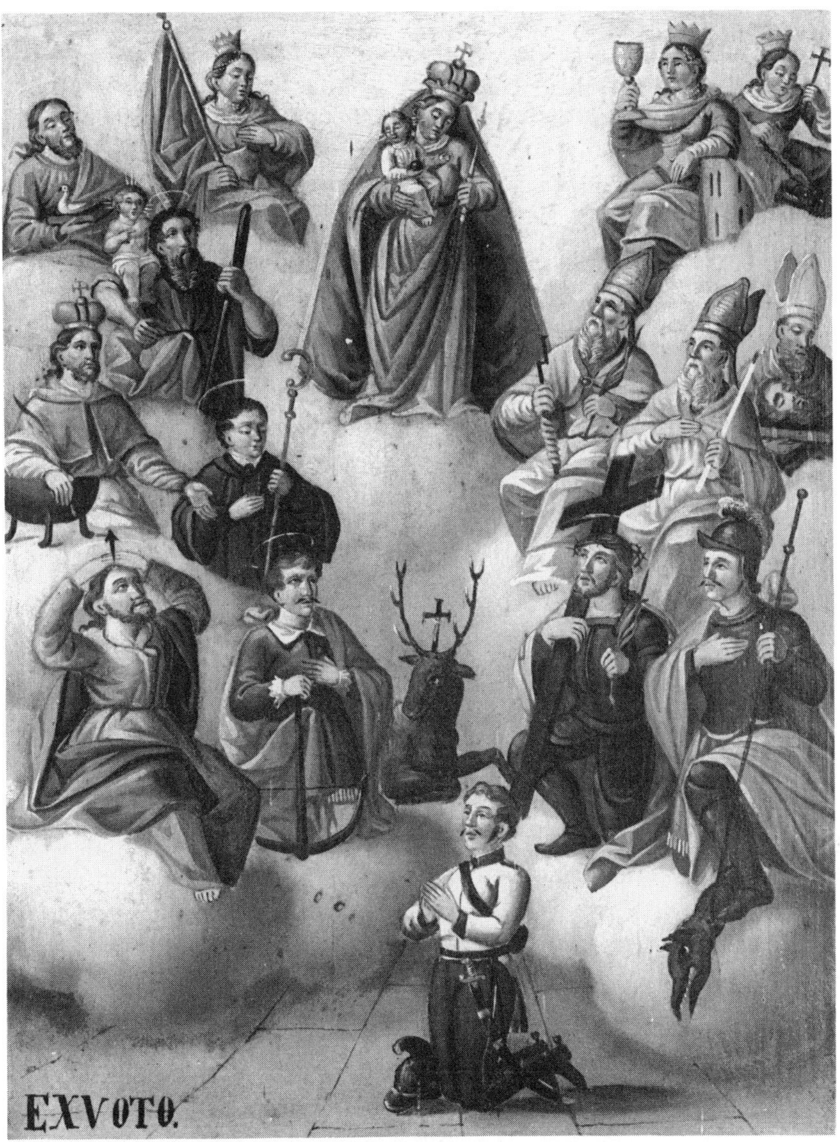

Figure 14. The *Vierzehnnothelfer* Invoked: A Heaven Full of Saints. (Bayerisches Nationalmuseum, Munich)

regional and national shrines to which large numbers of pilgrims were drawn. Anna Nimerfall chose the Madonna from one such shrine, the Altötting Mary favored by the Wittelsbachs, to help her with her needle problem.[6] Furthermore, all the venerated holy figures of the Catholic faith, whether identified with a specific shrine or not, offered believers some sort of protection, either by their specialization in the resolution of specific ailments and problems or by their provision of such generalized oversight as guardianship of their namesakes.[7]

The *Gnadenbilder* or images identified with local and national shrines became centerpieces of a Catholic "religious folk life" in which "the focal point . . . was pilgrimage customs."[8] As religious figures, they played an iconic role, connecting believers to "ordered ideas as to the origins and the right nature of the universe."[9] Those ideas in turn shaped believers' perceptions and interpretation of the human life cycle and afterlife; of human relationships; of time and space; of the natural and the extraordinary; and of success and failure, creating the phenomenon described by Robert Scribner as "an 'economy of the sacred.' " He argues that the rituals of "the individual life-cycle and the annual calendrical cycle" were intended "to invoke divine power and blessing in constituting and reconstituting social and biological life."[10] Just how important these periodic rituals were perceived to be is revealed in the story of Saint Notburga discussed later in this chapter. But the holy figures also found their way into everyday Catholic living by providing insurance and "formulae for success" concerning a wide variety of practical problems.[11] Their supernatural powers were, of course, the crucial factor in this ability to extend protection and guarantee success to their followers. And their help could even come concentrated in the form of a miracle such as Anna's.

Because of the key role played by the *Gnadenbilder* in this cultural setting, it was customary for pilgrims to buy a personal copy at the shrine to carry home with them. Since pilgrimages were the major form of vacation travel in the days before the Industrial Revolution, it is not surprising that travelers would wish to capture their experience in a suitable remembrance.[12] Scribner claims that the very first woodcuts were these "mementos" of pilgrimages; badges too were popular consumer items.[13] Such images also provided the subject matter for religious glasspaintings and lithographs. When these paintings entered the homes of consumers, therefore, they forged a crucial link between the original statues or paintings venerated in local shrines and the everyday lives of believers. Moreover, the subsequent appearance of these localized images in large numbers of votive paintings, that is, in testimonial depictions of miracles delivered by grateful believers at the shrines of the miracle-working saints or doctrinal figures, suggests that this was a circular connection. For the presence of beloved holy figures in the home helped to shape the conceptualization of miracles as conducted by these same figures in their specific local forms. The circle closed when the hanging of votive offerings in the appropriate shrines in turn reinforced the faith of others in the efficacy of the protection offered by the *Gnadenbilder*.[14]

Because religious glasspaintings and lithographs were produced in response to the thriving demand for images of local *Gnadenbilder*, I turn now to analyze in depth the meaning of these images to a typical group of consumers, the southern Germans whose patronage of the glasspainters proved so central in developing their market. For although the *Gnadenbilder* of Catholic Europe seem familiar to us as part of the Western religious tradition and we can get a general idea of their meaning for consumers by placing them in the context of the flourishing pilgrimage culture of the early modern period, we must be exceedingly cautious in analyzing their specific significance for local cult followers. Such a study can best be guided by Roger Chartier's concept of the "appropriation" of cultural forms by specific cultural or socioeconomic groups. In particular, he attacks the "now classic use of the notion of popular culture" because it assumes that classes possess cultural objects and activities, whereas the reality is one of "blurred distinctions."[15] For Chartier "popular" usage is defined by "the specific ways in which . . . cultural sets are appropriated," and "cultural types" are distinguished by "the relation each group has with shared objects, knowledge, or practices." He emphasizes, with good reason, Carlo Ginzburg's *The Cheese and the Worms,* since "the aggressive originality of Menocchio's reading" illustrates his point perfectly.[16] In this interpretation the same images take on varied meanings in the minds of distinct groups of users because of each group's unique cultural dispositions. This distinctness is clearly mirrored in the fragmentation of the Church's "catholic" images into their myriad local iconographical interpretations that we have observed peopling the localized shrines of the Catholic landscape.[17]

Analysis of the "appropriated" southern German form of a more general Catholic culture must therefore define the range of relationships between local *Gnadenbilder* and the cultural context to which they belonged. For these iconic images provided references extending from the practical to the inspirational, serving as what Victor Turner has called "dominant" symbols by compressing many meanings into one "multi-vocal" image.[18] On the one hand, the miraculous supernatural power provided by the subjects of glasspaintings and lithographs could be put to effective practical use as a protective force, intervening on behalf of the household while it dealt with the problems of daily life. On the other hand, the saints and biblical figures portrayed, who had themselves led natural lives and encountered the normal life experiences now facing household members, could serve as inspirational models for Christian living.[19] However, this broad multivocality was also curtailed by the same cultural context that invested it with such a breadth of meaning. So we must understand both the practical and the inspirational significance of the holy figures within the limits of possibility set by the cultural norms governing them. We need, therefore, to seek evidence for the many resonances of these symbols inside a framework of "thick description," treating the cultural context as "something within which they can be intelligibly—that is, thickly—described."[20] In addition, we must be careful to acknowledge cultural variations due to social divisions within the members of the cultural group and to sex-specific attitudes and concerns.

Reconstruction of this kind of contextualization involves using recently developed methods for establishing such material factors as demographic and economic conditions, as well as affective and normative codes. And this historical analysis can also include art-historical evaluation of the symbols themselves, in the tradition of the classic Erwin Panofsky studies of Father Time and Cupid.[21] For they were historically shaped forms. The inclusion or exclusion of attributes and other typifying features in their depiction can, therefore, help us to pinpoint the particular meanings that they had acquired by the historical period under consideration.

A symbol was not just subject to the limiting controls of its cultural context, however. The particular way in which it communicated its transcendent meanings to the viewer depended upon its position inside the painting and also on the painting's relationship to the *Herrgottswinkel* as a whole.[22] And when a painting contains several symbols, that too we must view as a composite of individual elements, important both individually and in relation to each other. This positional analysis requires both a syntactical and a structural approach. First, if we can identify the syntax within which each symbol relates to its fellows and to its viewers, this should clarify its potential significance within that particular context. Second, when several symbols are combined in one painting, the inclusion or exclusion of possible subjects and the internal arrangement of those chosen within the picture space are also significant in narrowing the number of possible meanings conveyed by each one. In addition, because of the normal arrangement of paintings in pairs, the consumer's choice of two balancing subjects also helps us to establish how one symbol or group of symbols becomes defined in terms of another.

The analysis that follows draws upon these theoretical approaches to elucidate the protective use and inspirational force of the religious images so popular with the consumers of glasspaintings and lithographs. It studies in turn four ways in which the holy figures were deployed within the home, or, in the case of votive paintings, outside it but with specific reference to the concerns of household members. Thus, we can observe the central role that religious art played in the lives of southern German Catholic households.

Glasspaintings and lithographs copied the many *Gnadenbilder* that peopled the local countryside, as we have seen. Included among the most popular of these *Gnadenbilder* were many variations on the figure of Mary. Indeed, the subject was such a popular one that it was the most prominent of all the themes portrayed in glasspainting. For "no other holy figure has ever appealed to and fascinated ordinary people more than the Mother of God."[23] Mary's son was of course of prime importance, as evidence provided by the accounts kept by the glasspainter Johann Baptist Reisbacher reveals; at least 82 votive paintings of the 275 commissioned from Reisbacher included variations on the theme of Christ's life and Passion, mostly Christ on the Cross. Yet at least 85 of these votive paintings included variations of the Mary motif, while the Holy Trinity trailed behind with a total of only 18 or so.[24] The central significance of these local Marian cult images in the lives of Catholic consumers makes them a suitable representative for the *Gnadenbild* category in general.[25]

We have already encountered Mary as she appeared in Father Bäumer's order for copies of the Holy Trinity *Gnadenbild* from his own parish that clearly incorporated the Mother of God as well, and was, therefore, of the type known as the Crowning of Mary. A Raimundsreuth version of this motif presents a popular version of the Holy Trinity in which the Father and Son sit side-by-side underneath a centralized and hovering Holy Ghost as dove. (See figure 15.) The reason for this choice of configuration becomes obvious when the viewer's attention turns to the also centralized figure of Mary standing between and beneath Father and Son, who together hold the crown over her head. This standard iconographical interpretation of the Trinity emphasizes its triadic nature with a triangular halo placed around the head of God the Father. Yet the inclusion of Mary into the group causes a quadratic, lozenge-shaped effect to predominate in the final image, balancing or even canceling the triadic suggestions of the Trinity itself.[26] Eva Hunt, in a fascinating book about Zinacantecan deities, has pointed to the tension between the triadic form of Roman Catholicism and the "problem of fitting a . . . quartet into a trio." For in agrarian societies, a quadratic "armature" is indicated by the seasonal nature of peasant life rhythms, and we have already seen how popular versions of the Four Seasons were for both middle and lower classes alike.[27] Mary provides the necessary squaring factor, and her prominence in the iconography of eighteenth- and nineteenth-century Bavaria suggests that in the minds of local believers she took her place alongside the Trinity in a position of special favor and grace, if not of equality, accorded no other holy figure.

There has been much scholarly speculation recently about the concept of Mary as "a symbol of the feminine component of the deity. She represents the human insight that the Ultimate is passionately tender, seductively attractive, irresistibly inspiring, and graciously healing."[28] Furthermore, Mary has repeatedly been connected with a variety of pre-Christian mother goddesses, often conceptualized as "the Goddess."[29] So her inclusion within the configuration of the male Trinity certainly suggests that her presence provides believers with a means of contemplating the role of feminine characteristics in the context of God's power. This role is, of course, predicated on Mary's intimate association with the Trinity by virtue of her motherhood of Jesus. And when we turn to examine a further instance in which we encountered Mary as her image hanging in the living room of the Wendlberger family was recorded after the death of the householder, we find that it is her motherhood that the family has considered significant; she appears on one side of the crucifix holding her infant son in her arms,

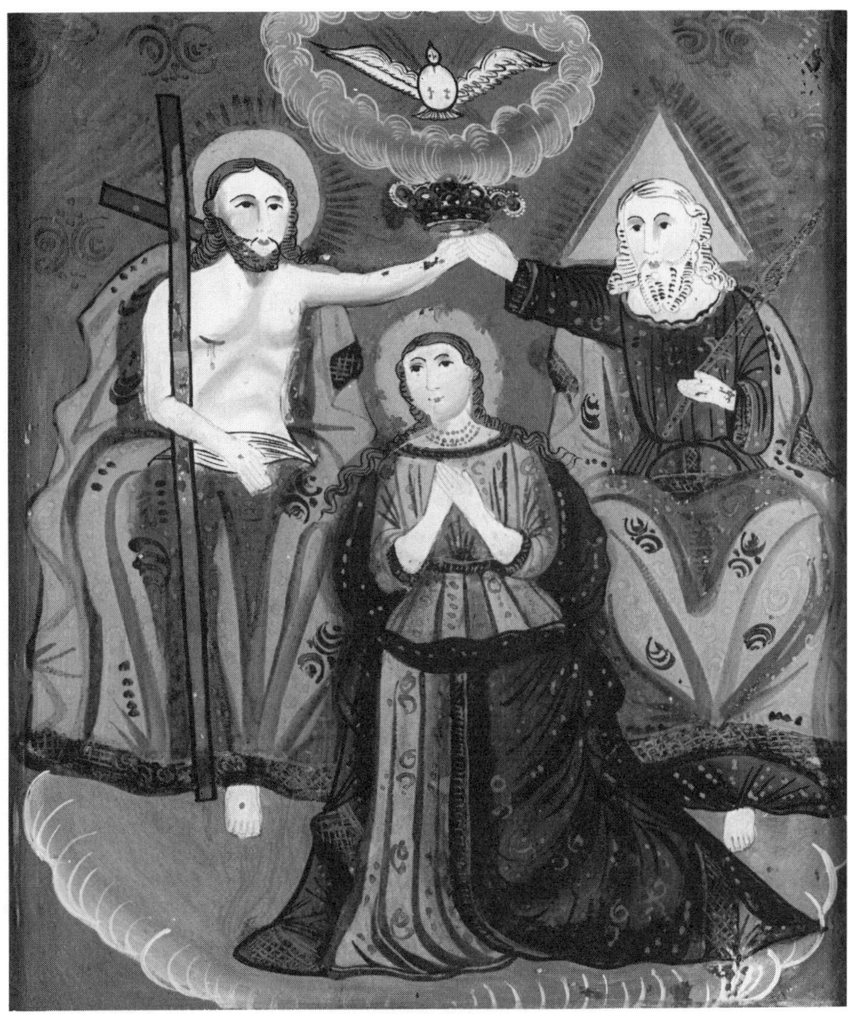

Figure 15. Mary as the squaring factor of the Trinity.
(Bayerisches Nationalmuseum, Munich)

while on the other side hangs the Holy Trinity to balance the arrangement. In this *Herrgottswinkel* the same quadratic implications as in the Bäumer *Gnadenbild* are present, but the concept of Mary as Mother is emphasized. Indeed, rather than calling Mary "Virgin," the Bavarian instinct was to call her *Mutter Gottes,* Mother of God. That is how she is listed in the Andreas Lang accounts, for example.

Mary's role as mother was expressed often in glasspaintings by her depiction as a human mother mourning the death of her son and, therefore, alone in her suffering. The usual pairing of the suffering Mary, however, was with the *Ecce Homo* that caused her state of grief; in addition, the two central figures of the Passion were often united by the *pietà* motif in which Jesus lies dead across the lap of his sorrowing mother. But the most popular thematic development in Bavaria of Mary's motherhood was the myriad of variations of the Madonna and infant child, including the version known as Mary the Helper that we encountered in Chapter 5 as chosen by the Wendlbergers. Indeed, this Mary the Helper motif was outstandingly popular throughout this period. In the Bodenmais inventories, only around 40 of the 542 glasspaintings listed could be identified by subject matter, but of those 40, 25 depicted Mary. Twenty-one referred in some way to her motherhood and 13 were specifically of Mary the Helper. Also, 40 of the 85 votive paintings commissioned from Reisbacher that depicted Mary were also specifically of Mary the Helper.[30]

The Madonna and Child motifs prominent in popular Catholic practice can be divided into two major theoretical categories, as typified by Mary the Helper and Mary of Loreto. These variations differ in their interpretations of Mary because the former emphasizes her humanity while the latter stresses her hieratic distance from all mortals, although the two types could often be blended and hybrid versions were not uncommon.[31] (See figures 16 and 17 for examples of these two major types.) On the one hand, the adaptations of detail in local presentations of Mary the Helper have never succeeded in disguising the original human scene of the Lucas Cranach painting, which has rightly been called an "idyll of family life."[32] By contrast, any sense of interactive warmth in the mother-child combination is lacking from the Mary of Loreto type with its royal clothing masking all but the faces, presented frontally, of both figures. Here, the majesty and immaculate nature of Mary as Mother of God takes precedence over her human relationship to the baby from whom she derives her special power and promi-

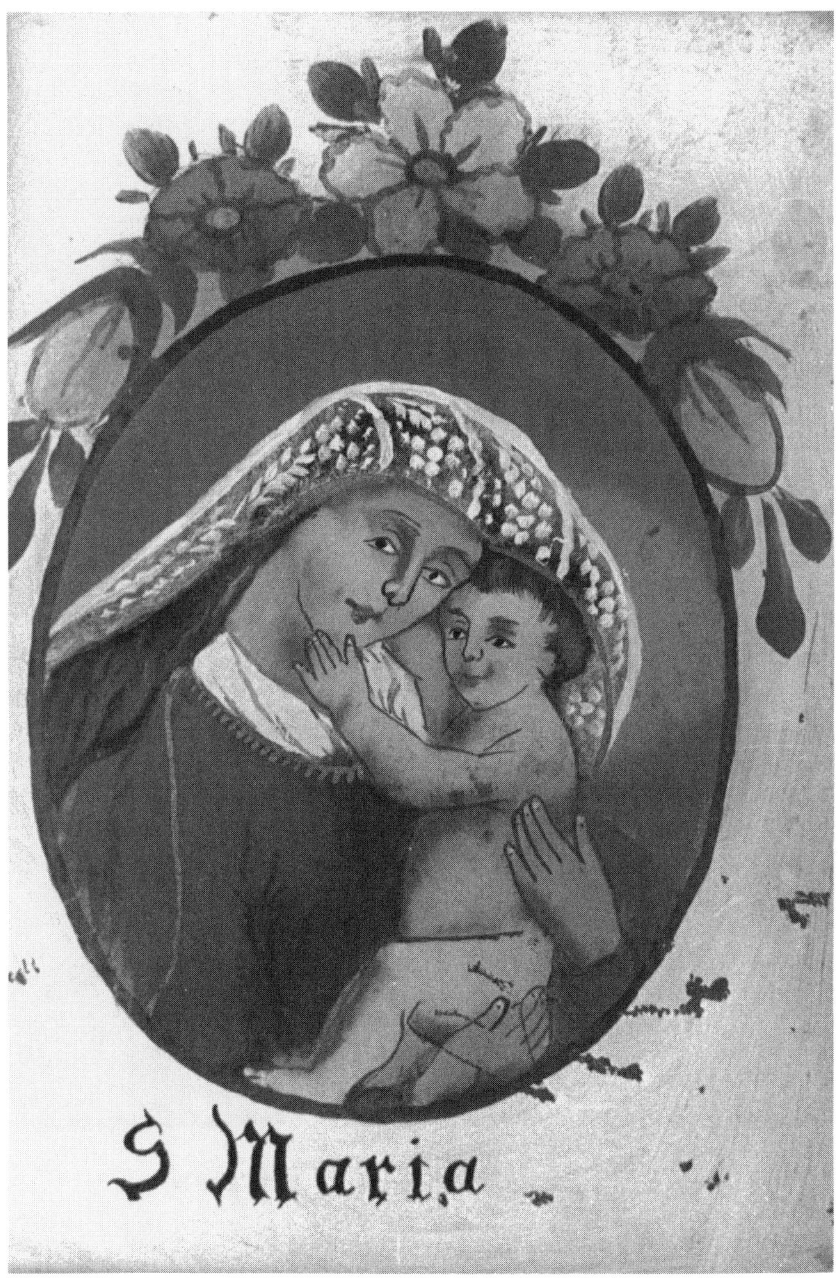

Figure 16. Mary the Helper. (Heimatmuseum, Oberammergau)

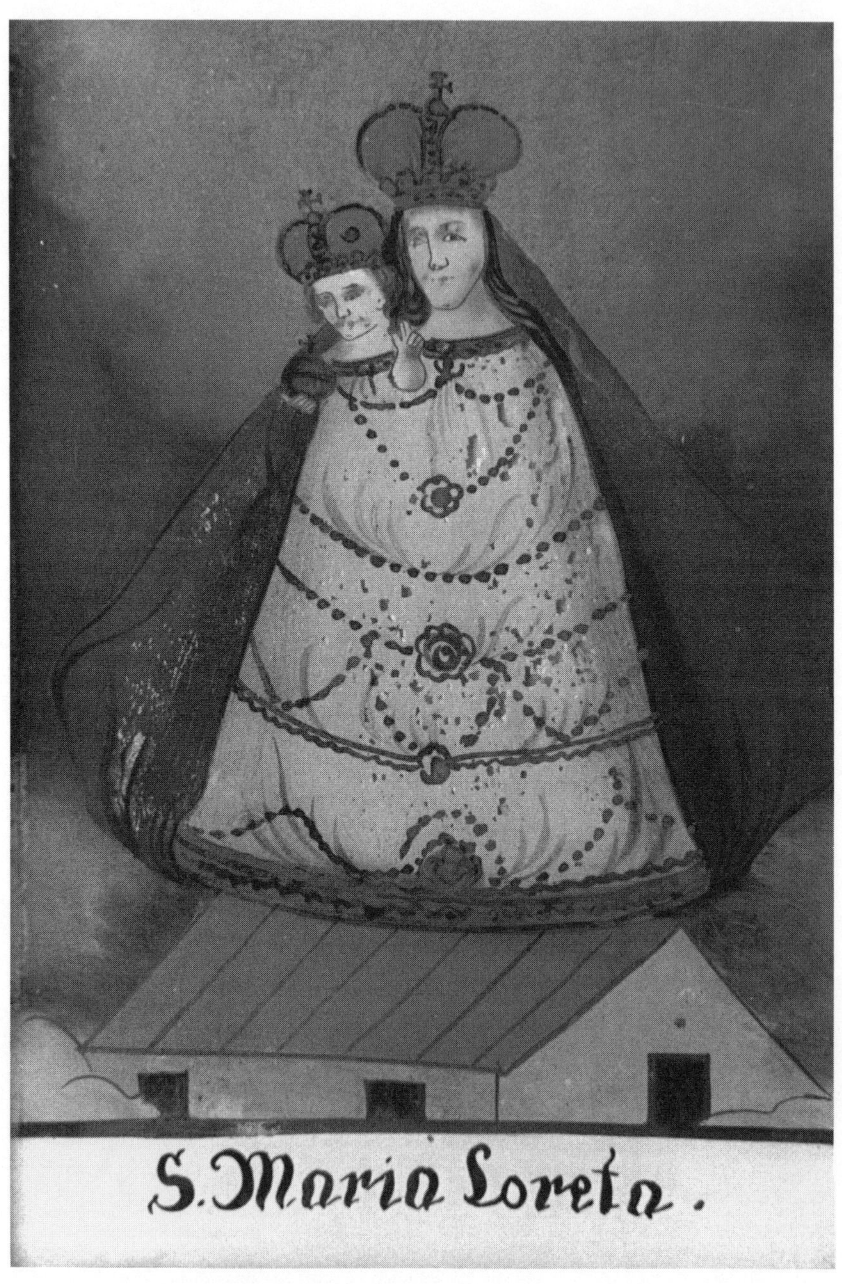

Figure 17. Mary of Loreto. (Heimatmuseum, Oberammergau)

nence. Yet this clear transference of power from the child as God to the mother who gave him birth makes Mary's motherhood a vehicle for her successful intercession with her resurrected son on behalf of the human beings for whose salvation he was sacrificed.

Despite these clear differences between the two types, even the Mary the Helper is related to cultish medieval depictions of Mary, still incidentally exemplified by the fifteenth-century Madonna revered at Hohenpeißenberg near Lake Staffel, in which Mary hands her child an apple symbolizing human sin.[33] Moreover, the very title "Helper" given the motif, which is derived from a cry for help, draws attention away from the playfulness of the scene toward the lovingly protective role of the mother. Indeed, Mary the Helper proved most popular during times of upheaval.[34] This need for loving shelter and aid is mirrored in other names given to local Marian cult figures, such as the versions named Mary "of Good Council" and Mary "of Solace," as it is also in the graphic depiction of the "Heart of Mary" prominently displayed on the Madonna's chest. Both prototypical images of Mary as Mother, therefore, serve the same essential purpose of expressing the protective power and intercessory efficacy of the Mother of God.[35]

The practical importance for consumers of this protective role provided by the many *Gnadenbilder* of Mary is further confirmed by the repeated depiction of these cult figures in votive paintings. Both pictorially and verbally, such paintings offer evidence for the effectiveness of Mary's intervention on behalf of believers in need. The thankful expression, "Mary has helped," is thus the corollary to the cry for help implied by her invocation, and the knowledge that she had proven her ability to stand by victims of disaster in the past has strengthened the faith of her cult followers for the future.[36] Moreover, the syntax suggested by the use of Marian images as protective devices lays greater emphasis on the viewer than on the child. Indeed, it seems to me that Jesus, albeit his role is implicitly central to the proceedings, is relegated to a dependent clause preceding the primary interplay of subject and object in the sentence. My reading of the Madonna's message goes as follows: "Because I am the mother of God (Jesus), I, Mary the Mother, can and will help and protect you (the viewer)." While, as we have noted, the past tense invoked by past performance makes an integral contribution to Mary's significance in the eyes of the consumer, the future promise of motherly protection is his or her focus of attention. As "the Virgin's children," to invoke the self-designation of twentieth-century Aztec believers in the maternal power of Mary, consumers might also identify with the baby in Mary's arms as protected child.[37]

Because it is as a mother that Mary promises to help her believers, her role as a female intercessor must be placed in the context of the male-female power relationships of the Catholic households where the habit of seeking her mediation was a significant behavioral pattern. For her activities as intercessor may well have reflected the social realities of Bavarian motherhood, as well as influencing them by the power of her example.[38] To establish the meaning of this sort of female mediation for household members, it is necessary to return to the combinations of paintings displayed in the *Herrgottswinkel*. There we have already seen Mary paired with the Trinity and with her son both as the Christ of the Passion and as an infant-in-arms. But we have not yet considered the very popular pairing of Mary with her husband Joseph, both in pendants intended as pairs and united in single paintings presenting variations on the theme of the Holy Family. Yet this reference to Mary's natural life offers interesting contributory evidence about the question of female power in the household. As a counterpoise to the all-powerful figure of God the Father, whose ultimate right to judge must be mitigated by the supplication of a host of intermediaries, Mary at the head of them, the figure of Joseph seems weak and approachable. While God the Father appears in his majesty in depictions of the Trinity, He is never to be seen alone as a source of protection in votive paintings or as a pendant in the *Herrgottswinkel*. The human Joseph, however, was frequently used as a pendant, and his derivation of power from wife and child, sometimes explicitly portrayed by the crown of flowers held by Jesus over his head, undermines the sense of authority that his position as male head of household should lend him.[39]

Thus, we find two contradictory images of the male role; this suggests that a hasty acceptance of the patriarchal supremacy derived from the legal, moral, and social power of the *Hausvater* or house father and implied by the need to find an intercessor on behalf of the God/father's "subject" family members might be unwise.[40] For Mary's power to protect her children as expressed in innumerable images might well have encouraged and also reflected independence and authority in the wives whose economic and domestic contributions to the household provided essential benefits for the family. The father's role might even at times appear as shadowy as God's in the votive paintings, where His concern for the favorable outcome of each disaster seems far less certain than that of the more active patron or patroness invoked. This would be particularly true of the households headed by a woman either temporarily or permanently; we have seen the frequency with which men set off from home to engage in commercial activities, and we have observed the widow of Johannes Noder managing her late husband's business, as many other widows also had to do. The recruitment of men into a business such as glasspainting through marriage would also tend to place the husband in a less authoritative position vis-a-vis his wife, as Goody has suggested, and so would age differences when the wife was substantially older than her husband.[41] Where rural industry had induced new familial relationships, in which the husband might be the parent responsible for child care and domestic duties, there too the image of the wife as protector might be enhanced. There is even a glasspainting in which Mary spins while the carpenter Joseph holds the child Jesus on his arm as he sits watching his wife at work, a painting that may well have reflected or influenced this revised setup.[42]

Despite these possibilities for a strong female role in the household, however, the constant resort to mediators does suggest that where patriarchal authority was strongly imposed, the role of the mother could be expected to be that of intercessor, as the one of the weak most likely to be successful in gaining the ear of the oppressor.[43] Indeed, by way of example, the diary of an English farmer's wife written in the 1790s illustrates the effectiveness of female manipulative powers in the similar context of a farming household. Anne Hughes conveys her almost motherly attitude to the male foibles of her very respectable husband when she tells us on the first page of her daily notations that "men be verry tiresome sometimes." She and her maid have well-established patterns of dealing with any problems that the head of the household's position of authority might put in their way. One can imagine the means by which this resourceful woman would have acted as intercessor for the child whose expected appearance ended her activity as diarist.[44]

Despite the possible ambiguity of Marian images as normative guides to the correct apportionment of power within familial relationships, her motherhood was, as we have noted, the key to her significance. As such, she was repeatedly depicted as the mother of an infant or small child, and thus as the nucleus of a family. In this context, her descent from pre-Christian fertility goddesses left Mary with strong reproductive implications, stressing the important role of the wife in each household as sole bearer of children in this "unit of production and reproduction."[45] In addition, her nutritive role as the mother of children was emphasized. Even her normative possibilities discussed above revolve around the role of the wife/mother in the survival of the household members, mostly the children. Mary's duties as mother would, therefore, center upon the nutritive function explicitly expressed both in elite art as the breast-feeding of the Infant Jesus and in popular art as the motif Mary Breast-feeding.[46] Here again, however, we meet with a challenge in the possible interpretation of Mary's significance for the consumers of glasspaintings. For in contrast to the breast-feeding mother of this motif and the methods of mothering that it suggests, Bavarian mothers had long followed the custom of hand-feeding infants, subjecting them to such alternatives as meal, maybe the "thick indigestible meal pap" used near Augsburg and "given in a sweetened form, cooked in milk, to children almost immediately after birth."[47] As a consequence, infant mortality remained high even during the nineteenth century in Bavaria.[48] The combination of this persistently high rate of infant deaths with culturally prescribed artificial feeding habits created mothering norms substantially different from those put forward in elite theories of responsible motherhood.[49] There were, therefore, two standards of motherhood united in the once again ambiguous cult figures of the Mother of God.

The popular conception of a mother's role is our primary concern here. We are reminded that it concerned not only the care of a live infant but also the duty owed to a dead one by numerous votive paintings of the dead babies. Their repeated depiction can thus provide supplementary evidence for a specifically southern Bavarian interpretation of Mary's relationship to her own baby in the Madonna theme. One of these *Totenbilder* or portraits of the dead can therefore represent the votive painting category in glasspainting (see figure 18). The absence of a protective supernatural figure in this painting makes it unusual as a votive offering, and we cannot pinpoint its destination in a specific cult shrine. Yet the same commitment of human beings to supernatural care that we have noted in other votive paintings is implied by this form of representation. In it, dead family members are depicted as they were last seen in life, but with crosses suspended above their heads. The swaddled infant lying on a cushion in the right foreground of the picture space is, therefore, dead, as may well be the two swaddled figures lying to the extreme right of the group and cut off by the frame. The

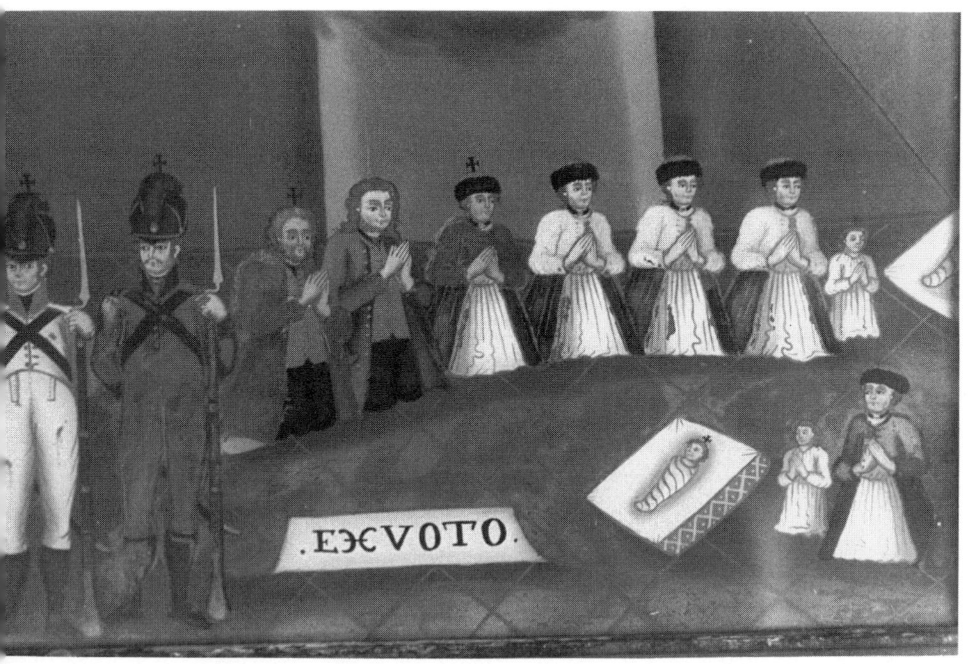

Figure 18. Anonymous *Totenbild.* (Heimatmuseum, Oberammergau)

entire extended family is here, including the old father and mother, now dead, and the two brothers whose involvement in the wars has led to their deaths also. Consequently, this painting reflects less a concern for the earthly welfare of the family than a desire to commit the souls of the dead to the care of God, appealing for their eternal peace.[50]

The tiny figure of the swaddled baby in our *Totenbild* thus represents both a duty to feed, clothe, and protect and a duty to care for an eternal soul. We have seen that the method used to feed a child such as this one might well have involved the hand-feeding of meal and other substitutes for breast milk that so often proved mortally threatening to its health. There is great poignancy, therefore, in the text of a similar votive painting in which Barbara Haimbmatnerin reports the death of "her beloved child, named Melchardt." For his illness appeared to be the *Fraiß* or digestive disorder so commonly fatal for infants and so clearly connected to their diet. We do not know if she consulted a doctor, but the likelihood is that she made use of folk remedies in her efforts to cure her son.[51] Ironically, the very nourishment and care she extended, in this case lovingly, may well have caused her child's early death.

The clothing of our infant example, as was sometimes the case with images of the Infant Jesus in cult figures as well, was the swaddling bands universally used to depict infants in votive paintings of this period. This reminds us that it was still a part of many a mother's duties to swaddle her baby. Indeed, it was not until well into the nineteenth century, or even later in some country areas of southern Bavaria, that this custom died out in southern Germany.[52] "Everyone saw firm swaddling as indispensable. It was not only to protect the tender nursling, whose limbs were like green branches, from hurts of all kinds, but people thought it would hold straight the back and extremities." For mothers whose duties in the household required long hours of work, the dual role of swaddling as corrective clothing and as protective device must have been significant indeed. It ranks with other such devices, leading-reins and similar items, as a precaution taken to prevent the life-threatening accidents so frequently described in votive paintings as befalling young children.[53]

Whether an infant was born alive or dead, it was necessary for the parents to care for its soul. They considered this duty so important that doctors often complained about the dangers of hurrying babies to a chilly christening service in bad weather. Moreover, some of the many votive paintings that depict dead infants such as the one in our example may be expressing gratitude for movements made by a stillborn child while at such a christening service. For the official reception of a living infant into the body of the Church would reassure the grieving parents that they had gained its soul access to the eternal rest they so desired both for themselves and for their offspring.[54] Their final duty in this case was consequently to fulfill the promise made during the crisis to commission and deliver a votive painting. The act of committing a dead child to supernatural care, however, could also include the hope explicitly expressed in a 1775 votive painting from Austria. Father and mother kneel beneath a *pietà* with eight dead babies lying between them. They offer up their prayer through the figure of the Mother of God: "Dear God, eight children are with Thee, so give the ninth to me."[55]

Knowledge of these customary duties and experiences of southern Bavarian mothers would form a subconscious background to the significance of Mary's motherhood in the minds of Bavarian glasspainting owners. That motherhood was, of course, directed toward the raising of a healthy infant such as the numerous depictions of fat, healthy babies held in Mary's arms. Nevertheless, evocation of the high infant death rates from which Bavarian mothers suffered would be contributed by the knowledge of Jesus's Passion lurking behind his healthy infant form. This combined message of life and death was familiar to Bavarian viewers as the repeatedly painted Child Jesus lying on the cross known as the Reclining Child. Mary too represented both life and death, as expressed by the *pietà* motif in which she receives back the dead body to which she first gave life.[56] For these reasons, it seems certain that any Bavarian owner of Marian cult images would bring an awareness of the frailty of the child in Mary's arms to his or her understanding of them.

The uncertainty of life for small southern Bavarian infants serves as a paradigm for the more general uncertainty about family and household safety experienced by their parents, an uncertainty for which the intervention of supernatural patrons like Mary provided a reassuring solution. If we look at surviving figures for the year-by-year experience of infant mortality in two glasspainting villages, Uffing and Oberammergau, presented in tables 8 and 9, we can see that the striking fact about the relationship between births and infant deaths is precisely its lack of predictability. This kind of uncertainty, undoubtedly perceived

Table 8 Uffing Vital Statistics, 1836–1861

Year	Deaths	Births	Infant Deaths*	Infant Mortality†
1836–37	16	22	9	40%
1837–38	17	16	8	50%
1838–39	18	14	7	50%
1839–40	11	13	5	38%
1840–41	9	18	3	17%
1846–47	14	19	5	24%
1847–48	17	19	8	39%
1848–49	20	19	8	39%
1849–50	15	22	5	23%
1850–51	22	24	13	54%
1856–57	13	20	8	40%
1857–58	19	20	14	66%
1858–59	25	16	12	75%
1859–60	20	16	9	56%
1860–61	16	13	5	38%

Sources: SAM, AR 1173/30, 1174/31, and 1174/35.
Note: The 1852 Census counted 498 inhabitants in Uffing and 123 families.
*Age one year old or younger.
†Infant mortality as a percentage of live births.

by the villagers themselves, who could observe the high death rate, for instance, in 1857–59, or the ample supply of babies born and surviving in the late 1860s, required the strongly supportive patterns of cultural response that Marian worship represented. Ironically, in a sense, the normative example implicit in the role of Mary as a southern Bavarian mother was a cause of these very uncertainties it was her primary function to provide protection against. But for her followers, Mary the nourisher and fertility symbol merged with Mary the intercessor and protectress in a complex multivocal symbol of unprecedented power and love.

Images of Mary were by no means the only biblical or doctrinal motifs chosen by Catholic consumers to hang in their homes. For not only were there the many variations on the story of Christ's life and Passion to select from but also there were a myriad of saints' portraits to buy singly or in combination as pairs as well. Many of these saints were popular with local consumers as their name saints, whose special pro-

Table 9 Oberammergau Vital Statistics, 1856–1875

Years	Deaths	Births	Infant Deaths*	Infant Mortality†
1856–57	29	24	10	37%
1857–58	37	31	15	50%
1858–59	33	28	13	46%
1859–60	48	32	11	33%
1860–61	34	25	12	48%
1866–67	26	40	8	20%
1867–68	23	37	6	16%
1868–69	40	34	6	17%
1869–70	44	45	17	38%
1874	45	49	23	47%
1875	36	47	12	25%

Sources: SAM, LRA 131474.
Note: The inhabitants of Oberammergau numbered 1,155 in 1840, 1,053 in 1855, and 1,121 in 1867. By 1875, the figure had climbed to 1,226.
*Age one year old or younger.
†Infant mortality as a percentage of live births.

tection reached out to their namesakes. And then there were the many saints whose patronage of specific interest groups or individuals rendered them useful as additional protective forces supplementing the doctrinal figures of the Holy Trinity, Jesus, and Mary.[57] Certainly, no saint could offer the all-embracing protection of these powerful religious symbols. But with a variety of well-defined problems went specialists whose expertise could be called upon in a moment of need and whose images were, therefore, a desirable addition to the household shrine. Sometimes such saints would be asked to support a doctrinal figure in its protective duties, and the patron invoked would then stand beside the cult image as they acted together in providing a miraculous solution to the problem at hand. When Mÿchael Purgmaÿr of Hohenkirchen, Upper Bavaria, fell beneath a wagon in 1748, for example, he called on both a local Madonna and a Tyrolean saint popular in Upper Bavaria, Saint Notburga. In the votive painting he later commissioned, the two women hover close together above the scene of disaster, and the rays extending from the Madonna are augmented by those emanating from Notburga's haloed and cloud-borne figure.[58] At other times, the saint would act alone, as Notburga did on behalf of the child with a nasal hemorrhage whose plight is recorded in a 1773 votive painting.[59] A victim could also invoke the aid of two or more saints in combination instead.

The repeated commitment of humans in need to the protection of patron saints confirms that their practical role for household members paralleled the Mother of God's role discussed above. Moreover, the specific duties that they could be called upon to perform as protectors were often related to their life stories and occupations in the same way that Mary's significance was a function of her motherhood of Jesus. This meant that individual saints could influence household concerns both by their supernatural contribution to the solution of problems arising out of the daily lives of the family and by their personal embodiment of a way of dealing with the issues themselves, played out in their own natural lives. Saint Notburga provides us with a good example, since her popularity as a local Alpine saint illustrates the way in which such saints served the needs of glasspainting customers. We can see at work the strong interconnection between her life story and her protective role that resulted in Purgmaÿr and others' inclusion of her in their pleas for help.

Notburga was a farm servant; she became the patroness of farm maids, but she also extended her protection to their employers, the farmers, as well as to the livelihood common to both maid and master, their cattle.[60] The chronicle of the Bavarian pilgrimage site dedicated to Saint Notburga at Weißling recorded over six hundred answers to prayers by the saint from 1749–91. Around two hundred of these cases involved problems with cattle, while the remaining two-thirds dealt with human sufferings. Mostly, Notburga cured illnesses, such as the twenty eye, eleven ear, and thirty-three foot diseases committed to her care, and in thirty-seven cases she aided women in childbirth, a function that surviving votive paintings from the Tyrol also attribute to her.[61] Grateful families would bring her such offerings as calves or butter and lard.[62] Even the gifts that expressed the thanks of her healed or protected cult followers could thus at times reflect the specialization of their patron, although her helping hand clearly reached beyond the narrow confines of farm management.[63]

Wolfgang Pfaundler has mapped out the extent of Notburga's influence, which was greatest in the Tyrol, western and southern Austria, and in Yugoslavia. Weißling was the only pilgrimage site to be established in Bavaria itself, although the saint could be called upon by Bavarians wishing to bolster the power of the local *Gnadenbild,* and her portrait was certainly produced by glasspainters. (See figures 8 and 9 for a Raimundsreuth example of a Saint Notburga and a comparable one probably executed in the Tyrol.) Notburga was born in Rattenberg, just over the border from Bavaria in that area of the Upper Inn Valley that once belonged to Lower Bavaria, so Notburga was considered a Bavarian saint as well.[64] Where she was not popular in the same general area, that is, in Switzerland and the Vorarlberg, Pfaundler suggests that division of properties excluded the problem of farm servants; the resulting landholdings were small enough to be worked by family members alone. Where the landholdings were passed on only to one son as in Bavaria, however, the need for servants could be acute, particularly since the continuing high infant mortality may have perpetuated a scarcity of extra hands available at harvest time.[65] In addition, the need for servants in the peasant households of central Europe could fluctuate with the family life cycle and fortunes.[66] Scarcity of farm labor and the consequent expense of attracting young men and women to the farm was often a source of complaint in Bavaria. Yet the number of servants in Bavarian employ was considerable throughout our period, particularly in comparison with other parts of Germany. Of the total population 15 percent were servants in 1771 and over 17 percent of the Upper Bavarian population were servants as late as 1840. Many may have been local farmers' children, even related to the landowner for whom they worked. Nevertheless, tensions between master and servant were common.[67]

Notburga's own story reflected the need for employing servants to take care of the farm animals and to bring in the harvest; it also highlighted the tensions that could result when employment of a faithful servant conflicted with the life of charity and devotion to God that such a servant might expect to lead. For she angered her employers on at least two famous occasions, when her duty to God and her fellowmen took precedence over her practical duties as servant or harvester. Although she was "an example of industriousness and loyalty, self-sacrificing charity and profound piety," her very charitable nature led to her dismissal from her post as kitchen maid at Castle Rottenburg.[68] She was forbidden to give extra food from the castle kitchens to local beggars, but she took them instead both her own food and the jug of wine customarily apportioned the Rottenburg servants. Consequently, her employers immediately dismissed her and she was obliged to find a new position with a farmer. When harvest time came, her help was needed in the fields, and she worked diligently until the sound of church bells informed her that a feast period had officially begun. As was expected of pious people, she wished to halt work, but her employer asked her to continue. She replied that she would cast her sickle in the air to ascertain God's will in the matter. If it stayed suspended, she was to observe the feast day, but if it fell to the ground, she must work on. Of course, it stayed in the air, and all harvesting ceased. Eventually, Notburga was invited back to the castle as housekeeper, and now she was encouraged in her charity toward the beggars, while she oversaw the Christian education of her employer's children as well until her death in 1313.[69]

The story of Saint Notburga stresses the value of good, loyal servants (and perhaps of considerate, sensible employers as well) who observed the Christian commandments inherent in the work rhythms and behaviors of traditional Bavarian life. Furthermore, her story serves to pinpoint the significance of the Christian example provided by her own and other saints' portraits as they hung in the homes of Bavarian farmers and craftsmen. For these paintings were not only many of them copies of local *Gnadenbilder* or of the famous *Gnadenbilder* revered in more distant Central European shrines; they also all served the purpose of illustrating the benefits of a Christian way of life. They were *Andachtsbilder* or devotional pictures and were intended to aid the viewer both in prayer and in shaping the pattern of his or her own behavior.[70] The paintings, therefore, had to remind their owners of relevant details in the history of the saint or saints portrayed, and attributes symbolizing their key significance were always provided to fulfill this need.

Consequently, in all paintings of her, Notburga is accompanied by the sickle associated with her saintly adherence to the commandments of God. She usually carries a tin container as well, reminiscent of the jug of wine she brought to the beggars, and sometimes she carries bread in her apron or the keys of a housekeeper around her waist.[71] The Raimundsreuth version reproduced in figure 8 shows her with both sickle and jug, but interestingly, the Tyrolean version omits the jug and includes a rosary instead. So it seems clear that she could conceivably be disassociated from her charitable acts but not from the miracle of the sickle that became her primary form of identification. Indeed, together with their adaptation to the needs of local believers, this kind of selection of attributes was a common practice. Only the most significant contributions of the saint were retained or emphasized, and in

Notburga's case, her connection to the farming household and its continued prosperity, albeit within the context of spiritual commitment that the sickle story provided, must have been most important to her followers. So the sickle sufficed to identify an unmarked image such as our Tyrolean example. Incidentally, the emphasis in the Raimundsreuth picture on the saint's figure and her two attributes illustrates that many customers made their purchases primarily because of the painting's content. For, as Herschel Chipp has pointed out, where the main significance of a painting lies in its "sacred meaning, . . . craftsmanship was necessary only to the point where it produced forms that adequately suggested or symbolized the all-important meaning."[72] Concessions to a need for decorative embellishment there are in this painting, but it is about as functional an image as one can possibly imagine. The protective powers of the saint are concentrated in a few hastily sketched lines, rather as the areas of the body radiating the protective powers of a flying witch are concentrated together on the Trobriand warrior's shield discussed in a fascinating article by Edmund Leach.[73]

Contemporaries did not overlook the spiritual messages emanating from Notburga's figure, however, and the association of the sickle with feast-day observance was certainly enough to confirm the motif's role as an *Andachtsbild*. Notburga moreover derived her protective powers from her sainthood, and her spiritual example was not unconnected with her ability to render practical assistance to her followers. In a votive painting dated 1818, the cult figure of Mary from Kirchenthal sends down the message to a woman still recumbent on her sickbed: "Your faith has helped you."[74] This reminder of the intimate relationship between sanctity and health serves to emphasize the impossibility of disentangling the various functions of a complex symbol like Notburga. For the spiritual example of her noble life of sacrifice, which can primarily be interpreted as a didactic and natural phenomenon, translates into a practical and supernatural phenomenon at the same time. Her own message is, therefore, an exhortation to the viewer: "If you want my protection, follow my example!" To those of her followers whose lives were patterned after her own high standards of faith and sanctity, health and good fortune were to be their rewards on earth, while a place in heaven and eternal rest were to be their final prize in death.

There is one complex image that illustrates separately the various fragments that we have found inextricably intertwined in the motifs discussed above. This final category, the *Haussegen* or *Haus Patronen*, protectors of the home, provides supporting evidence for my original contention that the images hanging in the *Herrgottswinkel* were intended to protect the household and that they communicated normative behavioral messages to household members as they fulfilled this primary role. In the two examples of Bavarian *Haus Patronen* in figures 19 and 20, the protective powers of four saints are combined with those of the Holy Trinity. Furthermore, examination of the patronage associated with each saint establishes that the coverage provided by the composite image extended well beyond the purely practical problems of the household to include those spiritual and doctrinal issues that were also, of course, the special concern of the Trinity itself.

At the center of both paintings, the artist has placed a popular, vertically arranged Holy Trinity motif, thus providing himself with a solidly doctrinal as well as protective centerpiece around which to group the four saints who fill the corners of the quadratic picture space. In the lower right-hand corner stands the long-venerated figure of Saint Sebastian, pictured, as was customary, undergoing the attempted martyrdom by arrows that he miraculously survived. His recovery from the wounds thus inflicted had led to his patronage of victims of the plague and other contagious diseases. His inclusion in our group of saints was, therefore, primarily intended to ensure the health of household members.[75] In the lower left-hand corner, Sebastian is joined by Saint Florian, whose ability to protect the house from fire had made him one of the most popular local saints in the area. Originally a patron of soldiers, his martyrdom by drowning had by the end of the fifteenth century suggested the possibility that he might make use of the water associated with his death to quench the fires so often threatening Bavarian towns and villages.[76] This adaptation of Florian's patronage to the needs of Bavarians whose fear of fire led them to seek out the most logical protector for their vulnerable wooden houses exemplifies the way in which particular saints were pressed into service by the people of a specific region. A further example of this common practice stands above Saint Florian in both our paintings, Saint Leonhard, the popular patron of livestock. Leonhard was originally the patron of prisoners, as the iron chains he holds suggest. Gradually, he became the protector of livestock as well, and his chain became the ordinary leading-chain used to guide cattle. For the "misunderstanding that plays a not insignificant role in representational art soon

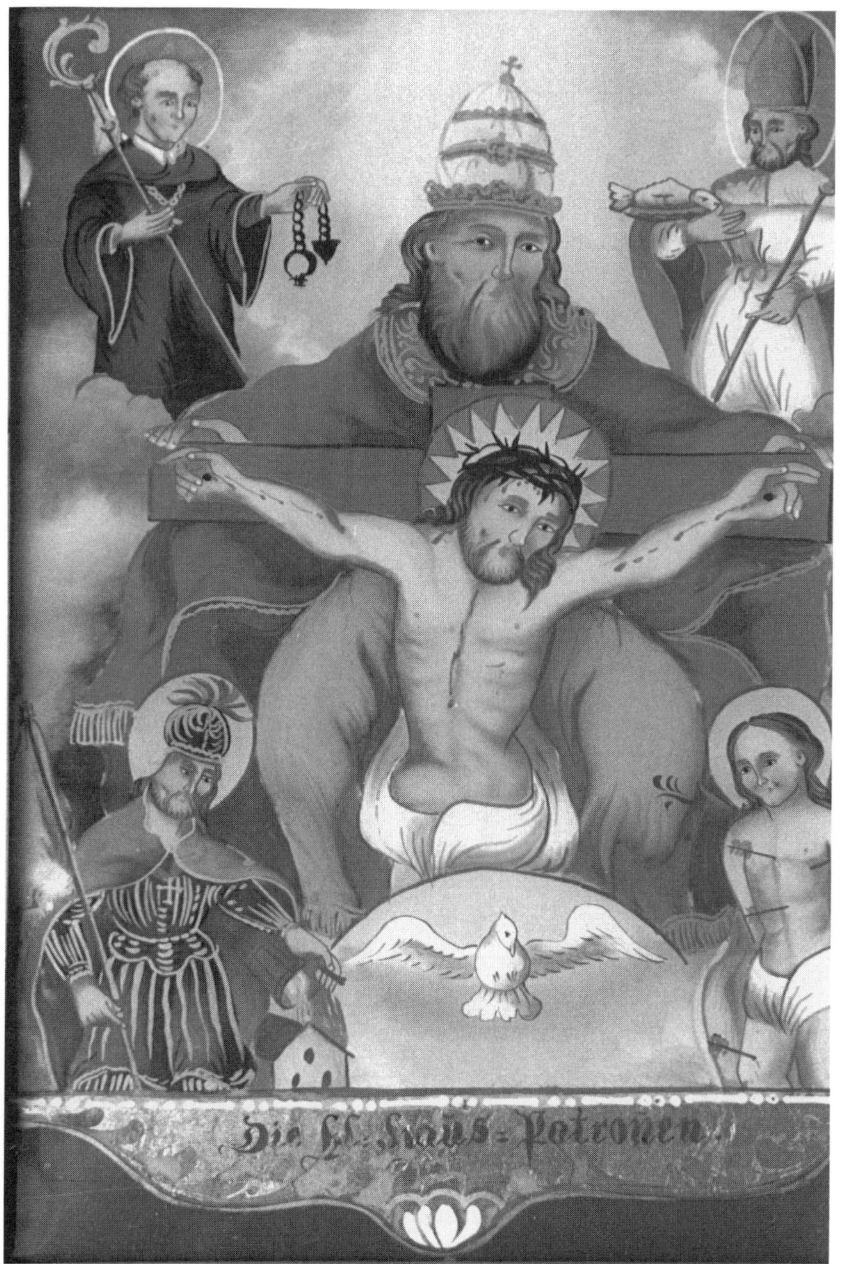

Figure 19. *Haus Patronen* by Gege. (Heimatmuseum, Oberammergau)

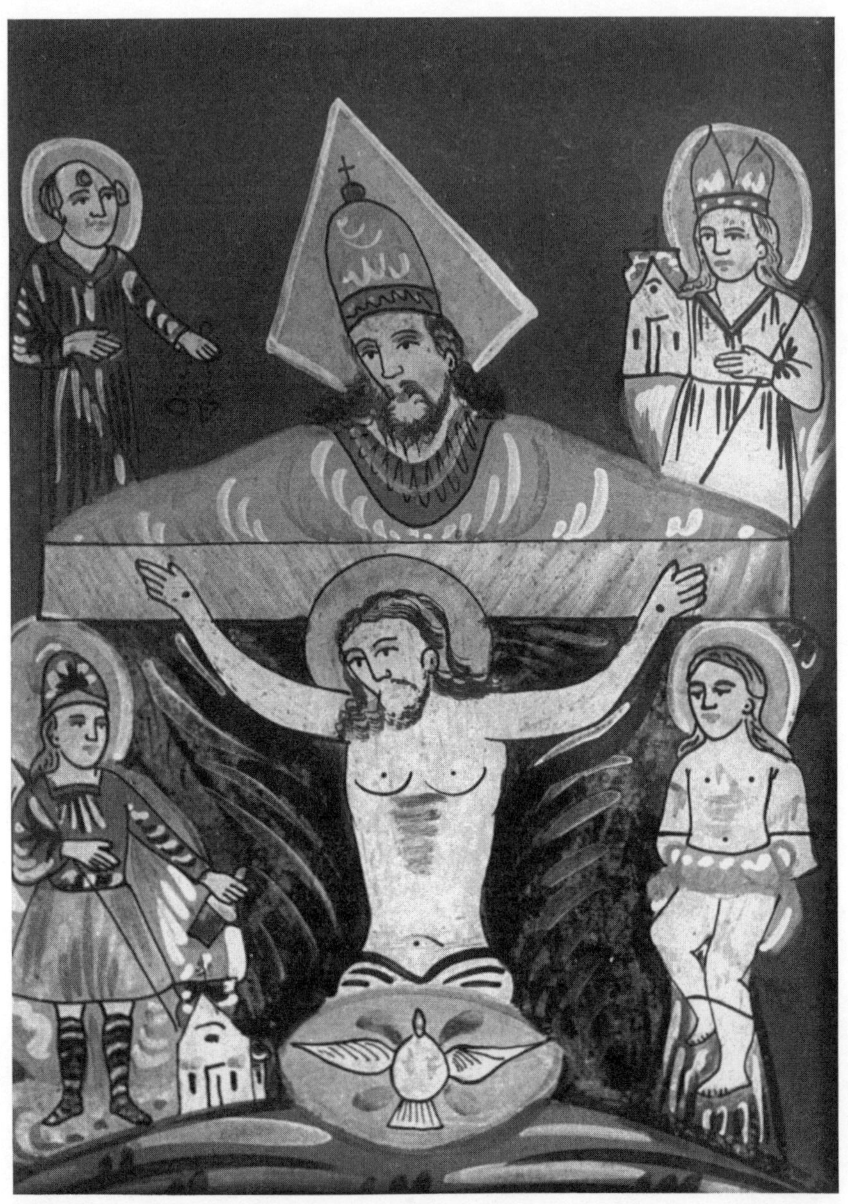

Figure 20. *Haus Patronen*, Raimundsreuth. (Herr Herbert Fastner, Zwiesel)

changed the prisoners' chains into cattle chains."[77] Even the order to which he is portrayed as belonging as a monk was altered from the Cistercians to the Benedictines, whose ability to cure animals had been established since the Middle Ages.[78] Leonhard thus contributes his particular ability to protect the livelihood of the production unit—that is, the cows and horses so important in the area—to the composite protective powers of the saintly group.[79]

The right-hand upper corner remains for our consideration, and it is here that this motif explicitly conveys the spiritual message implicit in the other motifs that we have already interpreted. While the Gege *Haus Patronen* includes Saint Ulrich in this corner of the painting, the Raimundsreuth painter has chosen to include Saint Wolfgang instead. The interchangeability of this fourth saint was due to his special role in the painting, which was to ensure the faith and sanctity of the household. For both men chosen were bishops and popular diocesan patrons, while they carry attributes that emphasize the rules and affairs of the church as well.[80] On the one hand, Ulrich's fish reminded his viewers that after he ate meat once by mistake as he sat beyond midnight one Thursday evening deep in conversation with another bishop, the offending remains brought by a disloyal servant to the Bavarian duke changed miraculously into the fish customarily eaten by the faithful on Fridays.[81] Thus, the bishop's saintly life compensated for this unwitting infraction of the church's rules. Saint Wolfgang's church, on the other hand, drew the viewer's attention to his construction of a small church in a remote area near Lake Aber. Wolfgang's minion in this holy enterprise was, as Moritz von Schwind reminds us in his delightful rendition of the bishop's famous story, the devil. The artist pictures Wolfgang's evil slave laboriously pushing a cart full of stones up the steeply winding path that leads to the construction efforts, while the figure of the bishop appears in the background, calmly at work on his project. In the verse that accompanies the painting, the artist tells us:

St. Wolfgang baut ein Kirchelein,
Der Teufel reißt ihm's immer ein.
Doch statt den heil'gen Mann zu irren,
Muß er ihm dienen und stein zu führen.
Ein Bild für jeden braven Mann,
Den dumme Teufel fechten an.

(Saint Wolfgang built a little church, which the devil kept tearing down again. But the saint became angry, and obliged the devil to serve him and carry stones, setting an example for every honest man to contest the stupid Devil.)[82]

Together, Saints Sebastian, Florian, Leonhard, and Ulrich or Wolfgang acted with the Holy Trinity to protect the household from illness, fire, starvation, and loss of faith. Their combined message as the plural subject of these paintings was, therefore, as simple as Saint Notburga's: "Have faith, and we will protect you (the viewer)." By incorporating the explicitly clerical patronage of the bishop and spiritual patronage of the central doctrinal figures into a painting that also provided physical protective patronage for the household, the artist has revealed the practical meaning of religious images. The presence of Bishops Ulrich and Wolfgang and of the Holy Trinity in the center of the paintings serves to underline the role played by church doctrine in the lives of Bavarian Catholics. But it is their practical guarantee of continued faith that best illuminates the way in which faith and health, faith and livelihood were but one and the same thing for the household members whose daily round was conducted under the protective eye of the saints and doctrinal figures looking down at them from their places in the *Herrgottswinkel.*

Epilogue

During the nineteenth century, all glasspainting families were faced with the destruction of their businesses because of the successful marketing of lithographs. This fundamental threat to their economic stability required a reorientation of each family's strategy for survival, a process that was shaped by the various situations in which the glasspainters found themselves when they began searching for other sources of income. In Upper Bavaria, this enforced adaptation coincided with the general reorientation of the region's artisanal work force that centered around service to tourists like the Blue Rider artists. Not surprisingly, therefore, local glasspainters resolved their economic problems in ways that illustrate well the process by which such areas took on a modern shape as "traditional" tourist centers.

In view of the fact that the challenge thrown at rural glasspainters came from the urban graphic arts centers, there was little chance of a reprieve. Industrialization in Bavaria generally took place around the urban centers and "deindustrialized" the countryside.[1] Moreover, the decline of glasspainting in the face of superior competition from chromolithography was rooted in the historical development of the graphic arts industry. The successful rural organizations established by glasspainters supplied the central European popular market by remaining in close touch with the demands of their rural customers; the hawking networks and the glasspainters' own cultural context ensured this. Yet the qualities that proved so important to the success of the glasspainting trading network discouraged any further development of the craft into a fully mechanized industrial procedure. The older techniques of the craftsmen, although potentially adaptable to change, suggested little exposure to the educational and technical advantages enjoyed by lithographers, who also enjoyed the patronage of wealthy members of court and professional circles from the start. Financial backing for this branch of the industry was assured by its initial attractiveness to such an audience. Similar opportunities were seldom available to the glasspainters, whose self-financing would hardly have stretched to the establishment of fixed plant.[2] In addition, the spread of lithography into the towns and cities of Europe assured its capacity to interpret the taste of a growing urban consumer market for colored prints, while both the versatility and the volume production of the mechanized procedure were necessary to exploit the expanding demands of nineteenth-century consumers. For all these reasons glasspainters found themselves redundant, at least in part because of their successful stimulation of an industrial development in their own field. Senefelder had written in 1818 that he would "not admit that lithography has made a great step toward the utmost perfection until the erring work of the human hand has been dispensed with as much as possible and the printing is done almost entirely by machinery."[3] This was a step that had certainly been achieved with the volume production of chromolithographs on steam presses in the second half of the nineteenth century.

Meanwhile, a few remaining glasspainters, located increasingly in the eastern parts of central Europe, did make a series of last-ditch attempts to stave off the threat posed by lithography. One strategy was to challenge the new lithographs with the production of "grisaille" glasspaintings that mimicked popular black and white prints. This shift in emphasis involved the revival during the 1850s of older gold and silver engraving techniques, as well as of a type of glasspainting known as a *Rußbild,* in which blacking was used to highlight the gold or silver motifs. The painters thus "robbed" the paintings of their greatest source of attraction, their vibrant color, which was so popular with the audience that was about to patronize chromolithographs. In Sandl, even the once-brilliant flowered borders were painted in grays.[4]

Glasspainters soon realized that this retreat from color had been a grave mistake, and they returned to the use of bright, but now factory-produced, colors. They frequently used lithographs to make patterns for their paintings. Wentzel prints provided *Risse;* indeed, one of his prints appears in the Blue Rider's *Almanac,* possibly a pattern used for a Saint George glasspainting. Chromolithographs were also used, such as the Madonna and Souls in Purgatory discovered by Haller that was copied in glass.[5] In 1912, when Hans Kyser visited Upper Bavaria, Josef Gege was still alive. Kyser's observation of the epigonal Staffelsee glasspainter led him to bemoan the fact that "his paintings seem like painfully executed copies of bad chromolithographs"; customers no longer wanted to pay out good money for such uninspiring work. The "smoothness and the motifs" of the new oil prints were the aim of glasspainters attempting to compete in the new market conditions of the early twentieth century.[6] Other glasspainters reduced their goals to the production of glass covers for chromolithographs, which could be stuck to the glass in place of painting it. Even votive painters drew inspiration from the new prints, and, in fact, votive paintings could even be constructed from framed chromolithographs. All these instances record desperate attempts to circumvent the inevitable death of glasspainting as a viable craft.[7]

As their businesses collapsed, individual glasspainting families responded in a variety of ways that ranged from emigration to successful integration into the new tourist economy, which included the adaptation of glasspainting to tourist demands as well. Johann Feyerabend, for example, gave up the struggle in 1869 by moving to Munich to become a photographer. His new profession was thus symptomatic of the general trend in the graphic arts during the nineteenth century. One of his counterparts in Raimundsreuth, Paul Janke, also appears to have chosen emigration, perhaps around the time when Franz Peterhansl felt obliged to lay aside the family glasspainting permit in 1875; conditions there during the late nineteenth century must have seemed discouraging indeed.[8] Wavering demographic statistics for the middle period of the nineteenth century suggest that emigration may also have been a favored response for other discouraged craftsmen such as Feyerabend and Janke at this key transitional moment. Table 10 captures in particular a drop in population measured in 1852 in all the Upper Bavarian communities save Uffing; Oberammergau and Seehausen still registered a figure lower than their 1840 total in 1861. Yet the absence in these villages of the pressure from an expanding population that so often caused large-scale emigration out of other declining centers of rural industry is remarkable. Indigenous population growth in the transition period was slow since infant mortality ensured stability.

Table 10 Population in Four Craft Villages, 1840–1985

Year	Murnau	Oberammergau	Seehausen	Uffing
1840	1,247	1,155	390	456
1852	1,163	1,032	381	498
1861	1,301	1,071	378	496
1871	1,414	1,198	374	555
1880	1,699	1,349	422	578
1885	1,630	1,246	413	621
1890	1,739	1,366	403	656
1900	2,040	1,559	423	707
1910	2,512	1,881	521	788
1919	2,439	1,897	618	822
1933	4,521	2,364	638	879
1939	4,521	3,640	712	877
1950*	5,427	5,325	1,866	1,638
1961	6,184	4,603	1,555	1,497
1970	6,860	4,661	1,582	1,495
1979	(10,418)†	4,800	(1,840)	(2,079)
1985	(11,029)	4,664	(2,025)	(2,229)

Sources: Beiträge zur Statistik Bayerns, vols. 192, 320, and 377 (Munich: Bayerisches Statistisches Landesamt, 1953, 1972, and 1980); *Gemeinde Daten, Ausgabe 1986* (Bayerisches Landesamt für Statistik und Datenverarbeitung, 1986).
*Includes refugees. †Parentheses denote a reformed area.

In Oberammergau, Daisenberger reckoned for the period from 1848–57, during which the 1852 census was taken, that 299 village births had been balanced by 286 deaths, leaving a net gain from that source of only 13. Deaths there exceeded births during the late 1850s, to be overtaken by a rising birth total in 1861–62 that receded again in the late 1860s. Immigration to Oberammergau, however, may have been substantial at times, while the figures are surely complicated by the absence of agents in the field.[9] And whatever the true demographic losses the glasspainting centers had suffered in the midcentury transition period they soon made up and more. By 1871 all Upper Bavarian centers but Seehausen had surpassed their 1840 total, and the trend continued upward, despite one further dip in the mid-1880s.[10]

These rising population figures reflect the fact that in Upper Bavaria there was much scope for adaptation within the context of the region's changing economy. We have observed, for example, the accumulation of landholdings by Johannes and Matthias Noder. Michael, from the next generation, could then hand over a substantial inheritance to his son Andreas, which included the original 1/16 holding in addition to the acquired agricultural properties.[11] Here was the reagrarianization process at work, as the Noder family contributed to the retention and even enhancement of Seehausen's agrarian nature. It was surely because of this creation of middle-sized farms, which could still benefit from an outside source of income, that so many Bavarian families began to provide the accommodations in which tourists could enjoy a "genuine" rural experience. Moreover, although large-scale farming would have been quite unappealing to the romantic imagination, these still small farming operations in a largely traditional setting remained delightfully quaint. Nothing could have been further removed from the crowded, noisy modernity of the city. And yet, while visitors re-created themselves in this rural paradise, their hosts supplemented their livelihood as farmers. For them the "modern" way of making ends meet was to permit strangers entry into their "traditional" existence.[12]

Another shift within this changing context was to the more long-lived village crafts, as the experience of Matthias Noder's brother Sebastian can illustrate. He moved to a house known as the *Schneider* or tailor's house, although his successor in the house, Johann Noder, is listed as both tailor and fisherman. Sebastian Gege's son Guntrum and granddaughter Klara married into fishing families as well. This traditional source of livelihood adapted well to vacationers' needs in the shape of boating services; as a 1912 booklet outlining the many attractions of the Lake Staffel area informed visitors, Seehausen fishermen provided boats and fishing opportunities as well. A fascinating Münter painting captures the Blue Rider artists enjoying these amenities.[13]

Yet another internal shift was to enter retail sales, as Feyerabend's mentor, the Murnau glasspainter Ignaz Schmid, was able to do. His father Johann Baptist moved from Uffing to Murnau by marrying the daughter of an artificial flower maker; there, he established himself as a glasspainter. By the late 1840s Ignaz had taken over his parents' business, but he had begun selling a wide variety of artistic products, including the traditional artificial flowers and glasspaintings. This shift into retail sales, often oriented specifically toward the tourists, was the general trend in Murnau, where the typical old-fashioned industries faced a gradual decline; there was, for example, only one brewery left in 1931. By 1912, consequently, Münter and Kandinsky could have shopped at Frieda Weiß's clothing store, across the street from the Griesbräu Inn out of which Kandinsky painted in 1908; they could have munched on Mathias Forster or A. Herrschmann's luscious pastries or browsed through Josef Rapp's collection of contemporary and antique jewelry and clocks. Visits to the epigonal glasspainter Heinrich Rambold would ironically have taken them by the Rambold shoe store where factory-made products of the highest quality were retailed.[14]

The tourists had begun arriving to help support this flourishing retail trade as early as 1865 in the wake of earlier forays by landscape painters.[15] For the Lake Staffel area provided access to enchanting and inspirational Alpine scenery; it also offered both summer and winter amusements, and a small winter sports industry even developed there. Furthermore, the wholesome waters of the lake attracted bathers in large numbers, 28,000–30,000 a year by 1912, up to 1,800 a day in the hot summer of 1921; mineral baths also provided therapy for invalids. In these new circumstances the accommodation of visitors could flourish as well as retailing. Indeed, the Gasthof zur Post, from which Carl Spitzweg sketched Murnau around 1830, was in 1865 "one of the friendliest inns of the uplands." And the accommodations grew apace, to include by the early twentieth century several sizeable hotels, often in former breweries like the Griesbräu, and even a fifty-bed "spa" hotel. "Most" private houses and villas also offered beds. By the 1930s one observer could argue that during summertime the Murnau area's population doubled! The 1928 drowning death there of a Belgian priest suggests that this influx of guests was drawing from a wide international pool.[16] Thus, Murnau continued to play its traditional role as the marketing and business center for the Lake Staffel region, while successfully assuring the prosperity of its growing population with the provision of the welcome additional income brought in by the tourist influx each year. On this basis, the town now enjoys a population (within expanded town limits) of over 11,000.[17]

Oberammergau too blossomed with retail outlets, both for tourists and for the continued production of the village's traditional crafts. There were roughly 120 woodcarvers and 6 colorers active there in the late 1850s.[18] And while some of the once-successful products, notably glasspaintings but also toys, were replaced by machine-made substitutes, in general these village craftsmen managed to survive factory competition. A mere 20 percent of the village's over three hundred households may have lived from woodcarving in 1905, but one mid-twentieth-century list calculates the craft work force at 121 woodcarvers and 44 apprentices, 11 painters and 4 apprentices, and 22 carpenters and 6 apprentices. The period after World War I was certainly discouraging and World War II was also bad for business. But a "boom" developed after the war, so that a 1960 guide book could argue that woodcarving was "for the majority of the inhabitants, the greatest source of income," with around three hundred families of the total population of around 4,600 living from it. Their craft, it claims, "today has more commissions than ever before, both at home and abroad." A current estimate of the craft's significance for the village argues that around half of the Oberammergau population still lives directly from tourism and woodcarving, a further third from retailing and other businesses.[19]

The great tourist attraction in Oberammergau is, of course, the Passion Play. Every ten years, "pilgrims" come to Oberammergau to assist the villagers in fulfilling their vow made in 1633 to perform a play as thanks for the salvation of the village from plague. Such pilgrims, recently as many as 520,000, have brought income into the village every ten years since at least the eighteenth century; 10,000 or so made their way to Oberammergau in 1760. The play gained special permission to continue after the general Enlightenment-inspired cessation of such "superstitious" performances. Already in 1840 it grossed 16,000 gulden, and in 1850 24,000 gulden when only fourteen rather than the more than eighty performances of the late twentieth century were given. Those moneys were divided between the community coffers and the performers, in 1850 464 individuals who shared 10,000 gulden, although the whole surrounding area benefited from the influx of play visitors.[20] In addition to bringing the tight-knit community of Oberammergau a welcome supplementary income, these visitors have perpetuated the international market for village crafts, woodcarving in particular.

Like Murnau, Oberammergau worked to entice both summer and winter visitors to the village every year. There were already seven inns in the village in the late 1850s, eleven in 1905 when 2,393 German visitors and 305 foreigners passed through Oberammergau in the summer months. By the summer of 1929 that number had grown to over 4,300, in addition to the 1,700 or so winter guests from the 1928–29 season; twenty-seven inns and lodging houses as well as private families offered them accommodation. By 1960 the village had the capacity to house around 2,500, a number which could swell to 5,000 in the years when the play was performed. One thousand or so visitors could fit into "hotels, inns and boarding houses and 1,500 in cultivated private residences." Current space for tourists is still about the same. To augment the many natural amenities of their locale, the community has developed both convention facilities and attractive recreational facilities such as the magnificent public bathing area and both summer and winter sporting opportunities.[21]

In the context of this burgeoning tourist presence in the Lake Staffel region, perhaps the most fascinating shift out of glasspainting was accomplished by the Geges of Seehausen, because it so clearly illustrates tourism's influence on the preservation of the "traditional" face in Alpine villages. Sebastian Gege became a decorative house painter when the family's glasspainting business could no longer bring in sufficient income. His son Josef carried on; he is listed in 1898 as a painter, employing two helpers.[22] The colorful façades created by painters like the Geges are one of the Alpine villages' most attractive features. The Gege home itself provides a fine example, as do the many Oberammergau façades. Frequently, these façades are religious in motif, and they add immeasurably to the quaint ambience of the recreational retreats. Moreover, the fact that locals perceived them to be of commercial value to the community is strongly suggested by the 1906 decision of Murnau's Beautification Committee, led by Emanuel von Seidl, to initiate a major renovation of the town's "look." Seidl argued successfully that "Murnau could be decorated by means of the painting of houses, tasteful painting of connected groups of buildings, characteristic craft emblems, . . . small architectural alterations, tree plantings, [and] windowbox adornments . . . according to a fixed, artistic plan." The town could then "become a prototype for how delightfully colored and cosy street paintings can be created." Work was soon in progress and included frescoes of King Ludwig and the local Marian cult figure on the walls of the Town Hall. Since Murnau, like other local communities, suffered from several massive fires even in the early nineteenth century, the town's appearance must in general have been a creation of the nineteenth and early twentieth centuries.[23]

The influx of tourists into rural Bavaria provided villagers with an ideal new source of subsidiary income. Now survival could depend on providing rooms, eventually even converting stalls into guest accommodation, running retail establishments for locals and visitors, offering recreational services, or maintaining the traditional appearance of the area. Within this general context even glasspainting began to enjoy a new popularity as part of the tourist market. By the 1870s

Sebastian Gege was already painting for tourists, and his work schedule reflected the tourist season. Even Heinrich Rambold has been described as working for tourists, despite the perhaps idealized description of his "traditional" business; he was joined in 1922 by Hedwig Schedler-Simet.[24] More recently, there has been a dramatic expansion of the craft, both in the production of commercial glasspaintings and in hobby activities. This revived interest in the craft is surely part of the intellectual trend begun by the Blue Rider artists; it favors either the "authentic" relics of a folk art tradition, both as antiques and as reproductions by a practitioner of the old school like Rambold, or paintings with nontraditional motifs that acquire their folksiness through the use of the traditional medium of glass.[25]

This attractiveness of "traditional" crafts such as glasspainting for "modern" practitioners and collectors illustrates well the ambiguous relationship of the glasspainting centers to the industrialized and urbanized world in which they have found a successful niche. For their appeal lies in that ambiguity; they have escaped much of the secularization process so clearly at work in the city, despite the many religious holdovers that remain even there.[26] Their new commercial activities clash no more with their Christian heritage than was true in the heyday of the pilgrimage era; rather, the shift to tourism has permitted them to leave in place a "quaint" cultural style that enchants visitors in search of change and perhaps spiritual inspiration. This was true for the Blue Rider group, as we have seen. Moreover, modern inventions, particularly of transportation, have encouraged the retention of religious practices like the decennial pilgrimages to the Passion Play.[27] As a 1950 press report argues, "Oberammergau in performing an obligation which is also a deep act of faith intends to carry out its high purpose and play its part in the renaissance of Western Christendom. Its popular Passion Play, . . . which has been preserved through changing times, seeks to draw pilgrims from far and wide."[28]

The striking success enjoyed by the glasspainting centers as tourist havens depended upon their relationship to similar centers of rural industry in Europe that later completed the transition to industrialization. For the searching out of recreational outlets by residents of these industrial centers encouraged a complementarity of occupation to develop that now permits both urban and rural inhabitants to coexist in a modern economy. This process, however, needs to be distinguished from the similar growth of a balance between commercialized and often large-scale agricultural units and their urban consumers that has provided other rural areas with a viable modern livelihood. For example, W. R. Lee imposes on nineteenth-century rural Bavaria a model that assumes the necessity of this kind of agricultural transformation when he assesses its agricultural picture pessimistically as the "model . . . probably the least suited for the effective support of long-term agricultural growth."[29] He also ends the story in midstream, for it was their very "backwardness" that was soon to serve the glasspainting centers so well. Turning adverse circumstances to advantage was, of course, nothing new for the region's inhabitants. And yet I am reminded of the experience of Grächen, a village lying on the shady side of the Visp valley in Switzerland, while its sunny neighbor Törbel enjoyed centuries of advantage in agricultural benefits. Then suddenly the tables turned, in one of those quirks of fate that changes tend to bring in their wake. For the winter sports industry has flourished in Grächen, leaving Törbel out in the cold![30] Nature and cultural history have similarly handed the glasspainting centers a chance to flourish anew in their twentieth-century guise.

Despite their ambiguous relationship to twentieth-century secular culture, the rural inhabitants of Bavarian tourist centers are by no means yokelish. On the contrary, their traditional appearance at least partially masks the fact that they are commercially gifted and draw imaginatively on their long tradition of involvement with the international commercial scene. We have traced the story of the glasspainters' contribution to the commercialization of their region, from the point of view of the producers and distributors whose livelihood was at stake, and also of the consumers whose increasing reliance on cash transactions for manufactured goods later contributed to the success of the Industrial Revolution. On that commercialization rests also the more modern economic health of the villages. For, because these nineteenth-century Bavarian peasants were already so integrally involved in the larger world of commerce beyond their mountainous retreat, they simply continued to balance both agricultural and commercial activities in piecing together a livelihood for their families. Only now their customers came to them from the cities of Europe and the world, put out by tourist agencies, as Schremmer has so aptly described the phenomenon.[31]

We began the story of *Hinterglasmalerei* with its discovery by the Blue Rider group, and it seems only fitting to end with them as well.

For with the sale of tradition to vacationers, we have come full circle back to their enchantment with the Lake Staffel area. It was, of course, their romantic fascination for the artistic crafts of Alpine Bavaria that was largely responsible for their contribution to the commercial health of the region in the early twentieth century. Clearly, we should not underestimate the role of the romantic revolution in rescuing such quaint areas from the collapse of their preindustrial economic base. Moreover, the Blue Rider artists stand as a fitting symbol for the transformation of rural Bavaria during the Industrial Revolution, for like the craftsmen they so admired, they too rooted their "modern" style firmly in the fertile soil of tradition.

Notes

Preface

1 I am using the terms *folk* and *art* loosely here to describe artworks massproduced by and for the "popular" classes for private display. That art was not, however, contained within local boundaries as the designation folk might seem to suggest because the "society of creation" was linked through international marketing networks with consumers who shared the producers' values, a crucial distinction that the subsequent discussion makes clear. Nor was it separated from national and even international iconographical traditions, as I explore in Part 2. See Nelson H. H. Graburn, ed., *Ethnic and Tourist Arts: Cultural Expressions from the Fourth World* (Berkeley: University of California Press, 1976), pp. 3–4.

2 Klaus Lankheit, ed., *The Blaue Reiter Almanac, Edited by Wassily Kandinsky and Franz Marc,* translated by Henning Falkenstein (New York: Viking, 1974), p. 40.

3 Mildred Lee Ward, *Reverse Paintings on Glass,* exhibition catalog, The Helen Foresman Spencer Museum of Art, University of Kansas, Lawrence, October 8–November 5, 1978, pp. 38–49, 102–22. On page 76 Ward reproduces a portrait by Greenleaf dated 1812. She concludes that "the American production of reverse paintings on glass was lively between 1800 and 1900, . . . that the subject matter in American glass paintings is the same as that found in American folk oils and watercolors of the period; and that distinct native influences affected the choice of subjects." These include the ever-popular portraits as well as patriotic symbols and memorials, and themes such as "trains and other modes of travel," "paintings . . . drawn from everyday life, such as . . . pictures of homes and public buildings," and "nature subjects," particularly flowers. In addition, "American historical themes, such as the Boston Massacre, are often found on glass panels of clocks and mirrors. Among other popular subjects are those of sea battles, interesting and historically important." Americans also bought glasspaintings imported from China.

Introduction: The "Discovery" and the Reality of Glasspainting

1 In the title of my introduction I am referring to the interest of intellectuals in "popular" mores as discussed in the first chapter, "The Discovery of the People," of Peter Burke's *Popular Culture in Early Modern Europe* (New York: Harper and Row, 1978). Jelena Hahl-Koch, ed., *Arnold Schoenberg–Wassily Kandinsky: Letters, Pictures and Documents,* translated by John C. Crawford (London: Faber and Faber, 1984), pp. 62–72.

2 See Hans K. Roethel and Jean K. Benjamin, eds., *Kandinsky: Catalogue Raisonné of the Oil Paintings: Volume One, 1900–1915* (Ithaca: Cornell University Press, 1982); Rosel Gollek, "Murnau im Alpenvorland," in *Deutsche Künstler kolonien und Künstlerorte,* ed. Gerhard Wietek (Munich: Thiemig, 1976), p. 179, mentions that Kandinsky had first seen Murnau in 1904 and admired it even then.

3 Hahl-Koch, *Arnold Schoenberg–Wassily Kandinsky,* p. 67, includes a comment by Kandinsky from 1914 that "Kochel is . . . fine. We just find Murnau more varied, freer."

4 Rosel Gollek, *Der Blaue Reiter in Lenbachhaus München: Katalog der Sammlung in der Städtischen Galerie* (Munich: Prestel, 1982), p. 261; see also Anne Mochon, *Gabriele Münter: Between Munich and Murnau,* exhibition catalog, Busch-Reisinger Museum, Harvard University, 1980, p. 39, for a very striking painting by Münter of the group rowing on the local lake, Lake Staffel.

5 See, for example, two vistas from Murnau by Carl Rottmann in the Lenbachhaus. G4448 is entitled *Vorgebirgslandschaft bei Murnau, 1843* and G4447 *Blick von der Höhe südlich Murnau auf das Wettersteinmassiv, 1843.*

6 See Roethel and Benjamin. eds., *Kandinsky: Catalogue Raisonné;* see also Kay Larson, "Two Arts Entwined: Gabriele Münter and Wassily Kandinsky in West Germany," *Architectural Digest* 43, no. 1 (January 1986): 80–81, for the view over to the church from Kandinsky's bedroom in the new house.

7 For the case of Murnau, see H.R., "Von den kinderjahren Murnaus als Sommerfrischort," *Land zwischen Lech und Isar* 9 (March 23, 1950): 67–68.

8 Peg Weiss, "Kandinsky und München: Begegnungen und Wandlungen," in *Kandinsky und München: Begegnungen und Wandlungen, 1896–1914,* edited by Armin Zweite (Munich: Prestel, 1982), pp. 60–63.

9 Rosel Gollek, *Gabriele Münter: Hinterglasbilder* (Munich: Piper, 1981), p. 14; Larson, "Two Arts Entwined," p. 78, mentions a "central oven between kitchen and living room" that provided heating. She describes the house on page 77 as a "tall, mansard-roofed, stoop-shouldered dwelling that projects the rustic dignity of farmhouses throughout the Alps."

10 See the reproductions of both furniture and staircase in Zweite, ed., *Kandinsky und München,* pp. 316–18, and in Larson, "Two Arts Entwined."

11 Gollek, *Der Blaue Reiter im Lenbachhaus München,* pp. 273, 380; Zweite, ed., *Kandinsky und München,* pp. 434–35; Ursula Glatzel, *Zür Bedeutung der Volkskunst Beim Blauen Reiter* (Diss., University of Munich, 1975), pp. 150–51. Glatzel interviewed a local artist in February 1974 who confirmed that Kandinsky was seen about dressed in peasant attire. Her dissertation stresses the "change in lifestyle" that the Murnau experience represented for Kandinsky and Münter.

12 Lankheit, ed., *The Blaue Reiter Almanac,* p. 40, argues that it was the most influential of the folk arts for the group. Of course, they were also fascinated by other folk media such as votive paintings and wooden carvings. See, for example, Münter's *Stilleben mit Heiligem Georg, 1911* and *Dunkles Stilleben (Geheimnis), 1911,* both in Gollek, *Der Blaue Reiter im Lenbachhaus München,* pp. 270–71, for Münter's use of wooden figures and the illustrations of votive paintings in the *Almanac.*

13 Glatzel, *Zür Bedeutung der Volkskunst Beim Blauen Reiter,* p. 140.

14 Weiss, "Kandinsky und München," p. 66.

15 See the catalog for the Solomon R. Guggenheim Museum's glasspainting exhibition held to commemorate the one hundredth anniversary of Kandinsky's birth: *Vasily Kandinsky: Painting on Glass (Hinterglasmalerei): Anniversary Exhibition,* New York, 1966.

16 See, for example, Rose-Carol Washton Long, *Kandinsky: The Development of an Abstract Style* (Oxford: Clarendon, 1980), pp. 81–82. She refers to an article by Eberhard Roters, "Wassily Kandinsky und die Gestalt des Blauen Reiters," *Jahrbuch der Berliner Museen* 5 (1963): 201–6, who argues for influence from Saint Martin as well. Hideho Nishida, "Genesis of the Blaue Reiter," in *Homage to Wassily Kandinsky,* edited by G. di San Lazarro (New York: Amiel, 1975), pp. 18–24, stresses the presence of representations of Saint George in Murnau, most particularly in one of Kandinsky's favorite churches, the Sainte-Marie de-Charité in Ramsach. It was also a favored theme in local glasspainting. See Glatzel, *Zür Bedeutung der Volkskunst Beim Blauen Reiter,* p. 217.

17 Lankheit, ed., *The Blaue Reiter Almanac,* pp. 147–87; Nishida suggests that a statue of Saint George that he reproduces in his article on the genesis of the Blaue Reiter "must have inspired" this still life. It seems clear, however, that the motif is directly derived from the glasspainting *St. Georgius* owned by Münter. See, for example, the reproduction of this painting in the front inside cover of Gollek, *Gabriele Münter: Hinterglasbilder.* Not only is the figure of the saint facing the same way in both glasspainting and painting (unlike the statue), but the iconographical details are very similar. The framing of the figure by an arch resembles far more closely the pictorial framing by the glasspainter than the arch of the niche in which the statue sits in the Nishida photograph. Gollek draws attention to Münter's use of her folk art collection in several still lifes when she discusses the painting on page 378 of *Der Blaue Reiter im Lenbachhaus München.* See also Glatzel, *Zür Bedeutung der Volkskunst Beim Blauen Reiter,* pp. 180ff.

18 Lankheit, ed., *The Blaue Reiter Almanac,* pp. 147, 169.

19 See Glatzel, *Zür Bedeutung der Volkskunst Beim Blauen Reiter,* p. 125, for the irony of this use of commercial products to exemplify spiritual expression.

20 Karola Sackel, "Der Letzte seiner Kunst: Heinrich Rambold, der Hinterglasmaler von Murnau," *Volkskunst macht Schule* 21 (1949): 9.

21 Hans Kyser, "Ueber eine sterbende Volkskunst," Berliner Tageblatt (September 6, 1912).

22 Gollek, *Gabriele Münter: Hinterglasbilder,* pp. 5–7.

23 Hans Konrad Roethel, *Gabriele Münter, 1877–1962,* exhibition catalog, Städtische Galerie im Lenbachhaus, Munich, October 13–December 2, 1962, quoting a note written by Münter for Dr. Johannes Eichner on February 10, 1933.

24 Gollek, *Gabriele Münter: Hinterglasbilder,* pp. 8–9 and illustration 1. See also *Gabriele Münter, 1877–1962: Gemälde, Zeichnungen, Hinterglasbilder und Volkskunst aus ihrem Besitz,* exhibition catalog, Städtische Galerie im Lenbachhaus, Munich, April 22–July 3, 1977, p. 123. The list of her glasspainting collection displayed in this exhibition includes several Rambolds (p. 137).

25 The word *popular* is fraught with ambiguity. I use it in the context of glasspainting to distinguish the rural peasants, laborers, and craftsmen who bought glasspaintings from urban, mostly middle- or upper-class consumers of paintings.

26 Mochon, *Gabriele Münter,* pp. 40–41, draws attention to the fact that the Münter house in Murnau had a similar *Tischecke* as shown in a photograph (ca. 1912) as well as in the *Kandinsky and Erma Bossi, 1910* painting. "Following the practice in Bavarian rural households, the suggestion of a votive corner with clusters of statues and glass paintings was created in the arrangement of objects in the room. Münter's painting of the interior limits the number of paintings and objects in order to clarify the composition and focus on the two figures at either end of the table. Yet again, Münter stresses the sense of context and environment in the lives of the artists around Kandinsky."

27 Sackel, "Der Letzte seiner Kunst," p. 10.

28 Edouard Roditi, "Interview with Gabriele Münter," *Arts Magazine* (January 1960): 39–40.

29 Gollek, *Gabriele Münter: Hinterglasbilder,* pp. 10–11 and illustration 2.

30 Weiss, "Kandinsky und München," p. 60, draws attention to Kandinsky's transferral of the lines and color washes of his woodcuts to his oil paintings. Similarly, Mochon, *Gabriele Münter,* p. 28, argues that "connections between methods of glass painting and the graphic processes [Münter] favored may have enticed her to try her hand in this medium."

31 See, for example, the *Paris Plate* at the Corning Museum of Glass, Corning, New York. It is dated as third to fourth century A.D. and listed as "reverse cold painted" in Donald B. Harden, *Glass of the Caesars,* exhibition catalog, Corning Museum of Glass, Corning; The British Museum, London; Römisch-Germanisches Museum, Cologne (Milan: Olivetti, 1987), p. 271.

32 Heinrich Büchner, *Hinterglasmalerei in der Böhmerwaldlandschaft und in Südbayern: Beiträge zur Geschichte einer alten Hauskunst* (Munich: Filser, 1936), p. 2; Herbert Wolfgang Keiser, *Die Deutsche Hinterglasmalerei* (Munich: Bruckmann, 1937), p. 15 and illustration 1.

33 See Franz L. Schott and Peter Volk, *Gemalt hinter Glas: Studioausstellung anläßlich der Restaurierung der Tischplatten aus dem Spiegelkabinett der Würzburger Residenz,* exhibition catalog, Bayerisches Nationalmuseum, Munich, February 26–April 24, 1988, and Residenz, Würzburg, April 29–June 26, 1988. The catalog also illustrates the beauty and intricacy of much elite glasspainting such as the Venetian *Anbetung der Könige* dated "after 1505" (pp. 34–35) and the exquisite South German workmanship in the painting *Maria, von zwei Engeln gekrönt* and a Crowning of Mary set into an altarpiece (pp. 23–25).

34 Gislind M. Ritz, "Die bürgerlich-handwerkliche Hinterglasmalerie des 18. Jahrhunderts in Augsburg," *Bayerisches Jahrbuch für Volkskunde* (1964–65): 47. Ritz's article is particularly valuable for its reproduction of the primary records that she uses in her examination of the Augsburg glasspainters.

35 Glasspainting was also practiced in other European countries for a middle-class public, notably in France and England. See Edith Mannoni, *Fixés et peinture sous verre* (Paris: Massin, n.d.), for vivid color illustrations of this work. See also Harold G. Clarke, *The Story of Old English Glass Pictures, 1690–1810* (London: Courier, 1928).

36 On Ignaz Baur, painter of historical paintings and frescoes, see Ritz, "Die bürgerlich-handwerkliche Hinterglasmalerei," p. 65.

37 Gislind M. Ritz, *Hinterglasmalerei: Geschichte, Erscheinung, Technik* (Munich: Callwey, 1972), p. 13; Ward, *Reverse Paintings on Glass*, pp. 21, 69, gives examples of the graphic Baumgartner style of glasspainting. This combination of craft skills in the same craftsman had a long history reaching back to the medieval workshops in which both painting and graphic art were practiced. See, for example, *Gothic and Renaissance Art in Nuremberg, 1300–1550*, exhibition catalog, The Metropolitan Museum of Art, New York, and Germanisches Nationalmuseum, Nuremberg (Munich: Prestel, 1986), pp. 59, 69–70.

38 Ritz, "Die bürgerlich-handwerkliche Hinterglasmalerei," p. 66.

39 Ibid., pp. 51, 73, quoting Paul von Stettin, *Kunstgewerbe und Handwerksgeschichte der Reichsstadt Augsburg*, 2 vols. (Augsburg, 1779 and 1788), 1:359ff and 2:253; Büchner, *Hinterglasmalerei*, p. 74. Clarke, *The Story of Old English Glass Pictures, 1690–1810*, especially pp. 1–11, describes the English version of the transfer technique, which provided glasspaintings popular during the eighteenth and early nineteenth centuries as colorful substitutes for prints. Clarke considers the years 1690–1810 as the "good" period, since "an abundance of coarsely-executed and poorly-coloured examples" appeared in the nineteenth century (p. 4). G. Bernard Hughes, "Old English Glass Pictures," *Country Life* (December 23, 1965), dates the decline from the 1780s. Excellent examples of the transfer type of glasspainting can be found in the Colonial Williamsburg Collection, for example, a series of mezzotint engravings of the Twelve Months transferred to glass and hanging in the Governor's Palace (no. 1967-460, paintings 1–12). The collection also includes several religious print transfers.

40 Max Seidel, *Hinterglasbilder* (Stuttgart and Zürich: Belser, 1978), p. 20. The painting is reproduced in Lucas Heinrich Wüthrich, *Ältere Hinterglasmalerei, 1520–1780* (Bern: Paul Haupt, 1976), figure 17. On page 15 Wüthrich points out that the painting is reversed from the original, as is common in glasspainting.

41 Ritz, *Hinterglasmalerei*, p. 13. Graphic art in Augsburg was linked to a rich history of religious and secular printmaking that includes the role of prints in Reformation and Catholic Reformation propaganda. The translation of these compelling iconographical themes into glasspainting could only enhance their appeal. See, for example, Robert Scribner, *For the Sake of Simple Folk: Popular Propaganda for the German Reformation* (Cambridge: Cambridge University Press, 1981), and for Catholic propaganda after the Council of Trent, see Manfred Brauneck, *Religiöse Volkskunst: Votivgaben—Andachtsbilder—Hinterglas—Rosenkranz—Amulette* (Cologne: DuMont, 1978), pp. 16–18 and the prints encouraging pilgrimage included throughout the text.

42 Hans Karlinger, *Deutsche Volkskunst* (Berlin: Propyläen, 1938), p. 49; Ritz, "Die bürgerlich-handwerkliche Hinterglasmalerei," p. 65, quotes von Stettin, *Kunstgewerbe*, pp. 359ff, in which von Stettin argues that glasspainting is "very useful

for the decoration of room and study and for that reason very beloved in many places." He mentions Portugal, Spain, and the American colonies; their presence in the Colonial Williamsburg Collection bears him out. Büchner, *Hinterglasmalerei,* p. 63, calls it "fashionable art in the service of rococo." Clarke, *The Story of Old English Glass Pictures, 1690–1810,* p. 1, quotes Horace Walpole.

43 Ritz, "Die bürgerlich-handwerkliche Hinterglasmalerei," p. 51; Büchner, *Hinterglasmalerei,* pp. 66–67.

44 Büchner, *Hinterglasmalerei,* pp. 66, 71; Ritz, "Die bürgerlich-handwerkliche Hinterglasmalerei," pp. 56, 67.

45 Robert Muchembled, *Popular Culture and Elite Culture in France, 1400–1750,* translated by Lydia Cochrane (Baton Rouge: Louisiana State University Press, 1985), p. 285, states that "imagery was an exclusively urban art"; the rural glass-painters form a significant exception to this characterization. They were themselves typical of their rural customers.

46 Ibid., pp. 48–49; Büchner, *Hinterglasmalerei,* pp. 66–71.

47 Büchner, *Hinterglasmalerei,* pp. 66–67, 70; Ritz, "Die bürgerlich-handwerkliche Hinterglasmalerei," p. 71, quoting Malerakten 7 (1727–1804), fasc. 59.

48 Ritz, "Die bürgerlich-handwerkliche Hinterglasmalerei," pp. 48, 62, 67, 69; Büchner, *Hinterglasmalerei,* p. 71.

49 Friedrich Knaipp, *Hinterglas Bilder aus Bauern- und Bergmannsstuben des 18. und 19. Jahrhunderts,* 2d ed. (Linz: Wimmer, 1973), pp. 50–53, 154.

50 Ibid., pp. 13, 29; Büchner, *Hinterglasmalerei,* pp. 4, 9, 12–13, 68.

51 Büchner, *Hinterglasmalerei,* pp. 80–81, 86, 96–97; Ritz, "Die bürgerlich-handwerkliche Hinterglasmalerie," pp. 65, 67, 75.

52 Büchner, *Hinterglasmalerei,* p. 86; BHA, Kurbayern Hofkammer Hofanlagsbuchhaltung, 265; Gislind M. Ritz, "Beiträge zu einer Stilkunde der Hinterglasmalerei am Staffelsee," *Bayerisches Jahrbuch für Volkskunde* (1966–67): 96.

53 Büchner, *Hinterglasmalerei,* p. 95.

54 See the account book for the Aschau glass factory in the latter half of the eighteenth century now in the possession of the Oberammergau town council. A possible exception is that of Murnau, since glasspainters there appear to have ordered their glass from local glaziers. See Büchner, *Hinterglasmalerei,* p. 97.

55 It was not unusual for the city workforce to lose initiative to country craftsmen in this period. The stranglehold on growth held by the guilds could only encourage the breaking out of production outside the limits of guild authority. See Eckart Schremmer, "Standortausweitung der Warenproduktion im langfristigen Wirtschaftswachstum: Zur Stadt-Land-Arbeitsteilung im Gewerbe des 18. Jahrhunderts," *Vierteljahrschrift für Sozial- und Wirtschaftsgeschichte* 59 (1972): 14.

56 Alois Senefelder, *The Invention of Lithography,* translated by J. V. Muller (New York: Fuchs and Lang Manufacturing Company, 1911), p. 7.

57 Many nineteenth-century government documents in the Bavarian archives are duplicated in this way, using a cursive handwriting rather than print.

58 See Leopold Dussler, *Die Incunabeln der deutschen Lithographie (1796–1821)* (Heidelberg: Weissbach, 1955); R. Arnim Winkler, *Die Frühzeit der deutschen Lithographie: Katalog der Bilder von 1796–1821* (Munich: Prestel, 1975).

59 See, for example, Wolfgang Brückner, *Elfenreigen, Hochzeitstraum: Die Öldruckfabrikation, 1880–1940* (Cologne: M. DuMont Schauberg, 1974).

60 The Langs of Oberammergau did a thriving business in frames. David P. Jaffee, "An Artisan-Entrepreneur's Portrait of the Industrializing North, 1790–1860," in *Essays from the Lowell Conference on Industrial History, 1982 and 1983,* edited by Robert Weible (North Andover: Museum of American Textile History, 1985), pp. 165–84, discusses a similar stimulation in the U.S. portrait market. His "rural portraitists" commercialized their trade to create "a vast rural market . . . which ranged from mass-produced cheap paper silhouettes to stylized oil canvases." Like the glasspainters, they were "forwarding changes in the image industry that eventually would make their presence expendable. . . . But in the meantime they brought an era of mass production and consumption to the farmhouse door and diffused a taste for the wide range of newly available cultural commodities." Their nemesis was, of course, photography (pp. 165–66).

61 This is the period when similar "protoindustrial" developments all over Europe were contributing to the transformation of key industrial sites like Lancashire. The term is now a familiar one, after its introduction by F. F. Mendels in his path-breaking article "Proto-industrialization: The First Phase of the Industrialization Process," *Journal of Economic History* 32 (1972): 241–61. A great deal of literature has emerged on this subject, notably the theoretical work by Peter Kriedte, Hans Medick, and Jürgen Schlumbohm in *Industrialization Before Industrialization: Rural Industry in the Genesis of Capitalism,* translated by Beate Schempp (Cambridge: Cambridge University Press, 1981). Much criticism has also emerged, and a helpful summation of the state of the debate is provided by L. A. Clarkson, *Proto-Industrialization: The First Phase of Industrialization?* (Basingstoke and London: Macmillan, 1985). Initially, I analyzed the glasspainters as a "protoindustrial" workforce, since they shared many characteristics with other such rural workers. See Helena Waddy Lepovitz, "The Industrialization of Popular Art in Bavaria," *Past and Present* 99 (May 1983): 88–122. The glasspainters, however, shared with many other rural craftsmen the experience of lethal challenges from industrial competitors, in their case chromolithographers. So they fall into the category of the "deindustrialized" within the contours of protoindustrial theory. However, as I have laid out in detail in my article "Gateway to the Mountains: Tourism and Positive Deindustrialization in the Bavarian Alps," *German History* 7 (December 1989): 293–318, the theory fails to explain the particular way in which rural Bavaria moved into the modern industrial world. The concept of "deindustrialization" fails to provide us with a positive formulation with which to deal with this transformation, remaining a residual category that conceptualizes the process only in terms of what is actually a complementary development, that of industrialization elsewhere. This is a matter that I discuss in some detail in the Epilogue (and in the article), where I suggest that all deindustrialization was not negative. Similarly, the complexity of artisanal relationships with industrialization is explored in *Shopkeepers and Master Artisans in Nineteenth-Century Europe,* edited by Geoffrey Crossick and Heinz-Gerhard Haupt (London: Methuen, 1984). David Blackbourn's contribution, "Between Resignation and Volatility: The German Petite Bourgeoisie in the Nineteenth Century" (pp. 35–61), is particularly helpful in nuancing the German *Mittelstand*'s experience of industrial competition that was by no means entirely destructive. The name of the game was adaptation —"if we replace the notion of linear evolution with that of adaptation" (p. 23)

—and that is what the glasspainters and their communities had to do in order to survive and prosper in the twentieth century. The Epilogue focuses on the particular benefits of tourism in supporting a wide variety of their adaptive approaches, illustrative of the flexibility of artisans in general.

1 *The Rural Glasspainting Workshops: A Strategy for Survival and Advancement*

1 The ellipsis points mark the omission of specific instructions concerning the preparation of the paintings, which were of the same iconographical type as the glasspainting in figure 11. SAM, AR 2043/142a; Büchner, *Hinterglasmalerei,* pp. 88–89.

2 Lankheit, ed., *The Blaue Reiter Almanac,* pp. 50, 57, 69, 70, 93, 155, 188, 200, 205, 218, 267–80.

3 Knaipp, *Hinterglas Bilder,* p. 19.

4 Pankraz Fried, *Herrschaftsgeschichte der Altbayerischen Landgerichte Dachau und Kranzberg im Hoch- und Spätmittelalter sowie in der Frühen Neuzeit* (Kommission für Bayerische Landesgeschichte, 1962), pp. 190–91. In the Dachau administrative district of western Bavaria that Fried studied intensively, smallholdings had increased by several hundred in the years between 1500 and 1726, but the short span of time between 1726 and 1760 saw further growth, proportionately to the earlier period four times the average annual rate. Fried does not give measures during the long period from 1500 to 1726 with which to assess the rate of growth or decline in the various stages of this development, for example, during the Thirty Years' War. But in Hermann Hörger, *Kirche, Dorfreligion und bäuerliche Gesellschaft: Strukturanalysen zur gesellschaftsgebundenen Religiosität ländlicher Unterschichten des 17. bis 19. Jahrhunderts, aufgezeigt an bayerischen Beispielen,* part 1 (Munich: Seitz and Höfling, 1978), there is plenty of evidence for the fluctuations of population. See also the Oberammergau Passion Play, which was initiated in the terrible year of the plague, 1634, that devastated the whole region. Hörger's graphs give startling evidence of this dramatic drop in population. See also Schremmer, "Standortausweitung der Warenproduktion," pp. 5, 12; Gerhard Hanke, "Zur Sozialstruktur der ländlichen Siedlungen Altbayerns im 17. und 18. Jahrhundert," in *Gesellschaft und Herrschaft. Forschungen zu sozial- und landgeschichtlichen Problemen vornehmlich in Bayern* (Munich: C. H. Beck, 1969), particularly pp. 228, 243–44; Fried, "Historisch-statistische Beiträge zur Geschichte des Kleinbauerntums (Söldnertums) im westlichen Oberbayern," *Mitteilungen der Geographischen Gesellschaft in München* 51 (1966), p. 19; W. R. Lee, *Population Growth, Economic Development and Social Change in Bavaria, 1750–1850* (New York: Arno, 1977), p. 116. For Lower Bavaria, see *Der Landkreis Wolfstein* (Bayerischer Wald: Verlag Landkreis Wolfstein, 1968), pp. 41–46.

5 See SAL 80/525a, A. Schmeller, *Bayerisches Wörterbuch,* and the clarification by Fried, "Historisch-statistische Beiträge," pp. 12–13, largely based on the notions of Josef von Hazzi, quoted in Schmelzle, *Der Staatshaushalt des Herzogtums Bayern im 18. Jahrhundert* (Stuttgart, 1900), p. 287. See also Hanke, "Zur Sozialstruktur

der ländlichen Siedlungen Altbayerns," pp. 228–35. Despite this ambiguity, the *Hoffuß* designations do give a useful picture of the relative worth of each landholder, allowing us to establish both the relationship of individual smallholders to the land and the extent of their need for supplementary occupations.

6 Hanke, "Zur Sozialstruktur der ländlichen Siedlungen Altbayerns," pp. 232–34, 245–46; Fried, "Historisch-statistische Beiträge," pp. 13–14, quoting *Churb. Generaliensammlung,* 1:133ff.

7 Eckart Schremmer, *Die Wirtschaft Bayerns: Vom hohen Mittelalter bis zum Beginn der Industrialisierung: Bergbau, Gewerbe, Handel* (Munich: Beck, 1970), pp. 345ff, calls it the "territorializing" of industry. It seems clear that the sustained growth of smallholdings in Bavaria depended at least in part upon the initiatives taken by smallholders in finding craft income to supplement their holdings. Whether craft opportunities initiated the growth of population or the pressure of demographic increases drove smallholders to seek out craft outlets to sustain their livelihood are questions that lie outside the scope of this study and are probably impossible to answer.

8 Ibid., pp. 395, 434–35. See also Schremmer, "Standortausweitung der Warenproduktion," p. 23.

9 Schremmer, *Die Wirtschaft Bayerns,* pp. 436–37. Lee, *Population Growth,* pp. 163–64, calculates that in the 1820s full-time and part-time craftsmen, together with their families, laborers, and journeymen, reached 38.5 percent of the population in the Rezatkreis administrative district. In the Isarkreis they accounted for 31.8 percent, in the Obermainkreis 29.0 percent, in the Oberdonaukreis 27.5 percent, in the Regenkreis 25.4 percent, in the Unterdonaukreis 23.7 percent, and in the Untermainkreis 20.6 percent.

10 Lee, *Population Growth,* p. 156.

11 H. Lieberich, "Das ländliches Handwerk in Altbayern vom 16.–18. Jahrhundert," *Mitteilungen für die Archivpflege in Oberbayern* 27 (1947): 721; Schremmer, "Standortausweitung der Warenproduktion," pp. 4–5, 24, 36, 38–39; Hanke, "Zur Sozialstruktur der ländlichen Siedlungen Altbayerns," p. 224.

12 Schremmer, *Die Wirtschaft Bayerns,* pp. 375–76; Lee, *Population Growth,* pp. xxvi–xxvii.

13 Around 1780, 2,077 shoemakers and 1,846 tailors worked in the countryside; the respective urban workforce was 649 and 582. Yet the per capita relationship of craftsmen to their customers was generally greater for the urban workers. For every ten thousand urban inhabitants of the new Bavarian kingdom, 73 shoemakers and 64 tailors worked in the towns; 58 or 56 respectively were active in the country. Only saw and grain millers, weavers, wagoners, farriers, and construction workers of thirty-nine professions surveyed were proportionately more numerous in the countryside, as one might expect. Lieberich, "Ländliches Handwerk," pp. 721–22; Ernst Anegg, *Zur Gewerbestruktur und Gewerbepolitik während der Regierung Montgelas* (Diss., University of Munich, 1965), pp. 29–31, 185ff; Schremmer, "Standortausweitung der Warenproduktion," pp. 24–34. Schremmer distinguishes between cities and market towns in this article and suggests that the market towns were perhaps growing faster than the cities (p. 34).

14 Fried, "Historisch-statistische Beiträge," p. 29.

15 Lieberich, "Ländliches Handwerk," p. 724.

16 Eckart Schremmer, "Proto-Industrialisation: A Step Towards Industrialisation?" *Journal of European Economic History* 10 (1981): 661.

17 Edward Shorter, *Social Change and Social Policy in Bavaria, 1800–1860* (Diss., Harvard University, Cambridge, Mass., 1967), p. 357; Lee, *Population Growth,* p. 170.

18 Gay L. Gullickson, "Agriculture and Cottage Industry: Redefining the Causes of Proto-Industrialization," *Journal of Economic History* 43, no. 4 (December 1983): 831–50, provides good cautionary evidence that protoindustry was by no means confined to these inhospitable regions.

19 See, for example, the exhibitions of local crafts in the Waldmuseum in Zwiesel, Lower Bavaria, and in the Heimatmuseum in Oberammergau, Upper Bavaria.

20 See, for example, Arno Kunze, "Vom Bauerndorf zum Weberdorf: Zur sozialen und wirtschaftlichen Struktur der Waldhufendörfer der Südlichen Oberlausitz in 16., 17., und 18. Jahrhunderts," in *Oberlausitzer Forschungen,* edited by Martin Reuther (1961); Rudolf Braun, *Industrialisierung und Volksleben: Veränderungen der Lebensformen unter Einwirkung der verlagsindustriellen Heimarbeit in einem ländlichen Industriegebiet (Zürcher Oberland) vor 1800,* 2d ed. (Göttingen: Vandenhoeck und Ruprecht, 1979).

21 Fried, "Historisch-statistische Beiträge," pp. 18–19.

22 Joseph Albert Daisenberger, *Geschichte des Dorfes Oberammergau* (Munich: Dr. C. Wolf and Son, 1858), p. 139.

23 Karl Gröber, *Alte Oberammergauer Hauskunst,* 2d ed. (Rosenheim: Rosenheimer, 1980), pp. 8ff; Daisenberger, *Geschichte des Dorfes Oberammergau,* p. 139; *Führer durch das Verleger Lang'sche kunst- und kulturgeschichtliche Oberammergauer Museum* (Oberammergau: Gg. Lang sel. erben, n.d.), pp. 4–7; *Königlich-Baierisches Intelligenz-Blatt des Iller-Kreises* (1815–16), pp. 861–62. See also the toy horses, wagons, and stables so typical of Oberammergau woodcarving in the Oberammergau Museum; BHA, Kurbayern Hofkammer Hofanlagsbuchhaltung 168.

24 Daisenberger, *Geschichte des Dorfes Oberammergau,* pp. 156, 181–85, 189. A good example of an Alpine village in which mixed farming of this sort was practiced for centuries is Törbel, studied by Robert McC. Netting in *Balancing on an Alp: Ecological Change and Continuity in a Swiss Mountain Community* (Cambridge: Cambridge University Press, 1981). Netting discusses the demographic impact of the potato in a fascinating chapter that might have some relevance for the changes taking place in Upper and Lower Bavaria as well (pp. 159–68). Törbel, however, was far less linked into the economy of the outside world than Oberammergau in the eighteenth and early nineteenth centuries. There is an intriguing discussion of the social and economic differences among horse farmers, cow farmers, and humble goat farmers of German villages in Gerhard Wilke and Kurt Wagner's "Family and Household: Social Structures in a German Village Between the Two World Wars," in *The German Family: Essays on the Social History of the Family in Nineteenth- and Twentieth-Century Germany,* edited by Richard J. Evans and W. R. Lee (London: Croom Helm, 1981), pp. 120–47. Common rights appear in SAM, Kataster 8791 (1810), for example, the rights

enjoyed by Josef Mangold, glasspainter, to certain forest rights, fourth class, and also "cutting rights in the remaining alpine pastures and wasteground."

25 Büchner, *Hinterglasmalerei,* pp. 80–81; Franz von Paula Schrank, *Baierische Reise* (Munich, 1786), pp. 75–76; *Königlich-Baierisches Intelligenz-Blatt des Iller-Kreises,* p. 864.

26 *Königlich-Baierisches Intelligenz-Blatt des Iller-Kreises,* p. 865; *Chur-pfalz-baïerisches Regierungs- und Intelligenzblatt* (1800), p. 431.

27 Aschau glass factory account book.

28 Büchner, *Hinterglasmalerei,* pp. 82–84; Andreas Lang and Johann Evangelist Lang account books; Oberammergau Death Register, 1824–69; gravestones of Josef Mangold and Johann Jakob Zwink.

29 SAM, Kataster 8791.

30 Josef von Hazzi, *Statistische Aufschlüsse über das Herzogtum Bayern* (Nuremberg, 1802), 2:64.

31 SAM, Kataster 25154, 25155.

32 Uffing Christening Register, 1683–1761.

33 Uffing Marriage Register, 1734–1803.

34 Aschau glass factory account book; SAM, LRA 7423, Kataster 24987.

35 SAM, AR 2043/138; see also the occupation listings on Seehausen graves which show that fishing continued to be a significant occupation for the village into the twentieth century.

36 SAM, LRA 7550.

37 Lee, *Population Growth,* p. 390.

38 *Häuserbuch der Stadt München,* 5 vols. (Munich: Stadt München, 1977), 2:113, 5:119; Murnau Marriage Register, 1744ff; Ahnentafel in the possession of Frau Agi Olofs, Seehausen.

39 SAM, Kataster 24906.

40 Simon Baumann, *Geschichte des Marktes Murnau in Oberbayern* (Murnau, 1855), pp. 149, 188–90.

41 Hansjakob Gebhart, "Murnau einst und jetzt," *Bayerland* 40 (1929): 205–6; Büchner, *Hinterglasmalerei,* p. 97. The Staffelsee area was also originally under the control of the bishop of Augsburg.

42 J. von Obernberg, *Reisen durch das Königreich Bayern* part 1, vol. 1 (Munich, 1815), p. 48.

43 Baumann, *Geschichte des Marktes Murnau,* pp. 188–89.

44 It is possible that Jakob März and Dominikus Gastl were brothers-in-law. Jakob married a Katharina Gastl and Dominikus an Anna März. This would certainly fit the pattern of familial recruitment.

45 Büchner, *Hinterglasmalerei,* pp. 96–101; Murnau Marriage Registers, 1744–1879; Murnau Death Registers, 1743–1834; Murnau Christening Registers, 1802–1830; SAM, LRA 7332, AR 2043/138, Kataster 25181.

46 Hazzi, *Statistische Aufschlüsse über das Herzogtum Bayern,* pp. 94–95; SAM, LRA 7332, AR 2043/138.

47 SAM, AR 1173/26.

48 SAM, LRA 7423, 3229; Büchner, *Hinterglasmalerei,* p. 99; Munich Address Books, 1871–72.

49 *Beiträge zur Statistik Bayerns*, vol. 192 (Munich: Bayerisches Statistisches Landesamt, 1953). Oberammergau, Murnau, and Seehausen all show a decline in population after 1840. Recovery of lost population takes place at slightly different times for the three locations, but it is complete by 1875 for all of them, and they continue to grow thereafter. See Table 10 in the Epilogue.

50 Joan Thirsk, *Economic Policy and Projects: The Development of a Consumer Society in Early Modern England* (Oxford: Clarendon Press, 1978), p. 3.

51 *Häuserbuch der Stadt München*, 2:113, 5:119.

52 Jack Goody, "Inheritance, Property, and Women: Some Comparative Considerations," in *Family and Inheritance: Rural Society in Western Europe, 1200–1800*, edited by Jack Goody, Joan Thirsk, and E. P. Thompson (Cambridge: Cambridge University Press, 1976), pp. 10–36. The recruitment of males through such marriages was of course common in crafts. It offered them a wonderful opportunity to gain access to the rights exercised by the family into which they were marrying.

53 Ritz, "Beiträge," p. 105. Josef Mangold and Josef Anton Lang in Oberammergau were notable artists. Büchner, *Hinterglasmalerei*, pp. 83–84; Heimatmuseum in Oberammergau; an 1842 print after Josef Anton Lang in the collection of Alfred Zwink, Altenau.

54 In 1808, however, they were each listed as a ⅓ holding, although the tax assessed on them was surprisingly low for this classification. See SAL, Häuser- und Rustikal-Steuer-Kataster des Steuerdistrikts Schönbrunn (1808).

55 *Der Landkreis Wolfstein*, pp. 41, 43, 118–19; BHA, Repertorium CXIII, Verz. 3, Fasz. 255, No. 285; Ludwig Veit, *Historisches Atlas von Bayern: Teil Altbayern: Passau Hochstift*, vol. 35 (Munich: Kommission für Bayerische Landesgeschichte, 1978), pp. 137, 312; SAL, Häuser- und Rustikal-Steuer-Kataster des Steuerdistrikts Schönbrunn (1808); personal communication from Herr Herbert Fastner, Zwiesel; *Der Landkreis Freyung-Grafenau* (Freyung: Landkreis Freyung-Grafenau, 1982), pp. 180, 198.

56 *Der Landkreis Freyung-Grafenau*, p. 200, quoting Leopold Nusshart, *Beschreibung des Fürstenthums Passau Kursalzburgischen Antheils in topographischer, ökonomischer und physikalischer Hinsicht* (Passau, 1804).

57 *Der Landkreis Freyung-Grafenau*, p. 199.

58 Veit, *Historisches Atlas von Bayern*, p. 312. Two of the houses listed in 1788 have names that would appear to connect them with glassworking: "Sonnglasgütl" and "Lindenglasergut." The Dillingers appear to have lived in "Sonnglasgütl." Freyung Christening Register, 1736–68; Hohenau Christening Register, 1731–97; Joseph Hess, *Die Hinterglasbilder in Luxemburger Staatsmuseum* (Luxemburg, 1952), p. 9; SAL, Repertorium 168, Verz. 1, Fasz. 1521, No. 56; Häuser- und Rustikal-Steuer-Kataster des Steuerdistrikts Schönbrunn (1808).

59 For the Neumaÿr family connection back to the glasspainting families of the local glassworks, see Raimund Schuster, *Das Raimundsreuter Hinterglasbild: Geschichte der Raimundsreuter Hinterglasmalerei und ihres Einflußgebietes* (Grafenau: Morsak, 1984), pp. 13–14.

60 Ibid., p. 14. See also, for example, Josef Vydra, *Die Hinterglasmalerei: Volkskunst aus tschechoslowakischen Sammlungen* (Prague: Artia, 1957), pp. 39–42. My earlier discussion introduced the Wittmans of Neukirchen beim Heilig Blut.

61 In "Family and 'Modernisation': The Peasant Family and Social Change in Nineteenth-Century Bavaria," W. R. Lee argues that on smallholdings "most surviving children would be employed at a comparatively early age outside the family holding." He adds later, however, that "in every case . . . the position and function of the child was determined by immediate economic considerations" (*The German Family,* p. 97). In glasspainting the logic suggests that children could best have served the household as extra craftsmen rather than by leaving to become servants elsewhere. Their subsequent establishment of separate glass-painting households also substantiates this argument, as does the evidence for adult siblings working together within a household.

62 Aschau glass factory account book; Büchner, *Hinterglasmalerei,* p. 87.

63 Büchner, *Hinterglasmalerei,* p. 38.

64 Uffing Death Register, 1802–52; SAM, Kataster 24987.

65 Wolfgang M. Schmid, "Alte Glasbilder," *Niederbayrische Heimatglocken* 30 (August 1930): 119; SAL, Repertorium 164, Verz. 1, No. 4516.

66 See, for example, *Königlich-Baierisches Intelligenz-Blatt des Iller-Kreises,* p. 866, and the Hofdorf letter to Matthias Noder.

67 Alfred Fuchs, *Die Raimundsreuter Hinterglasmalerei* (Passau: Gogeissl, 1965), p. 9; Gudrun Miller, *Die Geschichte der Hinterglasmalerei im Staffelseegebiet (Ihre Entwicklung bis zur Gegenwart)* (Munich, 1977), p. 11.

68 I wonder, for example, whether the order for four thousand paintings to Matthias Noder in 1816 sent him recruiting the help of other Noder and even Gege households to help him in filling such a large-scale request. The establishment of several households from the same family clearly does not preclude their cooperation on orders pertaining to one household in particular.

69 Hazzi, *Statistische Aufschlüsse über das Herzogtum Bayern,* 2:96; Andreas Lang account book. I am indebted to Herr Theo Hahn for the observation that low numbers suggest quality work in this context.

70 Knaipp, *Hinterglas Bilder,* pp. 152–94.

71 Ibid., p. 194; Georg Lang account book, 1832–34; Herbert Wolfgang Keiser, *Die Deutsche Hinterglasmalerei* (Munich: Bruckmann, 1937), pp. 42–43.

72 Bedrich Stiss, "Hinterglasmalereien in Böhmen," *Bayerisches Jahrbuch für Volkskunde* (1972–75): 126.

73 *Statistisch-topographische Beschreibung des Landgerichtes Wolfstein im Unterdonaukreise* (1830), p. 41.

74 Josef Meßner, *Ausgewählte Werke* (Vienna, 1897), pp. 287–88.

75 Josef Blau, *Böhmerwälder Hausindustrie und Volkskunst. Part 2, Frauen-Hauswerk und Volkskunst* (Prague, 1918), pp. 276–77.

76 Reinhard Haller, *Armenseelentaferl: Hinterglasbilder aus Bayern, Österreich und Böhmen* (Grafenau: Morsak, 1980), p. 22.

77 Robert Staininger, "Sandl und seine Einwohner," *Heimatgaue* 9, no. 3 (1928): 150–51.

78 Raimund Schuster, *Risse zu Hinterglas-bildern aus den 18. und 19. Jahrhundert* (Rosenheim: Rosenheimer, 1978), pp. 10–11; SAL, Repertorium 164, Verz. 1, No. 4516.

79 Johann Baptist Reisbacher, probably a student of Andreas Stoiber of Haibühl,

unfortunately had to sell his *Meisterstück* when he started business in Kollnburg, thus leaving a record of its existence. See Siegfried Seidl, "Der volkstümliche Maler Johann Bapt. Reisbacher sen. in Kollnburg bei Viechtach (Bayer. Wald)," *Bayerisches Jahrbuch für Volkskunde* (1980–81): 24.

80 SAL, Repertorium 168, Verz. 1, Fasz. 1519, Lit. C; Büchner, *Hinterglasmalerei*, pp. 38, 43.

81 Büchner, *Hinterglasmalerei*, p. 99, for the description of the *Meisterstück;* SAM, AR 1173/26.

82 SAM, AR 2043/138, LRA 7332, Kataster 25151.

83 SAM, LRA 7423.

84 BHA, GR 830/1-2 (1792); SAM, AR 2043/138; Schremmer, *Die Wirtschaft Bayerns*, p. 424. Hanke, "Zur Sozialstruktur der ländlichen Siedlungen Altbayerns," pp. 246, 261–62, places the tailors above the builders on the social scale.

85 Anegg, *Zur Gewerbestruktur und Gewerbepolitik*, pp. 63–66; *Königlich-Baierisches Intelligenz-Blatt des Iller-Kreises*, pp. 866–67; *Chur-pfalz-baïerisches Regierungs- und Intelligenzblatt*, pp. 430–31.

86 SAL, Repertorium 168, Verz. 1, Fasz. 1766, No. 125; Büchner, *Hinterglasmalerei*, pp. 34–38.

87 It is possible that these land purchases caused indebtedness that would burden the families of the purchaser. Johann Evangelist Lang was certainly borrowing thousands of gulden in the late 1830s and 1840s to help him finance real property acquisitions. SAM, LRA 131441. The substantial cash earnings of some glasspainters, however, might well have allowed for outright cash purchases of the holdings that appear as purchases in the records.

88 Curiously, by 1785 Johannes was selling his land to a Murnau smith at the original purchase price, despite substantial improvements that he had made to the property. Staffelseeisches Pfarrbuch, 1636–1780; BHA, KL 204/38.

89 SAM, Kataster 24906, 24987.

90 SAM, AR 3989/804. He paid around 78 gulden for his land; most of the other purchases were for under 10 gulden.

91 SAM, Akten der Verlassenschaft 75 (1879); AG Weilheim NR 1863/4/214. The Noders appear to have held state bonds of some sort.

92 SAM, Akten der Verlassenschaft 215 (1863–64), Kataster 24915.

93 SAM, AR 3977/416; Uffing Death Register, 1802–52; SAM, LRA 7423, Kataster 8791, 9034, and 24643 and 25181.

94 SAL, Häuser- und Rustikal-Steuer-Kataster des Steuerdistrikts Schönbrunn (1808), Urkataster 22/39 Vol. II (1843).

95 Lee, *Population Growth*, pp. 115–20. The restrictions on sale of *Hoffuß* land appear to have been lifted after February 1805. See also Pankraz Fried, "Reagrarisierung in Südbayern seit dem 19. Jahrhundert," in *Agrarisches Nebengewerbe und Formen der Reagrarisierung im Spätmittelalter und 19./20. Jahrhundert*, edited by Hermann Kellenbenz (Stuttgart: Fischer, 1975), pp. 177–93. See also, for example, a sale of land by the government in the Staffelsee area in 1841 (SAM, AR 3989/804) and the division of the Murnau commons in 1805 (Baumann, *Geschichte des Marktes Murnau in Oberbayern*, pp. 189–90). Hörger, *Kirche, Dorfreligion und bäuerliche Gesellschaft*, p. 23. Hanke identifies a slow increase

in the accretion of land to the smaller farming units from the end of the seventeenth century on that became more dramatic in the nineteenth century ("Zur Sozialstruktur der ländlichen Siedlungen Altbayerns," pp. 267–68). His table on pages 232–34 gives an excellent picture of the varied sizes of groundholdings of the occupiers of smallholdings measured by the *Hoffuß* system.

96 Age at marriage was generally lower in the first generation of glasspainters. Jakob März, the elder Dominikus Gastl, Sebastian Seiz, and Matthias Landes all married at around twenty-two, while Johannes Noder and Franz Xaver Eder married at twenty; the merchant Nemesi Schmid, grandfather of Nemesi, Jakob, and Johann Baptist, also married at twenty-three. Michael Kirchmayr, however, delayed his marriage until he was twenty-six, and Tobias Peterhansl was over thirty by the time he married, as was Josef Lang, the founder of the Oberammergau Lang family. By contrast, few of the younger generation married under the age of twenty-five, and several married when they were thirty or older. For poorer glasspainters, marriage might well have been delayed because of that poverty. Staffelseeisches Pfarrbuch, 1636–1780; Murnau Marriage Registers, 1744–1879; Uffing Marriage Registers, 1683–1879; Murnau Christening Registers, 1702–1830; Uffing Christening Registers, 1683–1813; Hohenau Marriage Register, 1786ff; Hohenau Death Register, 1787–1840; SAL, Urkataster 22/39 Vol. II (1843); Ahnentafel in the possession of Frau Agi Olofs, daughter of the last Seehausen painter; Fuchs, *Die Raimundsreuter Hinterglasmalerei,* p. 7; Adolf Roth, *Zwölf Oberammergauer Ahnentafeln* (Munich, 1934), p. 7; Uffing Death Register, 1734–1803; SAM, Akten der Verlassenschaft 215 (1863–64). For marriage variants, see E. A. Wrigley, "Marriage, Fertility and Population Growth in Eighteenth-Century England," in *Marriage and Society: Studies in the Social History of Marriage,* edited by R. B. Outhwaite (New York: St. Martin's Press, 1981). A very sensible and cautious assessment of the multiple pressures on marriage decisions appears in Michael Anderson, "Historical Demography After *The Population History of England,*" in *Population and Economy: Population and History from the Traditional to the Modern World,* edited by Robert I. Rotberg and Theodore K. Rabb (Cambridge: Cambridge University Press, 1986), pp. 44–45.

97 Büchner, *Hinterglasmalerei,* p. 86; SAM, LRA 131441. I noted earlier the extra holdings of Josef Anton Lang and Josef Mangold, the two most "artistic" glasspainters.

98 SAM, LRA 7332, AR 2043/138, LRA 7550, Akten der Verlassenschaft 75 (1879); *Königlich-Baierisches Intelligenz-Blatt des Iller-Kreises,* p. 867.

99 For examples of the analysis of Bavarian villagers by class, see Hanke, "Zur Sozialstruktur der ländlichen Siedlungen Altbayerns," pp. 225, 243–45, 247ff; Hörger, *Kirche, Dorfreligion und bäuerliche Gesellschaft,* pp. 35–63; Fintan Michael Phayer, *Religion und das Gewöhnliche Volk in Bayern in der Zeit von 1750–1850* (Munich: Neue Schriftenreihe des Stadtarchivs München, 1970), pp. 90ff, including an interesting pie chart illustrating the social distinctions in the parish he studies. See Kriedte, Medick, and Schlumbohm's *Industrialization Before Industrialization* (pp. 38–73) for Medick's well-known assessment of the noncapitalistic nature of both peasant and rural-industrial households. On pages 48–49 he describes the purchase of real estate by craftsmen as "exclusively

geared toward preserving the domestic subsistence unit" and as a "striving for independence." On pages 64–73 he describes any efforts beyond the assurance of survival as aimed at fulfilling "additional material or cultural needs which always took precedence over an expenditure of work to gain a purely monetary surplus." They were "primarily oriented toward cultural expenditure for status, prestige and luxury consumption." I do not find this orientation surprising, since profit was surely expended even by capitalists on luxuries, estates, and so forth. The view that "pre-industrial farmers were concerned chiefly with conventional levels of subsistence and were therefore little involved with the market" is dismissed by Clarkson, *Proto-Industrialization,* p. 42. Oberammergau agents abroad returned periodically to their wives and children resident on their landholdings in the village. They also retired there with their plots and assets to support them. For example, Daisenberger describes the return of Sebastian Hohenleutner from Cadiz to retire from business. He lived there "off his business assets and a small farm." The assets were substantial, almost 30,000 gulden (*Geschichte des Dorfes Oberammergau,* pp. 94, 142).

2 *Industrial Competition from the Graphic Arts: The Development of Chromolithography*

1 Jean Adhémar, *Graphic Art of the Eighteenth Century,* translated by M. I. Martin (London: Thames and Hudson, 1964), p. 91; Michael Twyman, *Lithography: 1800–1850: The Techniques of Drawing on Stone in England and France and Their Application in Works of Topography* (London: Oxford University Press, 1970), p. 3; Gerhard Langemeyer and Reinhart Schleier, *Bilder nach Bildern: Druckgrafik und die Vermittlung von Kunst,* exhibition catalog, Westfälisches Landesmuseum für Kunst und Kulturgeschichte, Münster, 1976, p. 297, quoting J. W. von Goethe, *Schriften zur Kunst,* part 1, vol. 33 (Munich: Deutscher Taschenbuch, 1962), pp. 69ff.

2 Franz Maria Ferchl, *Geschichte der Errichtung der Ersten Lithographischen Kunstanstalt bei der Feiertagsschule für Künstler und Techniker in München* (Munich, 1862), pp. 104–5.

3 Felix H. Man, *Artists' Lithographs: A World History from Senefelder to the Present Day* (London: Studio Vista, 1970), p. 29. See the copy of the *Lithographische Kunstprodukte* in the Handschriftenabteilung, Bayerische Staatsbibliothek in Munich.

4 Franz Maria Ferchl, "Uebersicht der einzig bestehenden, vollständigen Incunabeln-Sammlung der Lithographie," *Oberbayerisches Archiv* 17, no. 2 (1856): 157–59; Wolfgang Wegner, "'Les Oeuvres Lithographiques' und ihre Entstehungsgeschichte: Ein Beitrag zur Erforschung der Inkunabelzeit der Münchner Lithographie," *Oberbayerisches Archiv* (1965): 139–92.

5 Senefelder, *The Invention of Lithography,* p. 38.

6 See K470b in the Germanisches Nationalmuseum in Nuremberg.

7 Ferchl, "Uebersicht," pp. 166–67.

8 Ibid., pp. 167, 170; Winkler, *Die Frühzeit der deutschen Lithographie,* p. 438. A related project was the printing in colors of a family tree included in the 1808–9

edition of *Feyerbach-Gönner's Allgemeines bürgerliches Gesetzbuch für Baiern.* There is a copy in the Handschriftenabteilung, Bayerische Staatsbibliothek in Munich.

9 Winkler, *Die Frühzeit der deutschen Lithographie,* p. 438.

10 Ferchl, "Uebersicht," pp. 166–67; Carl Wagner, *Alois Senefelder, sein Leben und Wirken: Ein Beitrag zur Geschichte der Lithographie* (Leipzig: Giesecke und Devrient, 1914), pp. 85–86.

11 Twyman, *Lithography,* p. 128; Wegner, "Oeuvres Lithographiques," pp. 143, 148, 150–58.

12 Senefelder, *The Invention of Lithography,* p. 2.

13 Wegner, "Oeuvres Lithographiques," pp. 181–84; Senefelder, *The Invention of Lithography,* p. 77.

14 Wilhelm Weber, *A History of Lithography* (London, 1966), p. 79. Brückner makes the same connection between coloring and lower-class consumption in his *Elfenreigen, Hochzeitstraum,* p. 12.

15 Wegner, "Oeuvres Lithographiques," pp. 142–44, and a photograph of the title page from one of the earlier folios owned by the Bayerische Staatsbibliothek in Munich.

16 Senefelder, *The Invention of Lithography,* p. 22.

17 Ferchl, *Geschichte,* pp. 123–24.

18 See Chapter 4 for a detailed discussion of these relative prices.

19 Ferchl, *Geschichte,* p. 123; Heinrich Weishaupt, *Bayern's erste technische Schule* (Munich, 1865), p. 196; *Verzeichniß der bey der lithographischen Kunstanstalt an der Feyertags-Schule zu München erschienenen Kunstprodukte* (1818); Winkler, *Die Frühzeit der deutschen Lithographie,* p. 12.

20 Man, *Artists' Lithographs,* p. 52; Twyman, *Lithography,* pp. 128, 156, 159.

21 Wilhelm Zahn, *Die schönsten Ornamente und merkwürdigsten Gemälde aus Pompeji, Herkulanum und Stabiae nebst einigen Grundrissen und Ansichten nach den an Ort und Stelle gemachten Original zeichnungen* (Berlin: Georg Reimer, 1829). Joan M. Friedman, *Color Printing in England, 1846–1870* (New Haven: Yale Center for British Art, 1978), p. 42, also mentions an 1818 edition of poems decorated with "lithographed designs printed in up to six colors" by Johann August Barth.

22 Germanisches Nationalmuseum, Nuremberg, K1056C, LJ333; Weber, *A History of Lithography,* p. 80; I. Schwarz, *Zur Geschichte der Einführung der Lithographie in Wien* (Vienna, n.d.), pp. v–vi, describes a similar venture on a smaller scale by his colleague Peter Fendi. The various stages followed in the completion of a Lanzadelly print have been preserved, allowing one to observe the gradual emergence of the complete image as each color is added to the paper. Germanisches Nationalmuseum, Nuremberg, L1959–1961, L5505–5513. This print is entitled *Mummerei aus dem Freydal.*

23 Dr. Johann Baptist von Spix and Dr. Carl Fr. von Martius, *Reise in Brasilien,* 3 vols. (Munich, 1823, 1828, 1831), and Atlas, according to Man, *Artists' Lithographs,* p. 52.

24 Winkler, *Die Frühzeit der deutschen Lithographie,* p. 438; Senefelder, *The Invention of Lithography,* p. 89.

25 Germanisches Nationalmuseum, Nuremberg, L1764; Heinrich Weishaupt, *Verzeichniss der lithographischen Incunabeln-Sammlung* (Munich, 1884), p. 9; Wagner, *Alois Senefelder* (1914), pp. 91–92.

26 Ferchl, "Uebersicht," pp. 189–91; Senefelder collections in both the Germanisches Nationalmuseum, Nuremberg (L1951) and the Staatliche Graphische Sammlung, Munich (204174–204183). One of Senefelder's plates is included. See also BHA, MH 2845.

27 Senefelder, *The Invention of Lithography,* pp. 82–84; Wagner, *Alois Senefelder* (1914), p. 162; Ilse Mackenthun, *Joseph von Utzschneider: Sein Leben, sein Wirken, seine Zeit* (Diss., University of Munich, 1958), pp. 169–70; Handschriftenabteilung, Deutsches Museum, Munich, 5185 (Utzschneider diary).

28 *Anzeiger für Kunst- und Gewerbefleiß im Königreiche Baiern* 2, no. 39 (1816): 604.

29 Büchner, *Hinterglasmalerei,* p. 78.

30 Handschriftenabteilung, Deutsches Museum, Munich, 5184, 5185; Mackenthun, *Joseph von Utzschneider,* p. 170.

31 Sebastian Haindl, "Ueber den lithographischen Farbendruck in München," *Kunst- und Gewerbe-Blatt* 29, no. 3 (March 1843): 212–19. One further connection between glasspainting and lithography is certainly suggested by the reproduction of a seller of glasspaintings in the print *Market in Transylvania.*

32 Anonymous article entitled "Lithographischer Kunst-Farbendruck worauf sich Heinr. Weishaupt in München unter'm 23. August 1837 ein Privilegium auf 15 Jahre ertheilen liess," *Kunst- und Gewerbe-Blatt* 27, no. 2 (February 1841): 138–42.

33 Germanisches Nationalmuseum, Nuremberg, L3578, L3580, L1964, L1966, L2646.

34 A copy is in the possession of the Staatliche Graphische Sammlung in Munich (1967:124D).

35 SM, GA 178/49; BHA, MH 7150; Heinrich Weishaupt, *Theoretisch-praktische Anleitung zur Chromo-Lithographie oder zum lithographischen Farbendruck, so wie zum lithographischen Kunstdruck überhaupt, nach den neuesten, verbesserten Verfahrungsweisen, zur Herstellung des Vollendetsten, was diese Kunst zu liefern vermag* (Quedlinburg and Leipzig: Basse, 1848), especially p. 8.

36 BHA, MInn 13999.

37 BHA, MInn 14359, 14335; Germanisches Nationalmuseum, Nuremberg, L1968; Weishaupt, *Verzeichniss der lithographischen Incunabeln-Sammlung,* pp. 24, 41; Haindl, "Ueber den lithographischen Farbendruck in München," p. 217. Grosjean was also associated with the Cotta firm.

38 Weishaupt, *Theoretisch-praktische Anleitung,* pp. 6–7.

39 Man, *Artists' Lithographs,* pp. 53–54; Gustave von Groschwitz, "The Significance of Nineteenth-Century Color Lithography," *Gazette des Beaux-Arts* (1954): 247–49; *Le Lithographe* 1 (1838): 288; 2 (1839): 202–3; 3 (1842): 70–72; 4 (1845): 314.

40 Man, *Artists' Lithographs,* p. 53; Godefroy Engelmann, *Das Gesammtgebiet der Lithographie,* translated by W. Pabst and A. Kretzschmar (Chemnitz, 1840), pp. 32, 34.

41 Engelmann, *Das Gesammtgebiet der Lithographie,* pp. 33–34.

42 Léon Lang, "Godefroy Engelmann de Mulhouse, Imprimeur Lithographe," in *Trois Siècles d'Art Alsacien, 1648–1948* (Strasbourg-Paris: Istra, 1948), p. 177; *Le Lithographe* 5 (1846): 91, Bulletin Iconographique; H. Bouchot, *La Lithographie* (Paris, 1895), pp. 239–40. Peter C. Marzio calls it "one of the most advanced chromo houses in Europe" (*Chromolithography, 1840–1900,* p. 24).

43 Marzio, *Chromolithography, 1840–1900*, pp. 24–26, including quotations from the Philadelphia *Public Ledger,* March 4 and October 8, 1852, and *The Bulletin of the American Art-Union* (New York: George F. Nesbitt, 1850), pp. 26–27.

44 *Le Lithographe* 4 (1845): 314–15; 6 (1846):1; Twyman, *Lithography,* p. 235; Bouchot, *La Lithographie,* p. 241.

45 Hildebrand's was also mentioned by the Mühlhausen committee when they assessed the merits of Engelmann's discovery, while *Le Lithographe* included Hildebrand as a "printer in color" in their list of lithographers drawn up in 1838, together with the printers J. Storch, also of Berlin, and Dondorf from Frankfurt. Storch's work also appeared in the Zahn project, and Engelmann mentioned him too when he discussed Hildebrand's work in his account of the background to his discovery. *Le Lithographe* 1 (1838): xxxv, xxxvi, xxxviii; *Le Lithographe* 2 (1839): 203; Engelmann, *Das Gesammtgebiet der Lithographie,* pp. 32–33.

46 Other prints that were colored but not identified with the label *Farbendruck* were executed by Asmus, Gutschmidt, and the Royal Lithographic Institute. Asmus was later mentioned as a chromolithographer, and his prints for the 1829 edition were executed in association with Hildebrand. The Royal Lithographic Institute contributed chromolithographs to later editions of Zahn's book. There was even work from Louis Sachse and Company in the 1829 edition. Sachse had consulted with Senefelder in the 1820s, and he apparently experimented with the inventor's *Mosaikdruck,* although he did not make use of it in the Zahn project. H. E. Peschek, *Das Ganze des Steindrucks,* 3d ed. (Weimar, 1856), p. 147; Wagner, *Alois Senefelder,* pp. 164–66; Wilhelm Weber, *Aloys Senefelder zum 200. Geburtstag, 1771–1971: Lithographien, Bücher, Noten, Dokumente,* exhibition catalog, Stadtmuseum, Offenbach am Main, 1971, p. 7. Bouchot suggests in *La Lithographie* (p. 238) that stencils were used to color most of the prints in this first edition.

47 Wilhelm Zahn, *Ornamente aller Klassischen Kunstepochen, nach den Originalen in ihren eigenthümlichen Farben dargestellt,* 20 vols. (Berlin, ?1832–48); *Kayser's Bücher-Lexikon, 1833–1840* (Leipzig, 1841) covers volumes 2 through 5 of this work and lists each volume as containing five chromolithographs and an introductory page; Engelmann, *Das Gesammtgebiet der Lithographie,* p. 32. The State Library in Munich was able to acquire a complete copy of all twenty volumes, and, therefore, of the full one hundred plates, that have unfortunately since been destroyed.

48 The third edition appeared in 1852 and 1859. The printer A. Dettmers was prominently involved in the provision of colored plates for this edition.

49 Joseph Cramer, *Die Entwicklung des Steindruck-gewerbes in Deutschland* (Leipzig, 1918), p. 34; Wilhelm Weber, *Saxa Loquuntur* (Berlin, 1961), p. 133. Surviving Storch prints include: Germanisches Nationalmuseum, Nuremberg, L4251; Divi-

sion of Graphic Arts, National Museum of American History, U.S.A., 1215, 1280. *Katalog der Kunst- und Kunstindustrie-Ausstellung alter und neuer deutscher Meister sowie der deutschen Kunstschulen im Glaspalaste zu München* (1876), pp. 92, 94–95, 230.

50 Friedman, *Color Printing in England,* pp. 48–54; Bouchot, *La Lithographie,* pp. 239ff.

51 Twyman, *Lithography,* pp. 138, 159, 186, 199, 202.

52 Friedman, *Color Printing in England,* pp. 47–48. But see also Man, *Artists' Lithographs,* p. 54, for a contrary opinion. Man argues: "They were not three- or four-colour printings in imitation of another technique by printing colours on top of one another, but artists' lithographs with each colour standing on its own, separated and balanced, a principle used some decades later by Chéret and Toulouse-Lautrec."

53 Twyman, *Lithography,* pp. 160–61.

54 Friedman, *Color Printing in England,* p. 55; Peschek, *Das Ganze des Steindrucks,* pp. 147ff; Gustav Ballerstedt, *Beschreibung der Art und Weise, den lithographischen Buntdruck mittels eines Steins mit einem Abdruck zu bewirken. Erste Manier: Schablonen-Druck. Zweite Manier: Iris Druck* (Quedlinburg and Leipzig: Basse, 1839). This book is mentioned in Carl Wagner, *Alois Senefelder: Sein Leben und Wirken und die weitere Entwicklung der Lithographie,* 2d ed. (Leipzig, 1943), p. 273. Wagner suggests that the author traces his idea back to Engelmann.

55 BHA, MH 7150; Cramer, *Die Entwicklung des Steindruck-gewerbes in Deutschland,* p. 34.

56 See, for example, the striking numbers of *Brevet d'Invention* taken out in France during the 1850s for various kinds of chromolithographic procedures. They are listed in Charles Lorilleux, *Traité de Lithographie: Histoire, Theoríe, Practique* (Paris, 1889), pp. 358–59.

57 BHA, MH 7150.

58 Friedman, *Color Printing in England,* pp. 22–23; C. T. C. Lewis, *George Baxter: The Picture Printer* (London: Sampson Low, Marston and Co., 1924), pp. 31, 87.

59 Ulrike Eichler, "Münchener Bilderbogen," *Oberbayerisches Archiv* 99 (1974): x; R. Arnim Winkler, *Wie sammle ich Lithographien* (Munich, 1965), p. 32; Jean Mistler, François Blandez, and André Jacquemin, *Epinal et l'imagerie populaire* (Librairie Hachette, 1961), p. 107.

60 Hermann Dettmer, *Bilderbogen des 18. und 19. Jahrhunderts,* exhibition catalog, Westfälisches Landesmuseum für Kunst und Kulturgeschichte, Münster, 1976, pp. 5, 12–13; Weber, *A History of Lithography,* p. 76.

61 Dettmer, *Bilderbogen des 18. und 19. Jahrhunderts,* p. 6; Theodor Kohlmann, *Neurippiner Bilderbogen,* exhibition catalog, Berlin, 1981, p. 70.

62 Adolf Spamer and Mathilde Hain, *Der Bilderbogen von der "Geistlichen Hausmagd": Ein Beitrag zur Geschichte des religiösen Bilderbogens und der Erbauungsliteratur im populären Verlagswesen Mitteleuropas* (Göttingen: Schwartz, 1970), pp. 2–5.

63 Ibid., p. 17.

64 Ibid., pp. 10–11, 14; Klaus Lankheit, "Aus der Frühzeit der Weissenburger Bilder-

fabrik," *Kölner Zeitschrift für Soziologie und Sozial-psychologie* 21 (1969): 586, 594–95. Lankheit has analyzed the range of titles offered by the firm in the years 1853–57, as reflected in a French Colportage Commission's survey published in 1860. He concludes that by this time Wentzel was no longer concentrating on the normal type of broadsheet typified by Neurippin products. Rather, the titles suggest that he was stressing the market for *Wandschmuck*. For a more cautious view on the use of varnishing before the 1870s, see Brückner, *Elfenreigen, Hochzeitstraum*, pp. 144, 146.

65 Christa Pieske, *Bürgerliches Wandbild, 1840–1920: Populäre Druckgraphik aus Deutschland, Frankreich und England*, exhibition catalog, Goltze, Göttingen, 1975, p. 6.

66 Brückner, *Elfenreigen, Hochzeitstraum*, p. 16. Brückner also mentions prints from Frankfurt and Berlin.

67 Pieske, *Bürgerliches Wandbild*, pp. 6, 8.

68 Wolfgang Brückner, *Die Bilderfabrik* (Frankfurt am Main, 1973), pp. 41–42, 90, 101; Brückner, "Trivialer Wandschmuck der Zweiten Hälfte des 19. Jahrhunderts: Aufgezeigt am Beispiel einer Bilderfabrik," *Anzeiger des Germanisches Nationalmuseums* (1967): 120–21; and Brückner, *Elfenreigen, Hochzeitstraum*, p. 16.

69 Marzio, *Chromolithography, 1840–1900*, p. 53; Brückner, "Trivialer Wandschmuck der Zweiten Hälfte des 19. Jahrhunderts," p. 123; Cramer, *Die Entwicklung des Steindruck-gewerbes in Deutschland*, p. 72; Brückner, *Elfenreigen, Hochzeitstraum*, pp. 146–47; Ernst von Destouches, *Fünfzig Jahre Münchener Gewerbe-Geschichte, 1848–1898, Part 3* (Munich, 1898), pp. 89–90; *Statistik des Deutschen Reichs, Neue Folge* 6, no. 2 (Berlin, 1885): 14, 94; Christa Pieske, "Aus der Berliner Luxuspapierfabrikation um 1900: Produktion, Umsatz und Herstellerfirmen von Oblaten," *Volkskunst* 1, no. 3 (August 1978): 192.

70 Twyman, *Lithography*, p. 25; Marzio, *Chromolithography, 1840–1900*, p. 114, quoting *Art Interchange* (December 8, 1881): 215; *Bamberger Zeitung* 86 (March 27, 1859); Adolf Spamer, *Das kleine Andachtsbild vom XIV. bis zum XX. Jahrhundert* (Munich, 1930), p. 270.

3 A Market Shared: The Distribution of Glasspaintings and Lithographs

1 Hansjakob Gebhart, *Staffelsee-Chronik: Ein Heimatbuch* (Riedhausen, 1977), pp. 54, 68, 89–91; Schremmer, *Die Wirtschaft Bayerns*, pp. 616–18; Gebhart, "Murnau einst und jetzt," p. 205. Uta Lindgren, *Alpenübergänge von Bayern nach Italien, 1500–1850: Landkarten—Straßen—Verkehr* (Munich: Hirmer and Deutsches Museum, 1986), pp. 155–56, gives a very detailed picture of the Venice to Augsburg journey as reported in 1604 by two merchants. Map 1 is also derived from: Schremmer, *Die Wirtschaft Bayerns*, pp. 179, 622, 633; *Der Landkreis Wolfstein*, p. 35; Johann Brunner, *Das Postwesen in Bayern in seiner geschichtlichen Entwicklung von den Anfängen bis zur Gegenwart* (Munich, 1900), p. 72.

2 Raimund Schuster, *Hinterglasbilder aus Außergefild im Böhmerwald* (Grafenau: Morsak, 1980), p. 11; *Der Landkreis Wolfstein*, p. 35; Hans Becker, "Welschtiroler Hausierer in Vergangenheit und Gegenwart," *Der Schlern* 41 (1967): 328;

Friedrich Knaipp, "Über die Südtiroler Hausierer mit bayrischen, Böhmerwälder und oberösterreichischen Hinterglasbildern," *Der Schlern* 28, no. 10 (1954): 533–40.

3 Gebhart, *Staffelsee-Chronik*, p. 22.

4 See, for example, Brauneck, *Religiöse Volkskunst*, color illustrations 5 and 10; Edgar Harvolk, *Votivtafeln aus Bayern und Österreich aus dem Museum für Deutsche Volkskunde* (Berlin: Gebr. Mann, 1977), pp. 20–21, 28, 40. For the dangers of winter travel, see Lenz Kriss-Rettenbeck, *Das Votivbild* (Munich: Hermann Rinn, 1958), pp. 29, 31, 35. Uta Lindgren, *Alpenübergänge von Bayern nach Italien,* pp. 165–66, is also helpful. Furthermore, the visitor to the Oberammergau museum can find both wagons and horses reproduced as toys.

5 Johann Evangelist Lang Account Book, 1832–34; Johann Brunner, *Das Postwesen in Bayern in seiner geschichtlichen Entwicklung von den Anfängen bis zur Gegenwart* especially pp. 125ff. In *Geschichte des Dorfes Oberammergau,* pp. 189–90, Daisenberger mentions that the road through Oberammergau had become a postal route in 1851. See also Fernand Braudel, *Civilization and Capitalism: Fifteenth–Eighteenth Century, Vol. 2, The Wheels of Commerce,* translated by Siân Reynolds (London: Collins, 1982), pp. 352–57.

6 Fernand Braudel, *Civilization and Capitalism,* 2:350, quoting Werner Sombart, *Der moderne Kapitalismus,* vol. 2, 15th ed. (1928), pp. 357ff; Schremmer, *Die Wirtschaft Bayerns,* pp. 617–18; Georg Lang Account Book, 1797–1806; Knaipp, "Über die Südtiroler Hausierer," p. 536. Votive paintings again offer visual documentation of river transports of the sort that the glasspainters must have used. See Brauneck, *Religiöse Volkskunst,* color illustration 6, for one such case, in which a potential drowning is averted by the assistance of Mary the Helper. Klaus Beitl, *Votivbilder: Zeugnisse einer Alten Volkskunst* (Munich: Hugendubel, 1982), illustration 18, gives an example of the dangers of lake travel in an open boat on rough seas. A charming woodcut of the horse-drawn boat traffic on the Danube is provided in an article entitled "Ein Schiffszug auf der Donau," *Niederbayerische Hefte* 18 (1969): 26–27. Moreover, we can get an excellent idea of the hazards of raft travel such as März may have used from an article entitled "Aus der Geschichte der Isarflößerei," *Oberbayerisches Archiv* 109, no. 1 (1984): 111–12. In particular, the article describes an incident in 1660 that resulted in the death of all seventeen passengers of a raft driven by Joseph Pichlmayr as they journeyed on pilgrimage to Mamming. The following pages give excellent illustrations of such rafts from contemporary depictions. There was an *Ordinarifloß* that ran from 1623 between Munich and Vienna, on which "protective huts" were provided at extra charge. In 1823 the full voyage to Vienna cost 3 gulden. Whether März used this transport or the Murnau rafts past Munich we cannot know, although Baumann certainly mentions that Murnau raftsmen went as far as Vienna in the mid-nineteenth century. Around the same time, however, most rafts stopped at Munich. See also Brunner, *Das Postwesen in Bayern,* pp. 76–77, which includes an excellent illustration of a crowded raft with a hut for the wealthy traveler. Kriss-Rettenbeck, *Das Votivbild,* pp. 38–46, also chronicles the dangers of travel by water, including a rafting accident on the Isar.

7 Friedrich Knaipp, "Absatzgebiete und Handelswege der Hinterglasbilder darge-

stellt an Beispielen der wichtigsten Erzeugungsgebiete und Hausiererwohnsitze," *Österreichischer Volkskundeatlas* 15 (1959): 13; J. R. Bührlen, *Luftelmaler Franz Seraph Zwink von Oberammergau* (Oberammergau, 1921), p. 40ff; Daisenberger, *Geschichte des Dorfes Oberammergau,* pp. 140, 142; Schremmer, *Die Wirtschaft Bayerns,* pp. 616ff, which stresses the route to Venice and later to Trieste in his survey of major trading routes to the south of Bavaria; Hazzi, *Statistische Aufschlüsse über das Herzogtum Bayern,* p. 96. Again, votive paintings often describe the exigencies of international ocean travel. See, for example, Brauneck, *Religiöse Volkskunst,* color illustration 12, for a Bremen ship, the *Charlotte,* caught in a storm in 1838 on its way to North America.

8 *Chur-pfalz-baïerisches Regierungs-und Intelligenzblatt,* pp. 430–32.

9 *Königlich-Baierisches Intelligenz-Blatt des Iller-Kreises,* p. 863; Daisenberger, *Geschichte des Dorfes Oberammergau,* pp. 140–41; Oberammergau Death Registers. It is possible, of course, that at times the dead could have been merely visiting on business rather than established in trade at the place of their deaths.

10 Daisenberger, *Geschichte des Dorfes Oberammergau,* pp. 94, 141. Gröber, *Alte Oberammergauer Hauskunst,* 1930 ed., p. 19, suggests that the Gröden valley had 348 firms in 130 locations in the world by 1810. This long-term temporary migration seems to have been common for places like Oberammergau in which outside income had become essential to keep many families going. See, for example, Roland Sarti, *Long Live the Strong: A History of Rural Society in the Apennine Mountains* (Amherst: University of Massachusetts Press, 1985).

11 Andreas Lang Account Book, 1804ff; Johann Evangelist Lang Account Book, 1832–34; Georg Lang Account Books, 1797–1811; *Königlich-Baierisches Intelligenz-Blatt des Iller-Kreises,* p. 866. By the late 1840s Johann Evangelist could claim that he had developed trading connections with firms in "Prussia, Saxony, Frankfurt, Hamburg, Switzerland, France, Belgium, Holland, England, North and South America, and East India" (SAM, LRA 131441). And the Langs were not alone in establishing these sophisticated consumer networks. The Oberammergau merchant Andreas Bierling, for example, also shipped glasspaintings and other goods to many parts of Germany in the period 1833–56. Keiser, *Die Deutsche Hinterglasmalerei,* pp. 42–43.

12 Gislind M. Ritz, "Die bürgerlich-handwerkliche Hinterglasmalerei," p. 65, quoting Stettin, *Kunst-Gewerb- und Handwerksgeschichte der Reichsstadt Augsburg* (1779), pp. 359ff; Büchner, *Hinterglasmalerei,* p. 66; *Anzeiger für Kunst- und Gewerbefleiß im Königreiche Baiern* 2, no. 39 (1816): 599–605; Schrank, *Baierische Reise,* p. 76.

13 *Königlich-Baierisches Intelligenz-Blatt des Iller-Kreises,* p. 866; SAM, AR 1173/26.

14 Gröber, *Alte Oberammergauer Hauskunst* (1930 ed.), pp. 28–29; Daisenberger, *Geschichte des Dorfes Oberammergau,* p. 141. See also the discussion of international crises as typical for protoindustrial businesses in Kriedte, Medick, and Schlumbohm's *Industrialization Before Industrialization,* pp. 117–125.

15 Jonathan Sperber, *Popular Catholicism in Nineteenth-Century Germany* (Princeton: Princeton University Press, 1984), pp. 18–19, 64–68, discusses Kevelaer, and it is clear that it became increasingly popular until at least the 1870s.

16 SAM, Kataster 8829 and 8830.

17 Reinhard Haller, "Der Glasbildermaler Paulus Josephus Andreas Lohberger: Ein Beitrag zur Geschichte der Hinterglasmalerei in Niederbayern," *Beilage zum Amtlichen Schul-Anzeiger für den Regierungsbezirk Niederbayern* 6 (December, 1969): 12, 17–18; Becker, "Welschtiroler Hausierer in Vergangenheit und Gegenwart," pp. 326–27. The locals might also continue to act as hawkers, however. See Büchner, *Hinterglasmalerei,* pp. 22–23.

18 Haller, "Der Glasbildermaler Paulus Josephus Andreas Lohberger," pp. 17–18; SAA, Landgericht ä. O., PAR/686; Schuster, *Hinterglasbilder aus Außergefild im Böhmerwald,* p. 34; Knaipp, "Über die Südtiroler Hausierer," p. 534.

19 Oberammergau Death Register, 1762ff; Josef Blau, *Die Glasmacher im Böhmer- und Bayerwald in Volkskunde und Kulturgeschichte* (Regensberg, 1954), p. 102; Haller, "Ger Glasbildermaler Paulus Josephus Andreas Lohberger," p. 16.

20 Becker, "Welschtiroler Hausierer in Vergangenheit und Gegenwart," p. 328; SAA, Landgericht ä. O., PAR/686; Schuster, *Hinterglasbilder aus Außergefild im Böhmerwald,* pp. 20, 34; Büchner, *Hinterglasmalerei,* p. 22.

21 Büchner, *Hinterglasmalerei,* pp. 37, 90–91; SAM AR 2043/142a; Elfriede Grabner, *Hinterglasbilder: Geschichte, Technik, Ikonographie,* exhibition catalog, Steiermärkisches Landesmuseum Joanneum, 1982–83, p. 10; Johann Evangelist Lang Account Book, 1832–34; SAA, Landgericht ä. O., PAR/686; Knaipp, "Über die Südtiroler Hausierer," pp. 535ff; Raimund Schuster, "Von Kraxenträgern und Glasbilderhändlern im 19. Jahrhundert," *Volkskunst* 6, no. 2 (1983): 86.

22 Büchner, *Hinterglasmalerei,* pp. 37, 76, 88; SAA, Landgericht ä. O., PAR/686; Reinhard Haller, personal communication; Notice in the Church at Kreuzberg. In *Geschichte des baierischen Handels* ([Munich, 1817], p. 704), Roman Zirngibl discusses the right of access to all local markets granted the Oberammergau and Murnau craftsmen in 1759. See Wolfgang Brückner, *Die Verehrung des Heiligen Blutes in Walldürn: Volkskundlich-soziologische Untersuchungen zum Strukturwandel barocken Wallfahrtens* (Aschaffenburg: Paul Pattloch, 1958), pp. 80–83, gives an account of the economy that could grow up around a successful pilgrimage.

23 Shorter, *Social Change and Social Policy in Bavaria,* pp. 375–77; A. A. di Pauli, "Ueber die Tesineser und ihren Bilder-handel," *Der Sammler für Geschichte und Statistik von Tirol* 1 (1807): 36–47.

24 Dominique Lerch, *Imagerie et Société: L'imagerie Wentzel de Wissembourg au XIXe siècle* (Strasbourg: Istra, 1982), pp. 188–94; Spamer and Hain, *Der Bilderbogen von der "Geistlichen Hausmagd,"* p. 15; Rudolf Schenda, *Die Lesestoffe der kleinen Leute: Studien zur populären Literatur im 19. und 20. Jahrhundert* (Munich: Beck, 1976), pp. 47–49.

25 Spamer and Hain, *Der Bilderbogen von der "Geistlichen Hausmagd,"* pp. 16–17, quoting Karl Stieler, "Kunststudien aus den bairischen Bergen," in *Natur- und Lebensbildern aus den Alpen* (Stuttgart, 1886), p. 271; Brückner, *Die Bilderfabrik,* pp. 24–25; Becker, "Welschtiroler Hausierer in Vergangenheit und Gegenwart," p. 329; Brückner, "Trivialer Wandschmuck der Zweiten Hälfte des 19. Jahrhunderts," p. 122; Elke Hilscher, *Die Bilderbogen im 19. Jahrhundert* (Munich, 1977), p. 83.

26 SM, GA 178/49; SAA, Landgericht ä. O., PAR/686.

27 BHA, MH 7150; Blackbourn, "Between Resignation and Volatility," p. 41, draws attention to the "growing army of travelling salesmen—the 'itinerants in patent-leather shoes' as one critic called them." In general, the changing pattern of retailing discussed by Blackbourn is mirrored here, including shops, mail ordering, and sales representatives like Gerzabeck.

28 Lerch, *Imagerie et Société,* p. 160, suggests a rough estimate of 2 million prints for Wentzel shipments in 1869–70.

29 Brückner, *Die Bilderfabrik,* pp. 24–25; Hilscher, *Die Bilderbogen im 19. Jahrhundert,* p. 78.

30 Hilscher, *Die Bilderbogen im 19. Jahrhundert,* p. 78; Lerch, *Imagerie et Société,* pp. 151–74. It is interesting to note that there was no inevitable teleology about the development of agencies in key locations from family agents to businesses unconnected with the family or the village.

31 Hilscher, *Die Bilderbogen im 19. Jahrhundert,* p. 82; BHA, MH 7150; Friedrich Knaipp, "Hinterglasbildererzeugung: Produktion und Vertrieb bei Vinzenz Köck in Sandl, Oberösterreich, in den Jahren 1852–1864," *Österreichischer Volkskundeatlas* 15 (1959): pp. 10–13.

32 Karl Bücher, *Die Entstehung der Volkswirtschaft,* 14th and 15th eds. (Tübingen, 1920), pp. 183–84, provides this classification.

33 Seidl, "Der volkstümliche Maler Johann Bapt. Reisbacher," pp. 24, 28.

34 Kriedte, Medick, and Schlumbohm, *Industrialization Before Industrialization,* pp. 98–101. This concept has been criticized by Frank Perlin, "Proto-industrialization and Pre-colonial South Asia," *Past and Present* 98 (February 1983): 40–41, as providing a "catch-all" category for all the "residual" examples left over from the more complex *Verlagsystem* category that describes a full-fledged putting-out system of the kind so typical of the fully developed protoindustrial textile industry. Hazzi, *Statistische Aufschlüsse über das Herzogtum Bayern,* p. 67; SAM, LRA 7423; Büchner, *Hinterglasmalerei,* pp. 96, 99–100. See also a document concerning the retailing of glasspaintings and other decorative objects in the Amberg area in 1796, SAA Opf. Admin/5180. In the late nineteenth century, Josef Hetzenecker of Viechtach also retailed glasspaintings painted by a local craftsman, as recorded in his Einschreibe-Buch, 1867–1884/5, in the possession of the Grötz family of Viechtach, Lower Bavaria.

35 Kriedte, Medick, and Schlumbohm, *Industrialization Before Industrialization,* p. 99, describe the *Kaufsystem* as one that "gave rise to an economic dependence which gradually undermined the formal independence of the petty commodity producer." SAM, LRA 131441.

36 Büchner, *Hinterglasmalerei,* p. 82; Perlin, "Proto-industrialization and Pre-colonial South Asia," pp. 36, 40, expresses criticism of such "teleological" protoindustrial theories.

37 SM, GA 3853, 178/49; Brückner, *Die Bilderfabrik,* p. 22; Lerch, *Imagerie et Société,* pp. 38–49, 160; BHA, MH 7150, 7152.

38 See, for example, the Senefelder-Aretin partnership mentioned in Chapter 2 or the May-Wirsing partnership mentioned by Brückner in *Die Bilderfabrik,* p. 42. Government loans were sought by Senefelder, BHA MH 2845; Heinrich Weishaupt,

SM, GA 178/49; Thomas Driendl, BHA, MH 7152; and Karl Heindel, BHA, MH 7150. See also the Lang document, SAM, LRA 131441. Mendels, "Proto-industrialization," pp. 245–46.

4 *Paintings for the* Herrgottswinkel: *The Popular Market in Religious Art*

1 Raimund Schuster, *Hinterglasbilder und Risse aus dem Bayerischen Wald und anschließendem Böhmerwald* (Vilsbiburg: Der Storchenturm Sonderheft 3, 1979), pp. 7–8; SAM, AR 2043/142a; Büchner, *Hinterglasmalerei,* pp. 90–91. See examples of the tiny Oberammergau paintings in the Heimatmuseum there. Reinhard Haller, "Volkstümliche Hinterglasbilder in Verlassenschafts-inventaren des 18. Jahrhunderts: Aufgezeigt am Beispiel der Hofmark Bodenmais," *Verhandlungen des Historischen Vereins für Niederbayern* 99 (1973): 58; Spamer and Hain, *Der Bilderbogen von der "Geistlichen Hausmagd,"* p. 17, drawing from Karl Stieler, "Kunststudien aus den bairischen Bergen," in *Natur-und Lebensbildern aus den Alpen* (Stuttgart, 1886), pp. 271–74.

2 Winkler, *Die Frühzeit der deutschen Lithographie,* p. 436.

3 Lee, *Population Growth,* p. 159; Schremmer, *Die Wirtschaft Bayerns,* p. 432. There is a growing literature on the early development of consumerism in Europe. For the role of the graphic arts, see Chandra Mukerji, *From Graven Images: Patterns of Modern Materialism* (New York: Columbia University Press, 1983).

4 Haller, "Volkstümliche Hinterglasbilder in Verlassenschafts-inventaren des 18. Jahrhunderts," p. 55.

5 Lydia L. Dewiel, *Hinterglasmalerei in Bayern: 18. und 19. Jahrhundert* (Munich: Süddeutscher Verlag, 1986), p. 29, describes how she tried to establish the connection between prints and glasspaintings. She came up with a copper engraving by C. Galle of an *Agnus dei* and a glasspainting patterned after it. The glasspainting is illustrated on page 31, the engraving on page 32. *So Ruf Ich an Maria: Risse mit Wallfahrtsmotiven aus Schönstein,* exhibition catalog, Gäubodenmuseum Straubing, July 25–October 5, 1986, connects prints, patterns, and devotional paintings very well visually. See Büchner, *Hinterglasmalerei,* pp. 93–94, for the presence of Augsburg prints in the Gege collection of patterns.

6 See, for example, Jane Hayward, *Stained Glass Windows,* Bulletin of the Metropolitan Museum of Art, December 1971–January 1972, figure 3.

7 Ibid., pp. 33–36, of catalog of windows. On page 33 Hayward argues that "the sketchy, linear technique resembled that of the engraver rather than that of the painter. . . . The artists who designed such small, meticulously painted scenes were often printmakers by profession." See also Jenny Schneider, *Glasgemälde: Katalog der Sammlung des Schweizerischen Landesmuseums Zürich* (Zürich: Schweizerisches Landesmuseum, 1970), pp. 15, 21–22. Schneider points out that prints were used as patterns for these *Kabinettscheiben* as well, not always very faithfully. On page 16 she discusses the increasing popularity of grisaille panes; in the eighteenth century clear engraved glass panels captured the popular market as well. A direct connection between glasspaintings of this sort and reverse glasspainting is made in Wüthrich, *Ältere Hinterglasmalerei,* p. 5, where he discusses a 1521 reverse

glasspainting "in the style of a *Kabinettscheibe*." He argues that early reverse glasspaintings were executed by workers in stained glass.

8 Knaipp, *Hinterglas Bilder*, p. 31.

9 Fritz Bernhard and Fritz Glotzmann, *Fromme Bilderlust: Miniaturen auf kleinen Andachtsbildern* (Dortmund: Harenberg, 1980), give excellent examples of the variety of decor used in small contemplative paintings as well.

10 See, for example, Brauneck, *Religiöse Volkskunst*, illustrations 55–67, for the elaborate framing typical in eighteenth-century decor. Some vivid examples of paintings with highly decorative frames are included in Knaipp, *Hinterglas Bilder*, p. 110; Schmidt, *Hinterglas*, color illustration 8; Wolfgang Brückner, Hanswerfried Muth, and Hans-Peter Trenschel, *Hinterglasbilder aus Unterfränkischen Sammlungen* (Würzburg: Mainfränkische Hefte 79, 1983), pp. 57, 59–63, 70, 79, 91, 93, 103, 139, 151, 163, 219, 257, 261, 321.

11 I am grateful to Rudi Eswarin for his elaboration in a personal communication of this important proviso to the analysis of frames for glasspaintings. See also Wüthrich, *Ältere Hinterglasmalerei*, p. 4, where he argues that frames were "an absolute necessity" for glasspaintings.

12 A. Hyatt Mayor, *Prints and People: A Social History of Printed Pictures* (Princeton: Princeton University Press, 1971), illustration 90, shows a pinned print of Moses, "as tacked to a wall in The Annunciation, painting by Joos van Cleve, Antwerp, 1510–40." Mayor discusses the alterations in glass production that encouraged the framing of prints on the following page.

13 Ritz, *Hinterglasmalerei*, pp. 95, 100, 116–17, 138; Ward, *Reverse Paintings on Glass*, pp. 30–31, 102–22.

14 Lionel Rothkrug, "German Holiness and Western Sanctity in Medieval and Modern History," *Historical Reflections/Réflexions Historiques* 15, no. 1 (1988): in particular pp. 201–5, 245, discusses this longstanding role of the *Armenseelen* that existed even in the twentieth century in Bavaria. Haller, *Armenseelentaferl*, gives an excellent overview of the practices and beliefs associated with the images of *Armenseelen* produced both as prints and as glasspaintings. He illustrates both prints and paintings extensively and includes examples of chromolithographs later copied as glasspaintings as well. See pp. 158–59, 162–63.

15 Büchner, *Hinterglasmalerei*, p. 93. See also Josef Rosenegger and Edith Bartl, *Wallfahrten im Bayerischen Oberland*, 2d ed. (Freilassing: Pannonia, 1981).

16 The range of images available to consumers is captured in such studies of central European shrines as Rudolf Kriß, *Die Volkskunde der Altbayrischen Gnadenstätten*, 3 vols. (Munich: Filser, 1953–56), and Gustav Gugitz, *Das kleine Andachtsbild in den Österreichischen Gnadenstätten in Darstellung, Verbreitung und Brauchtum nebst einer Ikonographie* (Vienna: Hollinek, 1950) and *Österreichs Gnadenstätten in Kult und Brauch: Ein topographisches Handbuch zur religiösen Volkskunde in Fünf Bänden* (Vienna: Hollinek, 1955–58). A helpful overview of the paintings themselves is given in Brückner, Muth, and Trenschel, *Hinterglasbilder aus Unterfränkischen Sammlungen*.

17 Josef Hetzenecker, Einschreibe-Buch; Pieske, *Bürgerliches Wandbild*, p. 6; Brückner, *Die Bilderfabrik*, p. 32.

18 Haindl, "Ueber den lithographischen Farbendruck in München," p. 219.

19 *Verzeichniß der bey der lithographischen Kunstanstalt an der Feyertags-Schule zu München erschienenen Kunstprodukte* (1818), pp. 1–9; Hetzenecker, Einschreibe-Buch.

20 Dorothy Alexander and Walter L. Strauss, *The German Single-Leaf Woodcut, 1600–1700*, 2 vols. (New York: Abaris, 1977), 1:1–9.

21 Wolfgang Brückner, *Populäre Druckgraphik Europas: Deutschland vom 15. bis zum 20. Jahrhundert* (Munich: Callwey, 1975), p. 224, and his *Hinterglasmalerei* (Munich, Würzburg: Ethnologia Bavarica 3, 1976), p. 93.

22 Rudolf Schenda, "Ein französischer Bilderbogenkatalog aus dem Jahre 1860," *Schweizerisches Archiv für Volkskunde* 62 (1966): 52; Dominique Lerch, "Imagerie profane, Imagerie religieuse sous le second Empire, dans le Bas-Rhin: L'Imagerie Wentzel de Wissembourg," *Archives de l'Eglise d'Alsace*, n.s., 22 (1975): 335; Brückner, *Die Bilderfabrik*, p. 44. See also Lerch, *Imagerie et Société*, pp. 93–143, for the full range of and variations in Wentzel's production.

23 Schenda, "Ein französischer Bilderbogenkatalog aus dem Jahre 1860," p. 53; Christa Pieske, "Katalog der lithographischen Anstalt Eduard Gustav May," *Anzeiger des Germanischen Nationalmuseums* (1967): 134ff; Gugitz, *Das kleine Andachtsbild in den Österreichischen Gnadenstätten in Darstellung, Verbreitung und Brauchtum nebst einer Ikonographie*, pp. 109–13. Brauneck, *Religiöse Volkskunst*, p. 72, lists Maria Dreieichen and Maria Taferl as *Gnadenbilder* based on "old, prechristian cults." See also his color illustration 4. The growth of new Marian pilgrimages during the nineteenth and even twentieth centuries also stimulated the traditional devotional market.

24 Ferchl, "Uebersicht," pp. 144–45.

25 Weishaupt, *Verzeichniss der lithographischen Incunabeln-Sammlung*, pp. 24, 40; Haindl, "Ueber den lithographischen Farbendruck in München," p. 218; Germanisches Nationalmuseum, Nuremberg, L3435, 3436; Josef Vydra, *Die Hinterglasmalerei*, p. 21.

26 BHA, MInn 30104; F. Netto, *Das Geheimniß des Oelbilder-Drucks, erfunden vom Maler Liepmann in Berlin* (Quedlinburg und Leipzig: Basse, 1840), p. 5.

27 Schuster collection, Zwiesel; Reinhard Haller, personal communication. See also Brückner, *Elfenreigen, Hochzeitstraum*.

28 Joseph M. Ritz and Gislind M. Ritz, *Alte bemalte Bauernmöbel: Geschichte und Erscheinung—Technik und Pflege* (Munich: Callwey, 1984), pp. 42, 106; Burkhart Cording, *Volkskunst und Vergangenheit in den Museen des Bayerischen Waldes* (Grafenau: Morsak, 1977), p. 52; Wernher Scheingraber and Wilfried Bahnmüller, *Volkskunst im Bayerischen Oberland* (Freilassing: Pannonia, 1978), pp. 6–7.

29 Netto, *Das Geheimniß des Oelbilder-Drucks*, p. 5.

30 Haller, "Volkstümliche Hinterglasbilder in Verlassenschafts-inventaren des 18. Jahrhunderts," pp. 54, 58; Joseph M. Ritz, "Deutsche religiöse Volkskunst: Zu ihren Forschungsaufgaben: III. Hauskunst. (Der Herrgottswinkel)," *Volk und Volkstum: Jahrbuch für Volkskunde* 3 (1938): 259. See also Lenz Kriss-Rettenbeck, *Bilder und Zeichen religiösen Volksglaubens*, 2d ed. (Munich: Callwey, 1971), p. 15, in which he suggests that, despite their absence from inventories, small pictures probably were hung in other rooms of the house. They were perhaps not mentioned because of their primitive nature, and they may have been

unframed and fixed to the wall with a nail. Gislind Ritz mentions an alternate form used in the Bavarian and Bohemian Forest areas, in which the paintings were lined up along a ledge on the living-room wall (*Hinterglasmalerei,* p. 47).

31 See Haller, *Armenseelentaferl,* p. 50, for the cooling of saints in purgatory and Rudolf Kriß, *Die Volkskunde der Altbayrischen Gnadenstätten,* 3 vols. (Munich: Filser, 1953–56), 1:152 and 2:282, for discussion of the use of holy images pinned to stall doors as protectors. Ritz and Ritz, *Alte bemalte Bauernmöbel,* pp. 10–11, 30, 32, 48–49, 112, include examples of beds painted with religious images.

32 Spamer, *Das kleine Andachtsbild vom XIV bis zum XX Jahrhundert,* p. 267; Pieske, *Bürgerliches Wandbild,* pp. 7–8; for examples of paintings in nineteenth-century votives, see Emanuela Angiuli, ed., *Puglia Ex Voto* (Bari: Congedo, 1977), tables 6, 15, 19, 43, 52, 79, and p. 214; Iso Baumer, *Détresse et Confiance: Témoignages de piété populaire* (Porrentruy: Éditions Jurassiennes, 1984), pp. 182, 195; Angelo Turchini, ed., *Lo straordinario e il quotidiano: Ex voto, santuario, religione popolare nel Bresciano* (Brescia: Grafo, 1980), pp. 113 (landscape in living area), 120, 184, 191, 200–201, 233, 239; Gabriella Belli, ed., *Ex Voto: Tavolette votive nel Trentino: "Religione, cultura e società,"* exhibition catalog, Palazzo delle Albere, Trento, Autumn 1981–Spring 1982, pp. 227, 236, 252, 253, 276, 278, 280, 281, 287. See also illustrations of the use of religious pictures in the bedroom in Brückner, *Elfenreigen, Hochzeitstraum;* Ritz and Ritz, *Alte bemalte Bauernmöbel,* p. 31. Bernard Cousin, *Le Miracle et le Quotidien* (Aix-en-Provence: Sociétés, Mentalités, Cultures, 1983), p. 234, discusses the frequency of paintings included in nineteenth-century votive paintings. See also pages 112 and 226 for religious paintings in bedrooms; on p. 164 a framed landscape and a crucifix decorate a child's sleeping area.

33 I discuss this relationship in greater detail in my article "The Religious Context of Crisis Resolution in the Votive Paintings of Catholic Europe," *Journal of Social History* (June 1990). The fallacy of drawing a stark contrast between the two systems, "the standard religion/science conflict hypothesis," is discussed by Robert Wuthnow, "Science and the Sacred," in a collection of essays generally useful for this topic edited by Phillip E. Hammond, *The Sacred in a Secular Age: Toward Revision in the Scientific Study of Religion* (Berkeley: University of California Press, 1985). Wuthnow's article appears on pages 187–203, the quotation on page 192. Moreover, recent work by sociologists has suggested a general breakdown or at least a rethinking of "secularization theory." For example, Rodney Stark and William Sims Bainbridge, *The Future of Religion: Secularization, Revival and Cult Formation* (Berkeley: University of California Press, 1985), p. 529, conclude that "the scholars in the heart of Christendom who proclaim the death of God have been fooled by a simple change of residence. Faith lives in the sects and sectlike denominations, and in the hearts of the overwhelming majority of individual persons." See also David Lyon, "Rethinking Secularization: Retrospect and Prospect," *Review of Religious Research* 26, no. 3 (March 1985): 228–43; Stephen Sharot, "Secularization and the Diminishing Decline of Religion," *Review of Religious Research* 27, no. 3 (1986): 193–207; Jeffrey K. Hadden, "Toward Desacralizing Secularization Theory," *Social Forces* 65, no. 3 (1987): 587–611.

34 Wuthnow, "Science and the Sacred," p. 192. See also Rita H. Mataragnon, "Mod-

ernization and Religion: Must They Move in Different Directions?" in *The Many Faces of Religion and Society,* edited by Mataragnon and M. Darrol Bryant (New York: Paragon House Publishers, 1985), pp. 18–28.

35 Stark and Bainbridge, *The Future of Religion,* p. 262.

36 See, for example, Ritz and Ritz, *Alte bemalte Bauernmöbel.* Burke, *Popular Culture in Early Modern Europe,* pp. 244–50, discusses the increased production of luxury consumer goods for the rural classes and the interchange of what were once local folk arts in the eighteenth century. He cites, among other sources, the now classic article on peasant consumption by Jan de Vries, "Peasant Demand Patterns and Economic Development: Friesland 1550–1750," in *European Peasants and Their Markets,* edited by W. N. Parker and E. L. Jones (Princeton, 1975).

37 BHA, MInn 30104; Netto, *Das Geheimniß des Oelbilder-Drucks,* p. 5.

38 Ritz, "Deutsche religiöse Volkskunst," p. 257.

39 Ibid., p. 257; Reinhard Haller, personal communications; Haller, "Volkstümliche Hinterglasbilder in Verlassenschafts-inventaren des 18. Jahrhunderts," p. 55; Verlassenschaftsinventar aus dem Jahre 1754, Kurfürstliche Hofmark Bodenmais in Archiv Dr. Reinhard Haller, 8372 Zwiesel, West Germany.

40 Richard Trexler, "Florentine Religious Experience: The Sacred Image," *Studies in the Renaissance* 19 (1972): 7–41, discusses the image of Our Lady of Impruneta used in procession as a rain goddess, another good example of this ambiguity. The image leaves its strictly religious setting to fulfill a secular purpose in a secular setting but as a religious functionary.

41 David Warren Sabean, *Power in the Blood: Popular Culture and Village Discourse in Early Modern Germany* (Cambridge: Cambridge University Press, 1984), p. 109, stresses that eating together creates a "moral community." In this case, the saints partake of that community together with the members of the household.

42 See Wilhelm H. Riehl, *Die Familie* (Stuttgart: Cotta, 1861), pp. 187–88, in which he posits the dining table as a symbol of the household as a patriarchal unit.

43 Robert Redfield, "Art and Icon," in *Anthropology and Art: Readings in Cross-Cultural Aesthetics,* edited by Charlotte M. Otten (New York: Natural History Press, 1971), pp. 39–65.

44 Ibid., pp. 42–43.

45 Ibid., p. 48.

5 Spiritual Insurance: The Meaning of Glasspaintings and Lithographs

1 Edgar Harvolk, *Votivtafeln aus Bayern und Österreich,* p. 18. I explore the ramifications of this miracle and others recorded in European votive paintings in my article "The Religious Context of Crisis Resolution in the Votive Paintings of Catholic Europe."

2 See, for example, the votive painting on page 11 of Wilhelm Theopold, *Hab ein kostbar Gut erfleht: Ein Essay über Votivmalerei* (Munich: Thiemig, 1977). See also Karl Künstle, *Ikonographie der Heiligen* (Freiburg im Breisgau, 1926), pp. 469–74.

3 Kriß, *Die Volkskunde der Altbayrischen Gnadenstätten,* gives the reader a vivid feel for this sacralized landscape as he meanders from shrine to shrine in the first

two volumes of his study. Any walker in an area so dominated by local churches and shrines cannot fail to get a sense of their physical integration with the land.

4 *Lexikon für Theologie und Kirche,* 2d ed., vol. 5 (Freiburg: Herder, 1962), pp. 98–101, traces the growth of visual depictions of these holy figures, particularly from the late Middle Ages on. See also William A. Christian, Jr., *Local Religion in Sixteenth-Century Spain* (Princeton: Princeton University Press, 1981), p. 21.

5 Christian, *Local Religion in Sixteenth-Century Spain,* p. 20, discusses the "local, or localistic, religiosity" of Spanish villagers in Ciudad Real province. Particularly striking is his analysis of the priests who can both react suspiciously to the devotions of their parishioners and "when asked about the shrines of their home villages, . . . speak with tenderness, excitement, and pride. For them the religion learned at home, embedded in the home landscape, transcends the doctrinal attitudes learned in the seminary, which they may apply elsewhere." See also Georg Schreiber, *Wallfahrt und Volkstum in Geschichte und Leben* (Düsseldorf: L. Schwann, 1934), pp. 21–25; and Cousin, *Le Miracle et le Quotidien,* pp. 56–69, an analysis of the catchment areas of the 133 sites that he surveyed, most of which were exceedingly local. Rothkrug, "German Holiness and Western Sanctity in Medieval and Modern History," p. 245, sums up a lengthy argument about the differences between Bavarian and western European concepts of "the holy and its mobility" (p. 162) by suggesting that "an efflorescence of *Umritte* and more plebeian types of pilgrimages helped to transform villages and towns into networks of quasi-liturgical, encapsulated communities." There, "holiness remained earth-bound." See also his argument about *Ortsheilige,* the splitting of the same saint into different local variations (pp. 165–68). But was this not a general characteristic of popular Catholic identification with local shrines throughout Europe in this post-Reformation period? The role of spring and tree cults would have encouraged this earth-bound tendency, as his examples of the "wandering image" that returns to its place of origin illustrate (p. 166). Yet the images did wander, as they were carried in the minds of countless believers about their daily business, to act as protectors in miracles like Anna Nimerfall's outside the immediate purview of their shrines. Nevertheless, the connection back to the *place* of the image is retained because the recipients of miraculous intervention felt the need to give thanks to the protector involved by visiting the shrine on pilgrimage, usually depositing an expression of gratitude there as well.

6 William A. Christian, Jr., *Person and God in a Spanish Valley* (New York: Seminar Press, 1972), analyzes the local, regional, and national identifications with saints. *Wallfahrt kennt keine Grenzen,* exhibition catalog, Bayerisches Nationalmuseum, Munich, June 28–October 7, 1984, pp. 228–43, provides a good introduction to the Altötting shrine. The catalog also surveys several other key supraregional shrines, for example, the Austrian Mariazell connected with the Hapsburgs and the *Queen of Poland* at Tschenstochau (pp. 155–83). The origins of the Altötting cult, however, were connected with the legitimation of the Holy Roman Empire under Frederick III and Maximilian I. See, for example, Lionel Rothkrug, "Holy Shrines, Religious Dissonance and Satan in the Origins of the German Reformation," *Historical Reflections/Réflexions Historiques* 14, no. 2 (1987): 234–35, 246.

7 See, for example, Vera Schauber and Hanns Michael Schindler, *Die Heiligen und*

Namenspatrone im Jahreslauf (Munich: Delphin, 1985). In particular, the work of Steven Sargent on the names appearing in Miracle Books suggests that the Fourteen Helpers in Need provided a large proportion of namesake protection, at least in the late Middle Ages (paper delivered to the New York State Association of European Historians, October 1988). The exhibition catalog *Namenspatrone Hinter Glas* (OberÖsterreichische Landesmuseum, Linz, March 3, 1983–February 12, 1984) draws attention to the production of these name saints specifically on glass. Büchner's discovery of patterns for name saints in the Gege collection also emphasizes their production on glass (*Hinterglasmalerei,* p. 93). Of course, saints also afforded protection to groups of believers—to guilds, fraternal organizations, and the like—as well as to parishes.

8 Kriß, *Die Volkskunde der Altbayrischen Gnadenstätten,* 3:26.

9 Redfield, "Art and Icon," pp. 42–43.

10 Robert Scribner, "Cosmic Order and Daily Life: Sacred and Secular in Pre-Industrial German Society," in *Religion and Society in Early Modern Europe, 1500–1800,* edited by Kaspar von Greyerz (London: George Allen and Unwin, 1984), pp. 17–18. The chapter "Volksfrommes Jahr und Feiergestaltung" in Ludwig Veit and Ludwig Lenhart, *Kirche und Volksfrömmigkeit im Zeitalter des Barock* (Freiburg: Herder, 1956), pp. 130–74, gives a general picture of the intertwining of religious and secular in the Baroque lifestyle.

11 Scribner, "Cosmic Order and Daily Life," pp. 21ff.

12 John M. Theilmann, "Medieval Pilgrims and the Origins of Tourism," *Journal of Popular Culture* 20, no. 4 (1987): 93–102.

13 Scribner, *For the Sake of Simple Folk,* p. 5. See, for example, discussion and illustrations of mementos and badges in *Wallfahrt kennt keine Grenzen,* especially pp. 34–51. That glasspaintings had taken on the same function in the eighteenth and nineteenth centuries is well exemplified by the Bäumer Holy Trinity order.

14 Lenz Kriss-Rettenbeck, *Ex Voto: Zeichen, Bild und Abbild im christlichen Votivbrauchtum* (Zürich: Atlantis, 1972), pp. 303ff, calls this the "promulgation" effect of votive paintings.

15 Roger Chartier, *The Cultural Uses of Print in Early Modern France,* translated by Lydia G. Cochrane (Princeton: Princeton University Press, 1987), pp. 3, 7.

16 Steven L. Kaplan, ed., *Understanding Popular Culture: Europe from the Middle Ages to the Nineteenth Century* (New York: Mouton, 1984); in particular, see Roger Chartier, "Culture as Appropriation: Popular Cultural Uses in Early Modern France," pp. 229–53. Chartier discusses Carlo Ginzburg's *The Cheese and the Worms: The Cosmos of a Sixteenth-Century Miller,* translated by John and Anne Tedeschi (Harmondsworth: Penguin, 1982), especially p. 33. See also Sabean, *Power in the Blood,* especially pp. 94–95, for his emphasis on culture "as a series of arguments among people about the common things of their everyday lives."

17 Chartier, *The Cultural Uses of Print,* p. 17, draws attention to this distinction between "popular" and "catholic" behaviors. The former were "rooted in specific community customs" while the latter drew from "the Catholic spirit which was universal, officially backed, equal for all." Christian, *Person and God in a Spanish Valley,* p. 47, also draws attention to the "losing battle" fought by the Church

hierarchy against this fragmentation of what were supposed to be "generalized devotions."

18 Victor Turner, *The Forest of Symbols: Aspects of Ndembu Ritual* (Ithaca: Cornell University Press, 1967), p. 50.

19 Turner labels these two major groupings "orectic" and "normative"; that is, their meaning was at the orectic extreme "grossly physiological . . . relating to general human experience of an emotional kind" and at the normative extreme ethical, relating "to moral norms and principles governing the social structure." Ibid., p. 54. Turner also talks about the "operational meaning" of a symbol, or "how [people] act with reference to it, who so acts, and the social structural context of such action," in Victor Turner and Edith Turner, *Image and Pilgrimage in Christian Culture: Anthropological Perspectives* (New York: Columbia University Press, 1978), p. 146. See, for example, Emmanuel Le Roy Ladurie, *Carnival in Romans,* translated by Mary Feeney (New York: George Braziller, 1979), pp. 293–324, for his analysis of the multiple references of the symbols used during the carnival.

20 The term is of course the one now associated with Clifford Geertz's work. See Geertz, *The Interpretation of Cultures: Selected Essays* (New York: Basic Books, 1973), p. 14.

21 Erwin Panofsky, *Studies in Iconology: Humanistic Themes in the Art of the Renaissance* (New York: Harper and Row, 1962). Turner, *Image and Pilgrimage in Christian Culture,* p. 146, calls this the "exegetic meaning" of symbols. See also Scribner, *For the Sake of Simple Folk,* for his wide-ranging interpretations of Reformation imagery set in the context of what he calls "different kinds of shared cultural experience" (p. 244).

22 See Turner, *Image and Pilgrimage in Christian Culture,* p. 146, for the "positional" analysis of symbols. See also Scribner, *For the Sake of Simple Folk,* pp. 10–12, for his similar approach to the reading of complex images, based on semiology. On pages 211–16 Scribner discusses a particularly good example of a carefully structured multiple image.

23 Haller, "Volkstümliche Hinterglasbilder in Verlassenschafts-inventaren des 18. Jahrhunderts," p. 58. This observation is certainly substantiated by the growing scholarly literature on Mary. Her egalitarian and anti-hierarchical appeal was apparent from the start of her cult in the fifth century, when the crowd at Ephesus played a role in the decision-making process at the council that debated Mary's role as *Theotokos* or Mother of God. Geoffrey Ashe, *The Virgin* (London: Routledge and Kegan Paul, 1976), p. 191. Michael P. Carroll, *The Cult of the Virgin Mary: Psychological Origins* (Princeton: Princeton University Press, 1986), pp. 80–86, argues that the influx of "Roman poor," which official acceptance of Christianity had brought into the Church, accounts for the hierarchy's acceptance of Mary as cult figure, "giving them a type of Christianity that they wanted." That she remains a charismatically powerful figure in tension with hierarchical Christological emphases is well illustrated in Ronald L. Grimes, *Symbol and Conquest: Public Ritual and Drama in Santa Fe, New Mexico* (Ithaca: Cornell University Press, 1976), pp. 78–86. The coronation of Our Lady of the Conquest in 1973 at a special Mass in St. Francis Cathedral by the Fiesta Queen of Santa Fe symbolized her popular appeal, while the subsequent celebration of the Eucharist transferred

power and emphasis to the clerical hierarchy and their control over Christological ritual. This popular emphasis did not, however, preclude official crownings of the statue, such as the 1954 crowning by Francis Cardinal Spellman and the "papal" crowning in 1960 by a delegate of the Pope (pp. 51–52).

24 Kriss-Rettenbeck, *Bilder und Zeichen religiösen Volksglaubens* (1963), p. 57; Seidl, "Der volkstümliche Maler Johann Bapt. Reisbacher," p. 30. Mary Lee Nolan and Sidney Nolan, *Christian Pilgrimage in Modern Western Europe* (Chapel Hill: University of North Carolina Press, 1989), pp. 119–28, mention that "Christ-centered cultus, although nowhere extremely common, is primarily an Ibero-Germanic phenomenon."

25 See Brauneck, *Religiöse Volkskunst,* p. 72. Marian cults served also as a powerful Counter-Reformation propaganda tool. See, for example, Eva-Maria Bangerter-Schmid, *Erbauliche illustrierte Flugblätter aus den Jahren 1570–1670* (Frankfurt am Main: Peter Lang, 1986), p. 61.

26 Brückner, Muth and Trenschel, *Hinterglasbilder aus Unterfränkischen Sammlungen,* pp. 189, 198–99.

27 Eva Hunt, *The Transformation of the Hummingbird: Cultural Roots of a Zinacantecan Mythical Poem* (Ithaca: Cornell University Press, 1977), pp. 273–74. See also Scribner, "Cosmic Order and Daily Life," pp. 18–19, in which he calls attention to the centrality of "the annual calendrical cycle" of Church and community festivals, many of which "sought to invoke divine blessing on the material world," and, of course, were integrally intertwined with the biological cycle of the seasons.

28 Andrew M. Greeley, *The Mary Myth: On the Femininity of God* (New York: Seabury, 1977), p. 13.

29 See, for example, James J. Preston, ed., *Mother Worship: Theme and Variations* (Chapel Hill: University of North Carolina Press, 1982); Carroll, *The Cult of the Virgin Mary,* pp. 32–41, provides a cautious overview of the goddess connection.

30 Haller, "Volkstümliche Hinterglasbilder in Verlassenschafts-inventaren des 18. Jahrhunderts," p. 56; Seidl, "Der volkstümliche Maler Johann Bapt. Reisbacher," p. 30.

31 Brauneck, *Religiöse Volkskunst,* pp. 74–76, referring to Torsten Gebhard, "Die Marianischen Gnadenbilder in Bayern. Beobachtungen zur Chronologie und Typologie," in *Kultur und Volk: Festschrift für Gustav Gugitz,* edited by L. Schmidt (Vienna, 1954), pp. 93–116.

32 Karl Mindera, *Maria Hilf: Ein Beitrag zur religiösen Volkskunde* (Munich: Don Bosco, 1961), p. 12.

33 Ibid., p. 8; Rosenegger and Bartl, *Wallfahrten im Bayerischen Oberland,* pp. 6–7.

34 Mindera, *Maria Hilf,* pp. 12, 23; Brauneck, *Religiöse Volkskunst,* p. 75.

35 Preston, *Mother Worship,* p. 339, stresses that "everywhere the divine mother is a focus for [the] profound insecurity at the root of the human experience."

36 See Turner, *Image and Pilgrimage in Christian Culture,* p. 146, in this context.

37 William Madsen, *The Virgin's Children: Life in an Aztec Village Today* (Austin: University of Texas Press, 1960), p. ix.

38 See Preston, *Mother Worship,* p. 337, for the possible range of relationships between mother goddesses and empirical mothers. Recent studies of Mary have similarly placed her in the social contexts appropriate to the period and location

of their emphasis. See, for example, Penny Schine Gold, *The Lady and the Virgin: Image, Attitude, and Experience in Twelfth-Century France* (Chicago: University of Chicago Press, 1985), and Margaret R. Miles, *Image as Insight: Visual Understanding in Western Christianity and Secular Culture* (Boston: Beacon, 1985), especially pp. 63–93. Both authors stress the complexity of the relationship between the varied experience of real women and the multiple interpretations of the images they study.

39 His role as head of household was certainly one of the popular ways of interpreting him. See Cynthia Hahn, " 'Joseph Will Perfect, Mary Enlighten and Jesus Save Thee': The Holy Family as Marriage Model in the Mérode Triptych," *Art Bulletin* 68, no. 1 (March 1986): 54–66. Hahn argues that the Joseph depicted on this triptych reflected the desired image of the *pater familias.* He is "powerful and dignified," a "strong, capable head of his household." However, there was also a popular image of Joseph as "an old, tired buffoon, a butt of jokes." His age remains in this triptych, but in many popular glasspaintings he is substantially younger. See, for example, Brückner, Muth, and Trenschel, *Hinterglasbilder aus Unterfränkischen Sammlungen,* pp. 95, 111, 131, 133, 193, 219, 304, 316–19 (with exception of illustration 384). The versions on pages 109, 121, 127, 217, and 315 do include lines on his forehead, presumably suggesting age. But compare his hair to that of an Augsburg version of the elderly Joseph on page 81 or to that of Saint Mark on page 115 or of God on page 199. In Knaipp, *Hinterglas Bilder,* on page 90 Joseph is golden-haired, on page 113 he is dark-haired but with a wrinkled forehead, and on page 129 a Raimundsreuth version of the Holy Family includes a clearly white-haired Joseph. His relative youth and his ambiguous standing vis-à-vis wife and child in many glasspaintings suggest to me that his role as *Hausvater* is also ambiguous.

40 See Ingeborg Weber-Kellermann, *Die Familie: Geschichte, Geschichten und Bilder* (Frankfurt am Main: Insel, 1976), pp. 65–75. In Beitl, *Votivbilder,* Illustration 40, the special role of the *Hausvater* is highlighted by the special blue coat that he wears in a family votive painting. But the *Hausmutter* also played a key role, and she was the logical counterpoint to the *Hausvater,* as the pendant prints reproduced by Weber-Kellermann on page 73 emphasize. See Gullickson, *Spinners and Weavers of Auffay,* pp. 162–66, for an overview of historical interpretations of the male-female power structures in the household. She argues that female historians have tended to stress the "complementarity" of husband and wife rather than the hierarchy and role-separation of the male perspective. For an excellent and sensitive example of the complementarity thesis, see Martine Segalen, *Love and Power in the Peasant Family: Rural France in the Nineteenth Century,* translated by Sarah Matthews (Chicago: University of Chicago Press, 1983). On page 36 Segalen argues that "customs demonstrate that, beyond the framework of civil and Church law, the question of authority between the couple is still an open one." On pages 85–94 she describes the range of activities undertaken by the wife, which included the "privilege" of cooking, sex, and, of course, motherhood.

41 Jack Goody, *Production and Reproduction: A Comparative Study of the Domestic Domain* (Cambridge: Cambridge University Press, 1976), p. 63. He quotes a proverb: "Qui se marie par intérêt, de sa femme est le valet (Catalon)." Segalen,

Love and Power in the Peasant Family, pp. 58–72, illustrates many of these points, using proverbs as well.

42 Kriedte, Medick, and Schlumbohm, *Industrialization Before Industrialization,* pp. 61–62; B. H. Röttger, "Volkskunst im Bezirk Bogen," *Die ostbairischen Grenzmarken* 18, no. 4 (1929): 104. This image is similar to the depiction of Joseph in the Antwerp-Baltimore Diptych mentioned in Hahn, "Joseph Will Perfect," p. 55. There, "a very old Joseph sits on the ground with his bare feet comically protruding from beneath his robe while he sews, making stockings into swaddling clothes for the infant Jesus." The glasspainting lacks any humor and Joseph is young; however, the implications for upending the normal household relationships are surely the same. But see also Gullickson, *Spinners and Weavers of Auffay,* pp. 151–52. She challenges Medick's picture of family life from the vantage point of the Caux and argues that the picture worsened for women in the nineteenth century. This is a theme developed by Arthur E. Imhof in "Women, Family and Death: Excess Mortality of Women in Child-bearing Age in Four Communities in Nineteenth-Century Germany," in *The German Family,* edited by Evans and Lee, pp. 148–74. Lee, "Family and 'Modernisation,'" pp. 95–96, draws attention to the "economic exploitation" of Bavarian wives by their peasant husbands. He even cites evidence that suggests "wife-beating in Bavaria was . . . commoner than the ill-treatment of horses." It would be interesting to know whether much of the excess load borne by these women was actually self-exploitation out of a sense of responsibility for the well-being of the household.

43 This subordinate position, enforced by interpretations of Mary as humble receptor of God's will, is a clearly male reading of the lessons to be learned from Mary's motherhood. See, however, Bertram Schaffner, *Father Land: A Study of Authoritarianism in the German Family* (New York: Columbia University Press, 1948), pp. 31ff, for modern responses to the question, "A mother, who interferes when a father is punishing his son, is . . . ?" "Germans responded in terms of the threatened injury to the father's status or the effects of a possible interruption of an abstract conception of child-training. Seventy percent of the candidates felt that in one way or another she was transgressing an unwritten law." See also Christian, *Person and God in a Spanish Valley,* p. 177.

44 Anne Hughes, *The Diary of a Farmer's Wife, 1796–1797* (Harmondsworth: Penguin, 1981), especially p. 11. One might add here the concept of "Marianismo" as a moral counterweight to "Machismo." See Evelyn P. Stevens, "Marianismo: The Other Face of Machismo in Latin America," in *Female and Male in Latin America: Essays* edited by Ann Pescatello (Pittsburgh: University of Pittsburgh Press, 1973).

45 Greeley, *The Mary Myth,* p. 14; see also Hans Bleibrunner, "Andachtsbilder aus Niederbayern: Einleitung," *Beilage zum Amtlichen Schul-Anzeiger für den Regierungsbezirk Niederbayern* (December 1968): 52–53, in which he discusses the Schildthurn pilgrimage site where three maidens, Einbet, Warbet, and Wilbet, had been revered for centuries as the center of a mother cult. At the time of the Counter-Reformation, Mary was added to the cult, as Bleibrunner illustrates with a print in which both the Mother of God and the three maidens appear together in the clouds above the church.

46 Vincent Cronin, *Mary Portrayed* (London: Darton, Longman and Todd, 1968), pp. 42ff.
47 Lee, *Population Growth*, pp. 69–70.
48 Ibid., pp. 63, 70–73; Alfred Groth and Martin Hahn, "Die Säuglingsverhältnisse in Bayern," *Zeitschrift des königlichen Bayerischen Statistischen Landesamts* 42 (1910): 104ff.
49 See, for example, Johann Michael Sailer's injunction that "the healthy, strong mother obeys the call of nature, suckles, nurses her child herself, and certainly out of a feeling of love, enjoying a clear conscience and a feeling of composure and with fearless adherence to dietary prescriptions," in Georg Schreiber, *Mutter und Kind in der Kultur der Kirche: Studien zur Quellenkunde und Geschichte der Karitas Sozialhygiene und Bevölkerungspolitik* (Freiburg im Breisgau: Herder, 1918), pp. 121–22, quoting Johann Michael Sailer, *Handbuch der christlichen Moral*, vol. 3 (Sulzbach, 1834), pp. 130, 132.
50 Kriss-Rettenbeck, *Ex Voto*, pp. 206ff. This imagery was clearly related to the Souls in Purgatory motif discussed in Chapter 4. Both motifs express anxiety about the eternal happiness of the dead, as did also the continuing purchase of indulgences, particularly at special events such as Father Bäumer's Jubilee celebration.
51 Ibid., p. 206; Lee, *Population Growth*, p. 71; Robert W. Lee, "Medicalisation and Mortality Trends in South Germany in the Early Nineteenth Century," in *Mensch und Gesundheit in der Geschichte*, edited by Arthur E. Imhof (Husum: Matthiesen, 1980), pp. 92–93.
52 Reinhard Haller, personal communication; Christa Pieske, *Das freudige Ereignis und der jungen Kindlein Aufzucht*, 3d ed. (Munich: Bruckmann, 1981), p. 53; Edward Shorter, *The Making of the Modern Family* (New York: Basic Books, 1975), pp. 198–99. Netting, *Balancing on an Alp*, p. 130, found that swaddling infants for the first 2–3 months of their lives continued in Törbel up to the 1920s.
53 Ingeborg Weber-Kellermann, *Die Kindheit: Kleidung und Wohnen, Arbeit und Spiel: Eine Kulturgeschichte* (Frankfurt am Main: Insel, 1979), pp. 42–43. Wilhelm Theopold, *Das Kind in der Votivmalerei* (Munich: Thiemig, 1981), pp. 23, 109, shows examples of cradles furnished with knobs around which cloth bands are wound to hold the baby firmly inside, yet another example of the protective care taken of them.
54 Ibid., p. 38; Almut Amereller, *Votiv-Bilder: Volkskunst als Dokument menschlicher Hilfsbedürftigkeit, dargestellt am Beispiel der Votiv-Bilder des Klosters Andechs* (Munich: Heinz-Moos, 1965), p. 19.
55 Kriss-Rettenbeck, *Ex Voto*, p. 207.
56 See Greeley, *The Mary Myth*, pp. 185ff.
57 The functions of specialty protection and generalized protection of namesakes were combined for all the saints involved. See the discussions in Schauber and Schindler, *Die Heiligen und Namenspatrone im Jahreslauf*, of the protective specialties of the saints presented in the order of their Saint's Days. Wilhelm Theopold, *Votivmalerei und Medizin: Kulturgeschichte und Heilkunst im Spiegel der Votivmalerei* (Munich: Thiemig, 1978), p. 24, cites the particular specialties of the Fourteen Helpers in Need so popular as name saints.
58 Harvolk, *Votivtafeln aus Bayern und Österreich*, p. 21.

59 Theopold, *Hab ein kostbar Gut erfleht,* pp. 40–41.

60 Karl Künstle, *Ikonographie der Heiligen* (Freiburg im Breisgau, 1926), pp. 467–69, gives a general introduction to Notburga.

61 Beitl, *Votivbilder,* illustrations 22 and 23; Otto Aubry, *St. Notburga-Büchlein zum 200 jährigen Jubiläum der Wallfahrtskapelle in Weißling* (Pfaffenhofen-Am: Prechter, 1952), pp. 3–4.

62 Aubry, *St. Notburga-Büchlein zum 200 jährigen Jubiläum der Wallfahrtskapelle in Weißling,* p. 5.

63 Edgar Harvolk, *Votivtafeln: Bildzeugnisse von Hilfsbedürftigkeit und Gottvertrauen* (Munich: Callwey, 1979), pp. 69–70, 99, 128, and 143, contain examples of votive paintings delivered at Weißling.

64 Ibid., pp. 2, 6; Wolfgang von Pfaundler, *Sankt Notburga, Eine Heilige aus Tirol: Eine Bildgeschichte in drei Teilen* (Vienna, Munich: Herold, 1962), pp. 178–79.

65 Pfaundler, *Sankt Notburga, Eine Heilige aus Tirol,* pp. 178–79.

66 Lutz K. Berkner, "The Stem Family and the Developmental Cycle of the Peasant Household: An Eighteenth-Century Austrian Example," *American Historical Review* 77, no. 2 (April 1972): 413–15; Heinz Haushofer, "Ländliche Dienstboten in Altbayern," *Zeitschrift für Agrargeschichte und Agrarsoziologie* 23, no. 1 (April 1975): pp. 48–49.

67 Walter Hartinger, "Zur Bevölkerungs- und Sozialstruktur von Oberpfalz und Niederbayern in Vorindustrieller Zeit," *Zeitschrift für bayerische Landesgeschichte* 39, no. 3 (1976): 800; Lee, *Population Growth,* pp. 156–59; Haushofer, "Ländliche Dienstboten in Altbayern," p. 48. Berkner, "The Stem Family and the Developmental Cycle of the Peasant Household," pp. 412–13, 418, describes the expression of these tensions in local laws and local song.

68 Beitl, *Votivbilder,* illustration 22.

69 Aubry, *St. Notburga-Büchlein,* pp. 7ff.

70 See, for example, the discussion of Andachtsbilder in Bangerter-Schmid, *Erbauliche illustrierte Flugblätter aus den Jahren 1570–1670,* pp. 28–32. On pages 38–41 she discusses the context of Counter-Reformation propaganda efforts within which devotional materials like the *Andachtsbilder* were set.

71 Pfaundler, *Sankt Notburga,* pp. 156–58; Beitl, *Votivbilder,* illustration 23.

72 Herschel B. Chipp, "Formal and Symbolic Factors in the Art Styles of Primitive Cultures," in *Art and Aesthetics in Primitive Societies,* edited by Carol F. Jopling (New York: Dutton, 1971), p. 165.

73 Edmund R. Leach, "A Trobriand Medusa?" in *Art and Aesthetics in Primitive Societies,* edited by Carol F. Jopling (New York: Dutton, 1971), pp. 45–54.

74 Theopold, *Votivmalerei und Medizin,* p. 32.

75 Wilhelm Auer, *Goldene Legende: Leben der lieben heiligen Gottes auf alle Tage des Jahres* (Cologne, 1902), p. 48. See also Künstle, *Ikonographie der Heiligen,* pp. 524–28; Louis Réau, *Iconographie de l'Art Chrétien,* (Paris: Presses Universitaires de France, 1959), 3:1190–99. The association of plague with the symbol of the arrow is, of course, much older than Saint Sebastian. For example, Sophocles uses it in *Antigone.*

76 Bayerische Versicherungskammer, *St. Florian: Schutzpatron in Feuersnot* (Munich, 1977), p. 21; Florian Trenner, *Der heilige Florian* (Regensburg, 1981), p. 62.

See Beitl, *Votivbilder,* illustration 12, for one example of the many votive paintings that record these frequent disasters. See also Künstle, *Ikonographie der Heiligen,* pp. 232–36.

77 Künstle, *Ikonographie der Heiligen,* pp. 402–5; Günther Kapfhammer, *St. Leonhard zu ehren* (Rosenheimer, n.d.), p. 33, quoting Romuald Bauerreiss, no reference.

78 Ibid., p. 34. Steven D. Sargent, "Religious Responses to Social Violence in Eleventh-Century Aquitaine," *Historical Reflections/Réflexions Historiques* 12, no. 2 (1985): 219–40, discusses the origins of Saint Leonhard's cult. Sargent's dissertation also covers the early days of the cult in Bavaria (*Religion and Society in Late Medieval Bavaria: The Cult of St. Leonard, 1258–1500* (Ph.D. dissertation, University of Pennsylvania, 1982).

79 Sometimes Saint Leonhard is replaced by Saint Wendelin in this corner. Wendelin was a patron saint of sheep. See P. Alois Selzer, *St. Wendelin: Leben und Verehrung eines alemannisch-fränkischen Volksheiligen,* 2d ed. (Mödling bei Wien: St. Gabriel, 1962), pp. 210ff; Künstle, *Ikonographie der Heiligen,* pp. 590–91.

80 I am indebted to Herr Theo Hahn for the observation that these two saints are the patrons of local dioceses. See also Ritz, *Hinterglasmalerei,* p. 43. This argument is speculative, and it is possible that the two men are included for their patronage of practical concerns; Ulrich patronized believers inflicted with rats and mice or perhaps with fever, and Wolfgang was known as the patron of carpenters, timber workers, and miners, though they both had many interests. See Auer, *Goldene Legende,* p. 514; *Bischof Ulrich von Augsburg und seine Verehrung: Festgabe zur 1000. Wiederkehr des Todestages* (Augsburg, 1973); Gugitz, *Österreichs Gnadenstätten in Kult und Brauch,* 4:73; Franz C. Lipp, "Kult und volkstümliche Verehrung des heiligen Wolfgang," in *Der hl. Wolfgang in Geschichte, Kunst und Kult,* exhibition catalog, Ausstellung des Landes Oberösterreich, Linz, 1976, pp. 76–78; Réau, *Iconographie de l'Art Chrétien,* pp. 1348–49; Künstle, *Ikonographie der Heiligen,* pp. 564–65, 596–601. Knaipp, *Hinterglas Bilder,* p. 22, lists Wolfgang as the patron of woodworkers and the crippled. Schauber and Schindler, *Die Heiligen und Namenspatrone im Jahreslauf,* p. 33, suggest that Wolfgang was a "general helper in need," providing a very wide range of coverage from help in life-threatening moments to fire, plague, and a number of ailments to occupational groups. Nevertheless, both saints enjoyed strong links with the protection of faith.

81 Auer, *Goldene Legende,* p. 514; Gaby Steinbauer, *St. Ulrich—Patron des Bistums Augsburg: Untersuchungen zu Ulrichlegende* (St. Ottilien, 1981), pp. 40–41.

82 Rudolf Zinnhobler, *Der Heilige Wolfgang: Leben, Legende, Kult* (Linz, 1975), pp. 43ff and illustration 157. The Church was not his only common attribute, however.

Epilogue

1 Max Spindler, *Handbuch der Bayerischen Geschichte. Vol. IV, Das neue Bayern, 1800–1970,* part 2 (Munich: C. H. Beck, 1975), pp. 762–63. This is particularly true of the textile industry.

2 The patronage of Joseph von Utzschneider was exceptional for the glasspaint-

ers, and it does not seem to have been very effective. Johann Evangelist Lang did receive government money in the late 1840s.

3 Marzio, *Chromolithography, 1840–1900,* p. 81.

4 Brückner, *Elfenreigen, Hochzeitstraum,* p. 12; Knaipp, *Hinterglas Bilder,* pp. 31, 45–46, 52–53, 142–43; Raimund Schuster collection, Zwiesel; Ritz, *Hinterglasmalerei,* pp. 56, 60, and the illustrations on pp. 122–23.

5 Ritz, *Hinterglasmalerei,* p. 58; Haller, *Armenseelentaferl,* pp. 158–59 and personal communication; Knaipp, *Hinterglas Bilder,* p. 31; Lankheit, ed., *The Blaue Reiter Almanac,* pp. 81, 270.

6 Kyser, "Ueber eine sterbende Volkskunst."

7 Brückner, *Elfenreigen, Hochzeitstraum,* p. 26; Knaipp, *Hinterglas Bilder,* pp. 16, 46–48; Theopold, *Hab ein kostbar Gut erfleht,* p. 6.

8 SAL, Repertorium 164/22, No. 2407; Büchner, *Hinterglasmalerei,* p. 40; Schuster, *Das Raimundsreuter Hinterglasbild,* pp. 17, 20.

9 Daisenberger, *Geschichte des Dorfes Oberammergau,* pp. 139, 232.

10 See, for example, the growing house totals in Murnau, up from 220 houses in 1850 to around 300 in 1890 and 470 in 1930. "Villas," including Münter's, even appeared on the edges of the town. Gebhart, *Staffelsee-Chronik,* pp. 54, 64–68.

11 SAM, Akten der Verlassenschaft 75 (1879). The property subsequently left Noder hands. SAM, Kataster 24915.

12 See, for example, the booklet put out by the "Ferien- und Erholungsort Uffing am Staffelsee, Oberbayern." It is a "Wohnungsliste . . . mit Ortsplan," in which visitors can orient themselves in the village and locate suitable lodgings from offerings by a wide variety of households.

13 SAM, Kataster 25181, 24915; gravestones in Saint Michael's churchyard, Seehausen. The Introduction notes the Münter painting of the Blue Rider artists boating on the lake; Kandinsky mentions Seehausen and Uffing boating services in his correspondence with Schönberg, Hahl-Koch, *Arnold Schoenberg—Wassily Kandinsky,* p. 63. There was, however, tension between fishermen and shipping, at least in the mid nineteenth century. SAM, AR 3979/470. *Murnau am Staffelsee, Bayr. Hochland* (Murnau, 1912), p. 8, discusses Seehausen boating facilities. See also the advertisement for Seehausen as a "Fischerdorf."

14 SAM, LRA 7423; *Murnau am Staffelsee,* numerous advertisements; Gebhart, *Staffelsee-Chronik,* pp. 25, 34–35, 69–70, 106. Around 1910 Münter painted Master Brewer Schöttl of the Angerbräu in Murnau on glass, under the circumstances another "traditional" relic. Gollek, *Gabriele Münter: Hinterglasbilder,* color illustration 4. This is the shift discussed by Blackbourn, "Between Resignation and Volatility," p. 41. He argues that "industrialization provided an overall stimulus to the expansion of small retail outlets which outweighed its effects on craftsmen."

15 For example, Carl Rottmann painted the two landscapes of the view from Murnau now located in the Lenbachhaus, Munich, G4447 and G4448, in 1843.

16 Gebhart, *Staffelsee-Chronik,* pp. 21, 25, 34–35, 40, 69–70, 106; Charlotte Gampe, "Murnau war Ort des Wintersportes," *Schriften des Historischen Vereins Murnau am Staffelsee e. V.* 6, no. 10 (1985): 44–61; Gebhart, "Murnau einst und jetzt," pp. 205, 209–10; *Murnau am Staffelsee,* pp. 4–5, 7, the Bade-Anstalten advertisement and the advertisements for hotels such as the Bahnhof-Hotel with forty

beds, the Gasthof zum Stern in Seehausen with forty beds, the Post with fifty beds, and the Stahlbad and Kurhaus Staffelsee, among others. SAM, LRA 9547 (from the 1920s) lists the ski factory with around ten employees and fifteen inns.

17 *Firmen Handbuch Industrie* (Munich: Industrie- und Handelskammer für München und Oberbayern, 1984), pp. 125–27, lists only nine Murnau concerns, including a manufacturing plant for thermoplastic foil and the Karg brewery. There is no evidence to suggest that Murnau has even now taken any significant part in the postwar boom in industry enjoyed in Upper Bavaria. See *Die Wirtschaft Oberbayerns* (Munich: Industrie- und Handelskammer für München und Oberbayern, 1986).

18 Daisenberger, *Geschichte des Dorfes Oberammergau,* pp. 188–89.

19 Gröber, *Alte Oberammergauer Hauskunst* (1930), pp. 32–33; *Oberammergau damals und heute: Ein Dorfrundgang mit der Kamera* (Oberammergau: Freundeskreis Pilatushaus e. V., 1984), reproducing the 1905 Oberammergau Address Book; *Führer durch das Verleger Lang 'sche kunst- und kulturgeschichtliche Oberammergauer Museum,* pp. 8, 12. This booklet is unfortunately not dated but is probably of pre–World War II vintage. *Oberammergau and Environs* (Munich: Thiemig, 1960), pp. 12, 64; Roland Kaltenegger, *Oberammergau und die Passionsspiele, 1634–1984* (Oberammergau: Langen Müller, 1984), p. 29.

20 *The Passion Play House and the Local Museum* (Oberammergau: The Community of Oberammergau, 1963), pp. 3–7. Daisenberger, *Geschichte des Dorfes Oberammergau,* p. 177; Gebhart, *Staffelsee-Chronik,* pp. 22–23.

21 Daisenberger, *Geschichte des Dorfes Oberammergau,* pp. 188–89; SAM, LRA 62910; *Verein zur Förderung des Fremdenverkehrs in München und im bayer. Hochland (e. V.), Geschäfts-Bericht, 1905–6* (Munich: J. Schön, 1906), p. 14; *Oberammergau damals und heute,* reproducing the 1905 Oberammergau Address Book; *Oberammergau und Ammer-Gebirge Reiseführer* (Berlin: Grieben, 1930); *Die Ferien Schau Oberammergau* (Oberammergau: Verkehrsbüro der Arbeitsgemeinschaft Gemeinde Oberammergau, 1988), particularly pp. 8–13, 21–25, 29–37. Registered overnight stays in 1985–86 amounted to 139,539 Germans and 65,149 foreigners, according to the *Statistisches Jahrbuch 1987 für Bayern* (Bayerisches Landesamt für Statistik und Datenverarbeitung, 1987), p. 226. The average stay was 3.4 days. Possibly, these figures do not include the many guests staying in private homes.

22 E. Schropfer, "Der Glasmaler von Seehausen am Staffelsee," *Altbayerische Heimatpost* 42 (1954): 4; SAM, LRA 7341; epitaph of Josef Gege, Saint Michael's Church, Seehausen.

23 Gebhart, *Staffelsee-Chronik,* pp. 44, 54, 67–68. Daisenberger, *Geschichte des Dorfes Oberammergau,* p. 156, mentions a large fire in 1817. The whole process is reminiscent of the argument in Eric Hobsbawm and Terence Ranger, *The Invention of Tradition* (Cambridge: Cambridge University Press, 1983).

24 Schropfer, "Der Glasmaler von Seehausen am Staffelsee," p. 4; Knaipp, *Hinterglas Bilder,* p. 47; Eckhart Feuchtmayr, "Zur Geschichte der Hinterglasmalerei im Staffelseeraum (1750–1870)," *Schriften des Historischen Vereins Murnau am Staffelsee e. V.* 6, no. 10 (1985): 42; *Murnau am Staffelsee,* Rambold advertisement for his work "painted after old patterns."

25 See, for example, Nelson H. H. Graburn, "The Evolution of Tourist Arts," *Annals of Tourism Research* 11 (1984): 398–99, where he discusses the process "which occurs when outsiders, tourists, frequently attempt to buy examples of the functional embedded arts. The local people start to make near exact replicas just for sale, adhering to near traditional forms and designs which satisfy their own aesthetic traditions and guarantee some form of 'authenticity' to the buyers."

The production of glasspaintings for tourists rather than for the traditional popular markets, both Catholic and external—icons for Russian orthodox consumers, George Washingtons for Americans and so forth—grew out of the commercialization of production normal for Bavarian glasspainters. For meeting the demands of consumers was, of course, what they had always done, and so the interpretation of tourist interests in glasspaintings merely suggested a new orientation for their work. The use to which the resultant products were put, however, was clearly likely to be different than the customary use of religious images in particular. They were often destined for a context in which their cult significance would be lost when they were displayed as "folk" art, for example, by the Blue Rider collectors themselves. In this sense only, the transformation of glasspainting into a tourist art can be compared to the process going on in Third and Fourth World areas where ceremonial and family-oriented artworks strictly destined for the local community are adapted for sale to outsiders. See, for example, the discussions of this phenomenon in Graburn, ed., *Ethnic and Tourist Arts;* Benetta Jules-Rosette, *The Messages of Tourist Art: An African Semiotic System in Comparative Perspective* (New York: Plenum, 1984).

26 See the discussion of secularization theory and its pitfalls in Chapter 4. Examples of these holdovers appear in Stephen Wilson, "Cults of Saints in the Churches of Central Paris," in *Saints and Their Cults: Studies in Religious Sociology, Folklore and History,* edited by Wilson (Cambridge: Cambridge University Press, 1983), pp. 233–60; James J. Preston, "The Goddess Chandi as an Agent of Change," in Preston, ed., *Mother Worship,* especially p. 220. Preston stresses the increased reliance on the goddess induced by the multiple demands of life in a modern society.

27 We noted the advent of the train to Alpine Bavaria in the late nineteenth century. This was but the first stage in a modernization process that has culminated in airplane "pilgrimages" to shrines all over the world. Knock in Ireland, for example, gained an international airport on the basis of the pilgrimage center there.

28 *The Passion Play House and the Local Museum* p. 3.

29 Lee, *Population Growth,* pp. 124–25; Clarkson, *Proto-Industrialization,* p. 38, calls this "agriculturalization."

30 Netting, *Balancing on an Alp,* pp. 6–7.

31 Eckart Schremmer, "The Textile Industry in South Germany, 1750 to 1850: Some Causes for the Technological Backwardness During the Industrial Revolution; Investment Approach and Structure Approach," *Textile History* 7 (1976): 82. He also reminds us that "industrial backwardness, economic backwardness, social backwardness and poverty are not always synonyms" ("Proto-Industrialisation: A Step Towards Industrialisation?" p. 659).

Bibliography of Cited Works

Primary Sources

Bayerisches Hauptstaatsarchiv, Munich (BHA)
GR 830/1–2 (1792)
KL Fasz. 204/38
Kurbayern Hofkammer Hofanlagsbuchhaltung 126, 168, 265
Kurbayern Geheimes Landesarchiv 1229
MH 2845, 2846, 7150, 7152
MInn 13999, 14335, 14359, 30104
Repertorium CXIII, Verz. 3, Fasz. 255, No. 285
Staatsarchiv Amberg (SAA)
Landgericht ä O., PAR/686
Opf Admin/5180
Staatsarchiv Landshut (SAL)
80/525a
Häuser- und Rustikal-Steuer-Kataster des Steuerdistrikts Schönbrunn (1808)
Repertorium 164, Verz. 1, Fasz. –, No. 4516
Repertorium 164/22, No. 2407
Repertorium 168, Verz. 1, Fasz. 1519, Lit. C
Repertorium 168, Verz. 1, Fasz. 1521, No. 56
Repertorium 168, Verz. 1, Fasz. 1766, No. 125
Urkataster 22/39 Vol. II (1843)
Staatsarchiv München (SAM)
AG Weilheim NR 1863/4/214
Akten der Verlassenschaft 215 (1863–64), 75 (1879)
AR 1173/26, 2043/138, 2043/142a, 3977/416, 3979/470, 3989/804
Kataster 8791, 8829, 8830, 9034, 24643, 24906, 24915, 24987, 25151, 25154, 25155, 25181
LRA 3229, 62910, 7332, 7341, 7423, 7550, 9547, 131441

Stadtarchiv München (SM)
GA 178/49, 3851, 3853
Museums and Collections
Alte and Neue Pinakothek, Munich
Bayerisches Nationalmuseum, Munich
Bayerische Staatsbibliothek, Handschriftenabteilung, Munich
Colonial Williamsburg Collections, Williamsburg, Virginia
Corning Museum of Glass, Corning, New York
Deutsches Museum, Handschriftenabteilung, Munich
Dr. Raimund Schuster Sammlung, Zwiesel
Dr. Reinhard Haller Sammlung, Zwiesel
Germanisches Nationalmuseum, Nuremberg
Heimatmuseum, Garmisch-Partenkirchen
Heimatmuseum, Oberammergau
Herbert Fastner Sammlung, Zwiesel
Division of Graphic Arts, National Museum of American History, Washington, D.C.
Staatliche Graphische Sammlung, Munich
Waldmuseum, Zwiesel
Vital Statistics
Birth, marriage, and death records from the parishes of Murnau, Oberammergau, Seehausen, and Uffing in Upper Bavaria, Freyung and Hohenau in Lower Bavaria
Account Books
Aschau glass factory
Hetzenecker, Josef
Lang, Andreas
Lang, Georg
Lang, Johann Evangelist

Printed Sources

Adhémar, Jean. *Graphic Art of the Eighteenth Century.* Translated by M. I. Martin. London: Thames and Hudson, 1964.

Alexander, Dorothy, and Strauss, Walter L. *The German Single-Leaf Woodcut, 1600–1700: A Pictorial Catalogue.* 2 volumes. New York: Abaris, 1977.

Amereller, Almut. *Votiv-Bilder: Volkskunst als Dokument menschlicher Hilfsbedürftigkeit dargestellt am Beispiel der Votiv-Bilder des Klosters Andechs.* Munich: Heinz-Moos, 1965.

Anderson, Michael. "Historical Demography After *The Population History of England.*" In *Population and Economy: Population and History from the Traditional to the Modern World,* edited by Robert I. Rotberg and Theodore K. Rabb. Cambridge: Cambridge University Press, 1986.

Anegg, Ernst. *Zur Gewerbestruktur und Gewerbepolitik während der Regierung Montgelas.* Dissertation, University of Munich, 1965.

Angiuli, Emanuela, ed. *Puglia Ex Voto.* Bari: Congedo, 1977.

Anzeiger für Kunst-und Gewerbefleiß im Königreiche Baiern 2, no. 39 (1816): 599–605.

Ashe, Geoffrey. *The Virgin*. London: Routledge and Kegan Paul, 1976.

Aubry, Otto. *St. Notburga-Büchlein zum 200 jährigen Jubiläum der Wallfahrtskapelle in Weißling*. Pfaffenhofen-Am: Prechter, 1952.

Auer, Wilhelm. *Goldene Legende: Leben der lieben heiligen Gottes auf alle Tage des Jahres*. Cologne, 1902.

"Aus der Geschichte der Isarflößerei." *Oberbayerisches Archiv* 109, no. 1 (1984): 99–115.

Ballerstedt, Gustav. *Beschreibung der Art und Weise, den lithographischen Buntdruck mittels eines Steins mit einem Abdruck zu bewirken. Erste Manier: Schablonen-Druck. Zweite Manier: Iris Druck*. Quedlinburg and Leipzig: Basse, 1839.

Bamberger Zeitung 86 (March 27, 1859).

Bangerter-Schmid, Eva-Maria. *Erbauliche illustrierte Flugblätter aus den Jahren 1570–1670*. Frankfurt am Main: Peter Lang, 1986.

Baumann, Simon. *Geschichte des Marktes Murnau in Oberbayern*. Murnau, 1855.

Baumer, Iso. *Détresse et Confiance: Témoignages de piété populaire*. Porrentruy: Éditions Jurassiennes, 1984.

Bayerische Versicherungskammer. *St. Florian: Schutzpatron in Feuersnot*. Munich, 1977.

Becker, Hans. "Welschtiroler Hausierer in Vergangenheit und Gegenwart." *Der Schlern* 41 (1967): 325–37.

Beitl, Klaus. *Votivbilder: Zeugnisse einer Alten Volkskunst*. Munich: Hugendubel, 1982.

Beiträge zur Statistik Bayerns. Volumes 192, 320, and 377. Munich: Bayerisches Statistisches Landesamt, 1953, 1972, and 1980.

Belli, Gabriella, ed. *Ex Voto: Tavolette votive nel Trentino: "Religione, cultura e società."* Exhibition catalog, Palazzo delle Albere, Trento, Autumn 1981–Spring 1982.

Berkner, Lutz K. "The Stem Family and the Developmental Cycle of the Peasant Household: An Eighteenth-Century Austrian Example." *American Historical Review* 77, no. 2 (April 1972): 398–418.

Bernhard, Fritz, and Fritz Glotzmann. *Fromme Bilderlust: Miniaturen auf kleinen Andachtsbildern*. Dortmund: Harenberg, 1980.

Bischof Ulrich von Augsburg und seine Verehrung: Festgabe zur 1000. Wiederkehr des Todestages. Augsburg, 1973.

Blackbourn, David. "Between Resignation and Volatility: The German Petite Bourgeoisie in the Nineteenth Century." In *Shopkeepers and Master Artisans in Nineteenth-Century Europe*, pp. 35–61. Edited by Geoffrey Crossick and Heinz-Gerhard Haupt. London: Methuen, 1984.

Blau, Josef. *Böhmerwälder Hausindustrie und Volkskunst. Part 2, Frauen-Hauswerk und Volkskunst*. Prague, 1918.

———. *Die Glasmacher im Böhmer-und Bayerwald in Volkskunde und Kulturgeschichte*. Regensburg, 1954.

Bleibrunner, Hans. "Andachtsbilder aus Niederbayern: Einleitung." *Beilage zum Amtlichen Schul-Anzeiger für den Regierungsbezirk Niederbayern* (December 1968): 1ff.

Bouchot, H. *La Lithographie*. Paris, 1895.

Braudel, Fernand. *Civilization and Capitalism: Fifteenth–Eighteenth Century*. Volume

12, *The Wheels of Commerce*. Translated by Siân Reynolds. London: Collins, 1982.

Braun, Rudolf. *Industrialisierung und Volksleben: Veränderungen der Lebensformen unter Einwirkung der verlagsindustriellen Heimarbeit in einem ländlichen Industriegebiet (Zürcher Oberland) vor 1800*. 2d ed. Göttingen: Vandenhoeck und Ruprecht, 1979.

Brauneck, Manfred. *Religiöse Volkskunst: Votivgaben—Andachtsbilder—Hinterglas—Rosenkranz—Amulette*. Cologne: DuMont, 1978.

Brückner, Wolfgang. *Die Bilderfabrik*. Frankfurt am Main, 1973.

———. *Die Verehrung des Heiligen Blutes in Walldürn: Volkskundlich-soziologische Untersuchungen zum Strukturwandel barocken Wallfahrtens*. Aschaffenburg: Paul Pattloch, 1958.

———. *Elfenreigen, Hochzeitstraum: Die Öldruckfabrikation, 1880–1940*. Cologne: M. DuMont Schauberg, 1974.

———. *Hinterglasmalerei*. Volume 3. Munich, Würzburg: Ethnologia Bavarica, 1976.

———. *Populäre Druckgraphik Europas: Deutschland vom 15, bis zum 20. Jahrhundert*. Munich: Callwey, 1975.

———. "Trivialer Wandschmuck der Zweiten Hälfte des 19. Jahrhunderts: Aufgezeigt am Beispiel einer Bilderfabrik." *Anzeiger des Germanisches National-museums* (1967): 117–31.

Brückner, Wolfgang, Hanswernfried Muth, and Hans-Peter Trenschel. *Hinterglasbilder aus Unterfränkischen Sammlungen*. Würzburg: Mainfränkische Hefte 79, 1983.

Brunner, Johann. *Das Postwesen in Bayern in seiner geschichtlichen Entwicklung von den Anfängen bis zur Gegenwart*. Munich, 1900.

Bücher, Karl. *Die Entstehung der Volkswirtschaft*. 14th and 15th editions. Tübingen, 1920.

Büchner, Heinrich. *Hinterglasmalerei in der Böhmerwaldlandschaft und in Südbayern: Beiträge zur Geschichte einer alten Hauskunst*. Munich: Filser, 1936.

Bührlen, J. R. *Luftelmaler Franz Seraph Zwink von Oberammergau*. Oberammergau, 1921.

Burke, Peter. *Popular Culture in Early Modern Europe*. New York: Harper and Row, 1978.

Carroll, Michael P. *The Cult of the Virgin Mary: Psychological Origins*. Princeton: Princeton University Press, 1986.

Chartier, Roger. *The Cultural Uses of Print in Early Modern France*. Translated by Lydia G. Cochrane. Princeton: Princeton University Press, 1987.

———. "Culture as Appropriation: Popular Cultural Uses in Early Modern France." In *Understanding Popular Culture: Europe from the Middle Ages to the Nineteenth Century*, edited by Steven L. Kaplan. New York: Mouton, 1984.

Chipp, Herschel B. "Formal and Symbolic Factors in the Art Styles of Primitive Cultures." In *Art and Aesthetics in Primitive Societies*, edited by Carol F. Jopling. New York: Dutton, 1971.

Christian, William A., Jr. *Local Religion in Sixteenth-Century Spain*. Princeton: Princeton University Press, 1981.

———. *Person and God in a Spanish Valley*. New York: Seminar Press, 1972.

Chur-pfalz-baïerisches Regierungs- und Intelligenzblatt (1800), pp. 430–32.

Clark, Stuart. "French Historians and Early Modern Popular Culture." *Past and Present* 100 (August 1983): 62–99.

Clarke, Harold G. *The Story of Old English Glass Pictures, 1690–1810*. London: Courier, 1928.

Clarkson, L. A. *Proto-Industrialization: The First Phase of Industrialization?* Basingstoke and London: MacMillan, 1985.

Cording, Burkhart. *Volkskunst und Vergangenheit in den Museen des Bayerischen Waldes*. Grafenau: Morsak, 1977.

Cousin, Bernard. *Le Miracle et le Quotidien. Les ex-voto provençaux, images d'une société*. Aix-en-Provence: Sociétés, Mentalités, Cultures, 1983.

Cramer, Joseph. *Die Entwicklung des Steindruck-gewerbes in Deutschland*. Leipzig, 1918.

Cronin, Vincent. *Mary Portrayed*. London: Darton, Longman and Todd, 1968.

Crossick, Geoffrey, and Heinz-Gerhard Haupt, eds. *Shopkeepers and Master Artisans in Nineteenth-Century Europe*. London: Methuen, 1984.

Daisenberger, Joseph Albert. *Geschichte des Dorfes Oberammergau*. Munich: Dr. C. Wolf and Son, 1858.

Davis, Natalie Zemon. *Society and Culture in Early Modern France*. Stanford: Stanford University Press, 1975.

Der Landkreis Freyung-Grafenau. Freyung: Landkreis Freyung-Grafenau, 1982.

Der Landkreis Wolfstein. Bayerischer Wald: Verlag Landkreis Wolfstein, 1968.

Destouches, Ernst von. *Fünfzig Jahre Münchener Gewerbe-Geschichte, 1848–1898, Part 3*. Munich, 1898.

Dettmer, Hermann. *Bilderbogen des 18. und 19. Jahrhunderts*. Exhibition catalog, Westfälisches Landesmuseum für Kunst und Kulturgeschichte, Münster, 1976.

Dewiel, Lydia L. *Hinterglasmalerei in Bayern: 18. und 19 Jahrhundert*. Munich: Süddeutscher Verlag, 1986.

Die Ferien Schau Oberammergau. Oberammergau: Verkehrsbüro der Arbeitsgemeinschaft Gemeinde Oberammergau, 1988.

Diener, Christian, and Graham Fulton-Smith. *Franz Hanfstaengl: Album der Zeitgenossen*. Munich: Wilhelm Heyne, 1975.

Die Wirtschaft Oberbayerns. Munich: Industrie- und Handelskammer für München und Oberbayern, 1986.

Dussler, Leopold. *Die Incunabeln der deutschen Lithographie (1796–1821)*. Heidelberg: Weissbach, 1955.

Eichler, Ulrike. "Münchener Bilderbogen." *Oberbayerisches Archiv* 99 (1974): 1ff.

"Ein Schiffszug auf der Donau." *Niederbayerische Hefte* 18 (1969): 25–28.

Eisenbeiss, Wilhelm. *Briefe, Boten und Belege: Ein Beitrag zur Entwicklungsgeschichte des Botenwesens und der Post, dargestellt an der Geschichte der Stadt Regensburg bis zum Jahre 1920*. Regensburg, 1966.

Engelmann, Godefroy. *Das Gesammtgebiet der Lithographie*. Translated by W. Pabst and A. Kretzschmar. Chemnitz, 1840.

Ferchl, Franz Maria. *Geschichte der Errichtung der Ersten Lithographischen Kunstanstalt bei der Feiertagsschule für Künstler und Techniker in München*. Munich, 1862.

———. "Uebersicht der einzig bestehenden, vollständigen Incunabelin-Sammlung der Lithographie." *Oberbayerisches Archiv* 17, no. 2 (1856): 115–203.

Feuchtmayr, Eckhart. "Zur Geschichte der Hinterglasmalerei im Staffelseeraum (1750–1870)." *Schriften des Historischen Vereins Murnau am Staffelsee* 6, no. 10 (1985): 13–42.

Firmen Handbuch Industrie. Munich: Industrie- und Handelskammer für München und Oberbayern, 1984.

Fried, Pankraz. *Herrschaftsgeschichte der Altbayerischen Landgerichte Dachau und Kranzberg im Hoch- und Spätmittelalter sowie in der Frühen Neuzeit*. Kommission für Bayerische Landesgeschichte, 1962.

———. "Historisch-statistische Beiträge zur Geschichte des Kleinbauerntums (Söldnertums) im westlichen Oberbayern." *Mitteilungen der Geographischen Gesellschaft in München* 51 (1966): 5–39.

———. "Reagrarisierung in Südbayern seit dem 19. Jahrhundert." In *Agrarisches Nebengewerbe und Formen der Reagrarisierung im Spätmittelalter und 19./20. Jahrhundert*, edited by Hermann Kellenbenz. Stuttgart: Fischer, 1975.

Friedman, Joan M. *Color Printing in England, 1846–1870*. New Haven: Yale Center for British Art, 1978.

Fuchs, Alfred. *Die Raimundsreuter Hinterglasmalerei*. Passau: Gogeissl, 1965.

Führer durch das Verleger Lang'sche kunst- und kulturgeschichtliche Oberammergauer Museum. Oberammergau: Gg. Lang sel. erben, n.d.

Gabriele Münter, 1877–1962: Gemälde, Zeichnungen, Hinterglasbilder und Volkskunst aus ihrem Besitz. Exhibition catalog, Städtische Galerie im Lenbachhaus, Munich, April 22–July 3, 1977.

Gampe, Charlotte. "Murnau war Ort des Wintersportes." *Schriften des Historischen Vereins Murnau am Staffelsee* 6, no. 10 (1985): 44–61.

Gebhart, Hansjakob. "Murnau einst und jetzt." *Bayerland* 40 (1929): 205–11.

———. *Staffelsee-Chronik: Ein Heimatbuch*. Riedhausen, 1977.

Geertz, Clifford. "Deep Play: Notes on the Balinese Cockfight." *Daedalus* 101 (1972): 1–37.

———. *The Interpretation of Cultures: Selected Essays*. New York: Basic Books, 1973.

Geertz, Hildred. "An Anthropology of Religion and Magic." *Journal of Interdisciplinary History* 6, no. 1 (Summer 1975): 71–89.

Gemeinde Daten, Ausgabe 1986. Bayerisches Landesamt für Statistik und Datenverarbeitung, 1986.

Ginzburg, Carlo. *The Cheese and the Worms: The Cosmos of a Sixteenth-Century Miller*. Translated by John and Anne Tedeschi. Harmondsworth: Penguin, 1982.

Glatzel, Ursula. *Zür Bedeutung der Volkskunst Beim Blauen Reiter*. Dissertation, University of Munich, 1975.

Gold, Penny Schine. *The Lady and the Virgin: Image, Attitude, and Experience in Twelfth-Century France*. Chicago: University of Chicago Press, 1985.

Gollek, Rosel. *Der Blaue Reiter in Lenbachhaus München: Katalog der Sammlung in der Städtischen Galerie*. Munich: Prestel, 1982.

———. *Gabriele Münter: Hinterglasbilder*. Munich: Piper, 1981.

———. "Murnau im Alpenvorland." In *Deutsche Künstler kolonien und Künstlerorte*, edited by Gerhard Wietek. Munich: Thiemig, 1976.

Goody, Jack. "Inheritance, Property, and Women: Some Comparative Considerations." In *Family and Inheritance: Rural Society in Western Europe, 1200–1800*, edited by

Jack Goody, Joan Thirsk, and E. P. Thompson. Cambridge: Cambridge University Press, 1976.

———. *Production and Reproduction: A Comparative Study of the Domestic Domain.* Cambridge: Cambridge University Press, 1976.

Gothic and Renaissance Art in Nuremberg, 1300–1550. Exhibition catalog, The Metropolitan Museum of Art, New York, and Germanisches Nationalmuseum, Nuremberg. Munich: Prestel, 1986.

Grabner, Elfriede. *Hinterglasbilder: Geschichte, Technik, Ikonographie.* Exhibition catalog, Steiermärkisches Landesmuseum Joanneum, 1982–83.

Graburn, Nelson H. H., ed. *Ethnic and Tourist Arts: Cultural Expressions from the Fourth World.* Berkeley: University of California Press, 1976.

———. "The Evolution of Tourist Arts." *Annals of Tourism Research* 11 (1984): 393–419.

Greeley, Andrew M. *The Mary Myth: On the Femininity of God.* New York: Seabury, 1977.

Grimes, Ronald L. *Symbol and Conquest: Public Ritual and Drama in Santa Fe, New Mexico.* Ithaca: Cornell University Press, 1976.

Gröber, Karl. *Alte Oberammergauer Hauskunst.* 1st ed. (1930) and 2d ed. Rosenheim: Rosenheimer, 1980.

Groschwitz, Gustave von. "The Significance of Nineteenth-Century Color Lithography." *Gazette des Beaux-Arts* (1954): 243–66.

Groth, Alfred, and Martin Hahn. "Die Säuglingsverhältnisse in Bayern." *Zeitschrift des Königlichen Bayerischen Statistischen Landesamts* 42 (1910).

Gugitz, Gustav. *Das kleine Andachtsbild in den Österreichischen Gnadenstätten in Darstellung, Verbreitung und Brauchtum nebst einer Ikonographie.* Vienna: Hollinek, 1950.

———. *Österreichs Gnadenstätten in Kult und Brauch: Ein topographisches Handbuch zur religiösen Volkskunde in Fünf Bänden.* 5 vols. Vienna: Hollinek, 1955–58.

Gullickson, Gay L. "Agriculture and Cottage Industry: Redefining the Causes of Proto-Industrialization." *Journal of Economic History* 43, no. 4 (December 1983): 831–50.

———. *Spinners and Weavers of Auffay: Rural Industry and the Sexual Division of Labor in a French Village, 1750–1850.* Cambridge: Cambridge University Press, 1986.

Gutman, Myron P. *Toward the Modern Economy: Early Industry in Europe, 1500–1800.* New York: Alfred A. Knopf, 1988.

Haddon, Jeffrey K. "Toward Desacralizing Secularization Theory." *Social Forces* 65, no. 3 (1987): 587–611.

Hahl-Koch, Jelena, ed. *Arnold Schoenberg—Wassily Kandinsky: Letters, Pictures and Documents.* Translated by John C. Crawford. London: Faber and Faber, 1984.

Hahn, Cynthia. " 'Joseph Will Perfect, Mary Enlighten and Jesus Save Thee': The Holy Family as Marriage Model in the Mérode Triptych." *Art Bulletin* 68, no. 1 (March 1986): 54–66.

Haindl, Sebastian. "Ueber den lithographischen Farbendruck in München." *Kunst- und Gewerbe-Blatt* 29, no. 3 (March 1843): 212–19.

Haller, Reinhard. *Armenseelentaferl: Hinterglasbilder aus Bayern, Österreich und Böhmen*. Grafenau: Morsak, 1980.

———. "Der Glasbilder Paulus Josephus Andreas Lohberger: Ein Beitrag zur Geschichte der Hinterglasmalerei in Niederbayern." *Beilage zum Amtlichen Schul-Anzeiger für den Regierungsbezirk Niederbayern* 6 (December 1969): 1–25.

———. "Volkstümliche Hinterglasbilder in Verlassenschafts-inventaren des 18. Jahrhunderts: Aufgezeigt am Beispiel der Hofmark Bodenmais." *Verhandlungen des Historischen Vereins für Niederbayern* 99 (1973): 52–63.

Hammond, Phillip E. *The Sacred in a Secular Age: Toward Revision in the Scientific Study of Religion*. Berkeley: University of California Press, 1985.

Hanke, Gerhard. "Zur Sozialstruktur der ländlichen Siedlungen Altbayerns im 17. und 18. Jahrhundert." In *Gesellschaft und Herrschaft. Forschungen zu sozial- und landgeschichtlichen Problemen vornehmlich in Bayern*. Munich: C. H. Beck, 1969.

Harden, Donald B. *Glass of the Caesars*. Exhibition catalog, Corning Museum of Glass, Corning; The British Museum, London; Römisch-Germanisches Museum, Cologne. Milan: Olivetti, 1987.

Hartinger, Walter. "Zur Bevölkerungs- und Sozialstruktur von Oberpfalz und Niederbayern in Vorindustrieller Zeit." *Zeitschrift für bayerische Landesgeschichte* 39, no. 3 (1976): 785–822.

Harvolk, Edgar. *Votivtafeln aus Bayern und Österreich aus dem Museum für Deutsche Volkskunde*. Berlin: Gebr. Mann, 1977.

———. *Votivtafeln: Bildzeugnisse von Hilfsbedürftigkeit und Gottvertrauen*. Munich: Callwey, 1979.

Häuserbuch der Stadt München. 5 volumes. Munich: Stadt München, 1977.

Haushofer, Heinz. "Ländliche Dienstboten in Altbayern." *Zeitschrift für Agrargeschichte und Agrarsoziologie* 23, no. 1 (April 1975): 47ff.

Hayward, Jane. *Stained Glass Windows*. Bulletin of the Metropolitan Museum of Art, December 1971–January 1972.

Hazzi, Josef von. *Statistische Aufschlüsse über das Herzogtum Bayern*. Vol. 2. Nuremberg, 1802.

Hess, Joseph. *Die Hinterglasbilder in Luxemburger Staatsmuseum*. Luxemburg, 1952.

Hilscher, Elke. *Die Bilderbogen im 19. Jahrhundert*. Munich, 1977.

Hobsbawm, Eric and Terence Ranger. *The Invention of Tradition*. Cambridge: Cambridge University Press, 1983.

Hohenberg, Paul M., and Lynn Hollen Lees. *The Making of Urban Europe, 1000–1950*. Cambridge, Mass.: Harvard University Press, 1985.

Hörger, Hermann. *Kirche, Dorfreligion und bäuerliche Gesellschaft: Strukturanalysen zur gesellschaftsgebundenen Religiosität ländlicher Unterschichten des 17. bis 19. Jahrhunderts, aufgezeigt an bayerischen Beispielen*. Part 1. Munich: Seitz and Höfling, 1978.

H.R. "Von den kinderjahren Murnaus als Sommerfrischort." *Land zwischen Lech und Isar* 9 (March 23, 1950): 67–68.

Hughes, Anne. *The Diary of a Farmer's Wife, 1796–1797*. Harmondsworth: Penguin, 1981.

Hughes, G. Bernard. "Old English Glass Pictures." *Country Life* (December 23, 1965).

Hunt, Eva. *The Transformation of the Hummingbird: Cultural Roots of a Zinacantecan Mythical Poem*. Ithaca: Cornell University Press, 1977.

Imhof, Arthur E. "Women, Family and Death: Excess Mortality of Women in Childbearing Age in Four Communities in Nineteenth-Century Germany." In *The German Family: Essays on the Social History of the Family in Nineteenth- and Twentieth-Century Germany,* edited by Richard J. Evans and W. R. Lee. London: Croom Helm, 1981.

Jaffee, David P. "An Artisan-Entrepreneur's Portrait of the Industrializing North, 1790–1860." In *Essays from the Lowell Conference on Industrial History, 1982 and 1983,* edited by Robert Weible, pp. 165–84. North Andover: Museum of American Textile History, 1985.

Jules-Rosette, Benetta. *The Messages of Tourist Art: An African Semiotic System in Comparative Perspective.* New York: Plenum, 1984.

Kaltenneger, Roland. *Oberammergau und die Passionsspiele, 1634–1984.* Oberammergau: Langen Müller, 1984.

Kapfhammer, Günther. *St. Leonhard zu ehren.* Rosenheimer, n.d.

Kaplan, Steven L., ed. *Understanding Popular Culture: Europe from the Middle Ages to the Nineteenth Century.* New York: Mouton, 1984.

Karlinger, Hans. *Deutsche Volkskunst.* Berlin: Propyläen, 1938.

Katalog der Kunst- und Kunstindustrie-Ausstellung alter und neuer deutscher Meister sowie der deutschen Kunstschulen im Glaspalaste zu München. 1876.

Kayser's Bücher-Lexikon, 1833–1840. Leipzig, 1841.

Keiser, Herbert Wolfgang. *Die Deutsche Hinterglasmalerei.* Munich: Bruckmann, 1937.

Knaipp, Friedrich. "Absatzgebiete und Handelswege der Hinterglasbilder dargestellt an Beispielen der wichtigsten Erzeugungsgebiete und Hausiererwohnsitze." *Österreichischer Volkskundeatlas* 15 (1959): 13.

———. "Ein Querschnitt durch die neuesten Forschungen." *Oberösterreichische Heimatblätter* 2, no. 3 (1948): 214–26.

———. *Hinterglas Bilder aus Bauern- und Bergmannsstuben des 18. und 19. Jahrhunderts.* 2d ed. Linz: Wimmer, 1973.

———. "Hinterglasbildererzeugung: Produktion und Vertrieb bei Vinzenz Köck in Sandl, Oberösterreich, in den Jahren 1852–1864." *Österreichischer Volkskundeatlas* 15 (1959): 10–13.

———. "Über die Südtiroler Hausierer mit bayrischen, Böhmerwälder und oberösterreichischen Hinterglasbildern." *Der Schlern* 28, no. 10 (1954): 533–40.

Knodel, John, and Etienne Van de Walle. "Breastfeeding, Fertility and Infant Mortality: An Analysis of Some Early German Data." *Population Studies* 21, no. 2 (September 1967): 109–31.

Kohlmann, Theodor. *Neurippiner Bilderbogen.* Exhibition catalog, Berlin, 1981.

Königlich-Baierisches Intelligenz-Blatt des Iller-Kreises (1815–16), pp. 860–68.

Kriedte, Peter, Hans Medick, and Jürgen Schlumbohm. *Industrialization Before Industrialization: Rural Industry in the Genesis of Capitalism.* Translated by Beate Schempp. Cambridge: Cambridge University Press, 1981.

Kriß, Rudolf. *Die Volkskunde der Altbayrischen Gnadenstätten.* 3 volumes. Munich: Filser, 1953–56.

Kriss-Rettenbeck, Lenz. *Bilder und Zeichen religiösen Volksglaubens.* 1st and 2d editions. Munich: Callwey, 1963 and 1971.

———. *Das Votivbild.* Munich: Hermann Rinn, 1958.

———. *Ex Voto: Zeichen, Bild und Abbild im christlichen Votivbrauchtum*. Zürich: Atlantis, 1972.

Künstle, Karl. *Ikonographie der Heiligen*. Freiburg im Breisgau, 1926.

Kunze, Arno. "Vom Bauerndorf zum Weberdorf: Zur sozialen und wirtschaftlichen Struktur der Waldhufendörfer der Südlichen Oberlausitz in 16., 17., und 18. Jahrhunderts." In *Oberlausitzer Forschungen*, edited by Martin Reuther. 1961.

Kyser, Hans. "Ueber eine sterbende Volkskunst." *Berliner Tageblatt* (September 6, 1912).

Lang, Léon. "Godefroy Engelmann de Mulhouse, Imprimeur Lithographe." In *Trois Siècles d'Art Alsacien, 1648–1948*. Strasbourg-Paris: Istra, 1948.

Langemeyer, Gerhard, and Reinhart Schleier. *Bilder nach Bildern: Druckgrafik und die Vermittlung von Kunst*. Exhibition catalog, Westfälisches Landesmuseum für Kunst und Kulturgeschichte, Münster, 1976.

Lankheit, Klaus. "Aus der Frühzeit der Weissenburger Bilderfabrik." *Kölner Zeitschrift für Soziologie und Sozial-psychologie* 21 (1969): 585–600.

Lankheit, Klaus, ed. *The Blaue Reiter Almanac, edited by Wassily Kandinsky and Franz Marc*. Translated by Henning Falkenstein. New York: Viking, 1974.

Larson, Kay. "Two Arts Entwined: Gabriele Münter and Wassily Kandinsky in West Germany." *Architectural Digest* 43, no. 1 (January 1986): 76–83, 170–71.

Leach, Edmund R. "A Trobriand Medusa?" In *Art and Aesthetics in Primitive Societies*, edited by Carol F. Jopling. New York: Dutton, 1971.

Lee, Robert W. "Medicalisation and Mortality Trends in South Germany in the Early Nineteenth Century." In *Mensch und Gesundheit in der Geschichte*, edited by Arthur E. Imhof. Husum: Matthiesen, 1980.

Lee, W. R. "Family and 'Modernisation': The Peasant Family and Social Change in Nineteenth-Century Bavaria." In *The German Family: Essays on the Social History of the Family in Nineteenth- and Twentieth-Century Germany*, edited by Richard J. Evans and W. R. Lee. London: Croom Helm, 1981.

———. *Population Growth, Economic Development and Social Change in Bavaria, 1750–1850*. New York: Arno, 1977.

Le Lithographe. Volumes 1–6. 1838–48.

Lepovitz, Helena Waddy. "Gateway to the Mountains: Tourism and Positive Deindustrialization in the Bavarian Alps." *German History* 7 (December 1989): 293–318.

———. "The Industrialization of Popular Art in Bavaria." *Past and Present* 99 (May 1983): 88–122.

———. "The Religious Context of Crisis Resolution in the Votive Paintings of Catholic Europe." *Journal of Social History* (June 1990).

———. "Spiritual Insurance: A Strategy for Psychological Survival." *Notebooks in Cultural Analysis* 1 (1984).

Lerch, Dominique. *Imagerie et Société: L'imagerie Wentzel de Wissembourg au XIXe siècle*. Strasbourg: Istra, 1982.

———. "Imagerie profane, Imagerie religieuse sous le second Empire, dans le Bas-Rhin: L'Imagerie Wentzel de Wissembourg." *Archives de l'Eglise d'Alsace*, n.s., 22 (1975): 323–43.

Le Roy Ladurie, Emmanuel. *Carnival in Romans*. Translated by Mary Feeney. New York: George Braziller, 1979.

Lewis, C. T. C. *George Baxter: The Picture Printer.* London: Sampson Low, Marston, and Co., 1924.

Lexikon für Theologie und Kirche. 2d edition. Freiburg: Herder, 1962.

Lieberich, H. "Das ländliches Handwerk in Altbayern vom 16.–18. Jahrhundert." *Mitteilungen für die Archivpflege in Oberbayern* 27 (1947): 721–40.

Lindgren, Uta. *Alpenübergänge von Bayern nach Italien, 1500–1850: Landkarten—Straßen—Verkehr.* Munich: Hirmer and Deutsches Museum, 1986.

Lipp, Franz C. "Kult und volkstümliche Verehrung des heiligen Wolfgang." In *Der hl. Wolfgang in Geschichte, Kunst und Kult.* Exhibition catalog, Ausstellung des Landes Oberösterreich, Linz, 1976.

"Lithographischer Kunst-Farbendruck worauf sich Heinr. Weishaupt in München unter'm 23. August 1837 ein Privilegium auf 15 Jahre ertheilen liess." *Kunst- und Gewerbe-Blatt* 27, no. 2 (February 1841): 138–42.

Lorilleux, Charles. *Traité de Lithographie: Histoire, Theoríe, Practique.* Paris, 1889.

Lyon, David. "Rethinking Secularization: Retrospect and Prospect." *Review of Religious Research* 26, no. 3 (March 1985): 228–43.

Mackenthun, Ilse. *Joseph von Utzschneider: Sein Leben, sein Wirken, seine Zeit.* Dissertation, University of Munich, 1958.

Madsen, William. *The Virgin's Children: Life in an Aztec Village Today.* Austin: University of Texas Press, 1960.

Man, Felix H. *Artists' Lithographs: A World History from Senefelder to the Present Day.* London: Studio Vista, 1970.

Mannoni, Edith. *Fixés et peinture sous verre.* Paris: Massin, n.d.

Marzio, Peter C. *Chromolithography, 1840–1900. The Democratic Art: Pictures for a Nineteenth-Century America.* Boston: Godine, 1979.

Mataragnon, Rita H. "Modernization and Religion: Must They Move in Different Directions?" In *The Many Faces of Religion and Society,* edited by Mataragnon and M. Darrol Bryant. New York: Paragon House Publishers, 1985.

Mayor, A. Hyatt. *Prints and People: A Social History of Printed Pictures.* Princeton: Princeton University Press, 1971.

Mendels, F. F. "Proto-industrialization: The First Phase of the Industrialization Process." *Journal of Economic History* 32 (1972): 241–61.

Meßner, Josef. *Ausgewählte Werke.* Vienna, 1897.

Miles, Margaret R. *Image as Insight: Visual Understanding in Western Christianity and Secular Culture.* Boston: Beacon, 1985.

Miller, Gudrun. *Die Geschichte der Hinterglasmalerei im Staffelseegebiet (Ihre Entwicklung bis zur Gegenwart).* Munich, 1977.

Mindera, Karl. *Maria Hilf: Ein Beitrag zur religiösen Volkskunde.* Munich: Don Bosco, 1961.

Mistler, Jean, François Blandez, and André Jacquemin. *Epinal et l'imagerie populaire.* Librairie Hachette, 1961.

Mochon, Anne. *Gabriele Münter: Between Munich and Murnau.* Exhibition catalog, Busch-Reisinger Museum, Harvard University, 1980.

Muchembled, Robert. *Popular Culture and Elite Culture in France, 1400–1750.* Translated by Lydia Cochrane. Baton Rouge: Louisiana State University Press, 1985.

Mukerji, Chandra. *From Graven Images: Patterns of Modern Materialism.* New York: Columbia University Press, 1983.

Murnau am Staffelsee, Bayr. Hochland. Murnau, 1912.

Namenspatrone Hinter Glas. Exhibition catalog, OberÖsterreichische Landesmuseum, Linz, March 3, 1983–February 12, 1984.

Netting, Robert McC. *Balancing on an Alp: Ecological Change and Continuity in a Swiss Mountain Community.* Cambridge: Cambridge University Press, 1981.

Netto, F. *Das Geheimniß des Oelbilder-Drucks, erfunden vom Maler Liepmann in Berlin.* Quedlinburg and Leipzig: Basse, 1840.

Nishida, Hideho. "Genesis of the Blaue Reiter." In *Homage to Wassily Kandinsky,* edited by G. di San Lazarro. New York: Amiel, 1975.

Nolan, Mary Lee, and Sidney Nolan. *Christian Pilgrimage in Modern Western Europe.* Chapel Hill: University of North Carolina Press, 1989.

Oberammergau and Environs. Munich: Thiemig, 1960.

Oberammergau damals und heute: Ein Dorfrundgang mit der Kamera. Oberammergau: Freundeskreis Pilatushaus, 1984.

Oberammergau und Ammer-Gebirge Reiseführer. Berlin: Grieben, 1930.

Oberammergau und die Passionsspiele, 1634–1984. Oberammergau: Langen Müller, 1984.

Obernberg, J. von. *Reisen durch das Königreich Bayern.* Part 1, volume 1. Munich, 1815.

Panofsky, Erwin. *Studies in Iconology: Humanistic Themes in the Art of the Renaissance.* New York: Harper and Row, 1962.

The Passion Play House and the Local Museum. Oberammergau: The Community of Oberammergau, 1963.

Pauli, A. A. di. "Ueber die Tesineser und ihren Bilder-handel." *Der Sammler für Geschichte und Statistik von Tirol* 1 (1807): 36–47.

Perlin, Frank. "Proto-industrialization and Pre-colonial South Asia." *Past and Present* 98 (February 1983): 30–95.

Peschek, H. E. *Das Ganze des Steindrucks.* 3d ed. Weimar, 1856.

Pfaundler, Wolfgang von. *Sankt Notburga, Eine Heilige aus Tirol: Eine Bildgeschichte in drei Teilen.* Vienna, Munich: Herold, 1962.

Phayer, Fintan Michael. *Religion und das Gewöhnliche Volk in Bayern in der Zeit von 1750–1850.* Munich: Neue Schriftenreihe des Stadtarchivs München, 1970.

———. *Sexual Liberation and Religion in Nineteenth-Century Europe.* London: Croom Helm, 1977.

Pieske, Christa. "Aus der Berliner Luxuspapierfabrikation um 1900: Produktion, Umsatz und Herstellerfirmen von Oblaten." *Volkskunst* 1, no. 3 (August 1978): 185–95.

———. *Bürgerliches Wandbild, 1840–1920: Populäre Druckgraphik aus Deutschland, Frankreich und England.* Exhibition catalog, Goltze, Göttingen, 1975.

———. *Das freudige Ereignis und der jungen Kindlein Aufzucht.* 3d ed. Munich: Bruckmann, 1981.

———. "Katalog der lithographischen Anstalt Eduard Gustav May." *Anzeiger des Germanischen Nationalmuseums* (1967): 132–62.

Preston, James J. "The Goddess Chandi as an Agent of Change." In *Mother Worship,* edited by Preston.

———. *Mother Worship: Theme and Variations.* Chapel Hill: University of North Carolina Press, 1982.

Réau, Louis. *Iconographie de l'Art Chrétien.* 3 vols. Paris: Presses Universitaires de France, 1959.

Redfield, Robert. "Art and Icon." In *Anthropology and Art: Readings in Cross-Cultural Aesthetics,* edited by Charlotte M. Otten. New York: Natural History Press, 1971.

Riehl, Wilhelm H. *Die Familie.* Stuttgart: Cotta, 1861.

Ritz, Gislind M. "Beiträge zu einer Stilkunde der Hinterglasmalerei am Staffelsee." *Bayerisches Jahrbuch für Volkskunde* (1966–67): 95–111.

———. "Die bürgerlich-handwerkliche Hinterglasmalerei des 18. Jahrhunderts in Augsburg." *Bayerisches Jahrbuch für Volkskunde* (1964–65): 47–75.

———. *Hinterglasmalerei: Geschichte, Erscheinung, Technik.* Munich: Callwey, 1972.

Ritz, Joseph M. "Deutsche religiöse Volkskunst: Zu ihren Forschungsaufgaben: III. Hauskunst. (Der Herrgottswinkel)." *Volk und Volkstum: Jahrbuch für Volkskunde* 3 (1938): 256–62.

Ritz, Joseph M., and Gislind M. Ritz. *Alte bemalte Bauernmöbel: Geschichte und Erscheinung—Technik und Pflege.* Munich: Callwey, 1984.

Roditi, Edouard. "Interview with Gabriele Münter." *Arts Magazine* (January 1960): 36–41.

Roethel, Hans Konrad. *Gabriele Münter, 1877–1962.* Exhibition catalog, Städtische Galerie im Lenbachhaus, Munich, October 13–December 2, 1962.

Roethel, Hans K., and Jean K. Benjamin, eds. *Kandinsky: Catalogue Raisonné of the Oil Paintings. Volume One, 1900–1915.* Ithaca: Cornell University Press, 1982.

Rosenegger, Josef, and Edith Bartl. *Wallfahrten im Bayerischen Oberland.* 2d ed. Freilassing: Pannonia, 1981.

Roters, Eberhard. "Wassily Kandinsky und die Gestalt des Blauen Reiters." *Jahrbuch der Berliner Museen* 5 (1963): 201–6.

Roth, Adolf. *Zwölf Oberammergauer Ahnentafeln.* Munich, 1934.

Rothkrug, Lionel. "German Holiness and Western Sanctity in Medieval and Modern History." *Historical Reflections/Réflexions Historiques* 15, no. 1 (1988).

———. "Holy Shrines, Religious Dissonance and Satan in the Origins of the German Reformation." *Historical Reflections/Réflexions Historiques* 14, no. 2 (1987).

———. "Religious Practices and Collective Perceptions: Hidden Homologies in the Renaissance and Reformation." *Historical Reflections/Réflexions Historiques* 7, no. 1 (Spring 1980).

Röttger, B. H. "Volkskunst im Bezirk Bogen." *Die ostbairischen Grenzmarken* 18, no. 4 (1929): 100–107.

Sabean, David Warren. *Power in the Blood: Popular Culture and Village Discourse in Early Modern Germany.* Cambridge: Cambridge University Press, 1984.

Sackel, Karola. "Der Letzte seiner Kunst: Heinrich Rambold, der Hinterglasmaler von Murnau." *Volkskunst macht Schule* 21 (1949): 9–10.

Sargent, Steven D. *Religion and Society in Late Medieval Bavaria: The Cult of St. Leonard, 1258–1500.* Ph.D. dissertation, University of Pennsylvania, 1982.

———. "Religious Responses to Social Violence in Eleventh-Century Aquitaine." *Historical Reflections/Réflexions Historiques* 12, no. 2 (1985): 219–40.

Sarti, Roland. *Long Live the Strong: A History of Rural Society in the Apennine Mountains.* Amherst: University of Massachusetts Press, 1985.

Schaffner, Bertram. *Father Land: A Study of Authoritarianism in the German Family.* New York: Columbia University Press, 1948.

Schauber, Vera, and Hanns Michael Schindler. *Die Heiligen und Namenspatrone im Jahreslauf.* Munich: Delphin, 1985.

Scheingraber, Wersnher and Wilfried Bahnmüller. *Volkskunst im Bayerischen Oberland.* Freilassing: Pannonia, 1978.

Schenda, Rudolf. *Die Lesestoffe der kleinen Leute: Studien zur populären Literatur im 19. und 20. Jahrhundert.* Munich: Beck, 1976.

———. "Ein französischer Bilderbogenkatalog aus dem Jahre 1860." *Schweizerisches Archiv für Volkskunde* 62 (1966): 49–61.

Schmid, Wolfgang M. "Alte Glasbilder." *Niederbayrische Heimatglocken* 30 (August 1930).

Schneider, Jenny. *Glasgemälde: Katalog der Sammlung des Schweizerischen Landesmuseums Zürich.* Zürich: Schweizerisches Landesmuseum, 1970.

Schott, Franz L., and Peter Volk. *Gemalt hinter Glas: Studioausstellung anläßlich der Restaurierung der Tischplatten aus dem Spiegelkabinett der Würzburger Residenz.* Exhibition catalog, Bayerisches Nationalmuseum, Munich, February 26–April 24, 1988. Residenz, Würzburg, April 29–June 26, 1988.

Schrank, Franz von Paula. *Baierische Reise.* Munich, 1786.

Schreiber, Georg. *Mutter und Kind in der Kultur der Kirche: Studien zur Quellenkunde und Geschichte der Karitas Sozialhygiene und Bevölkerungspolitik.* Freiburg im Breisgau: Herder, 1918.

———. *Wallfahrt und Volkstum in Geschichte und Leben.* Düsseldorf: L. Schwann, 1934.

Schremmer, Eckart. *Die Wirtschaft Bayerns: Vom hohen Mittelalter bis zum Beginn der Industrialisierung: Bergbau, Gewerbe, Handel.* Munich: Beck, 1970.

———. "Proto-Industrialisation: A Step Towards Industrialisation?" *Journal of European Economic History* 10 (1981): 653–70.

———. "Standortausweitung der Warenproduktion im langfristigen Wirtschaftswachstum: Zur Stadt-Land-Arbeitsteilung im Gewerbe des 18. Jahrhunderts." *Vierteljahrschrift für Sozial- und Wirtschaftsgeschichte* 59 (1972): 1–40.

———. "The Textile Industry in South Germany, 1750 to 1850: Some Causes for the Technological Backwardness During the Industrial Revolution; Investment Approach and Structure Approach." *Textile History* 7 (1976): 60–89.

Schropfer, E. "Der Glasmaler von Seehausen am Staffelsee." *Altbayerische Heimatpost* 42 (1954): 4.

Schuster, Raimund. *Das Raimundsreuter Hinterglasbild: Geschichte der Raimundsreuter Hinterglasmalerei und ihres Einflußgebietes.* Grafenau: Morsak, 1984.

———. *Hinterglasbilder aus Außergefild im Böhmerwald.* Grafenau: Morsak, 1980.

———. *Hinterglasbilder und Risse aus dem Bayerischen Wald und anschließendem Böhmerwald.* Vilsbiburg: Der Storchenturm Sonderheft 3 (1979).

———. *Risse zu Hinterglas-bildern aus den 18. und 19. Jahrhundert.* Rosenheim: Rosenheimer, 1978.

———. "Von Kraxenträgern und Glasbilderhändlern im 19. Jahrhundert." *Volkskunst* 6, no. 2 (1983): 84–87.

Schwarz, I. *Zur Geschichte der Einführung der Lithographie in Wien.* Vienna, n.d.

Scribner, Robert. "Cosmic Order and Daily Life: Sacred and Secular in Pre-Industrial German Society." In *Religion and Society in Early Modern Europe, 1500–1800,* edited by Kaspar von Greyerz. London: George Allen and Unwin, 1984.

———. *For the Sake of Simple Folk: Popular Propaganda for the German Reformation.* Cambridge: Cambridge University Press, 1981.

Segalen, Martine. *Love and Power in the Peasant Family: Rural France in the Nineteenth Century.* Translated by Sarah Matthews. Chicago: University of Chicago Press, 1983.

Seidel, Max. *Hinterglasbilder.* Stuttgart and Zürich: Belser, 1978.

Seidl, Siegfried. "Der volkstümliche Maler Johann Bapt. Reisbacher sen. in Kollnburg bei Viechtach (Bayer. Wald)." *Bayerisches Jahrbuch für Volkskunde* (1980–81): 24–38.

Selzer, P. Alois. *St. Wendelin: Leben und Verehrung eines alemannisch-fränkischen Volksheiligen.* 2d ed. Mödling bei Wien: St. Gabriel, 1962.

Senefelder, Alois. *The Invention of Lithography.* Translated by J. V. Muller. New York: Fuchs and Lang Manufacturing Company, 1911.

Sharot, Stephen. "Secularization and the Diminishing Decline of Religion." *Review of Religious Research* 27, no. 3 (1986): 193–207.

Shepherd, William R. *Historical Atlas.* 9th ed. New York: Barnes and Noble, 1964.

Shorter, Edward. *The Making of the Modern Family.* New York: Basic Books, 1975.

Shorter, Edward. *Social Change and Social Policy in Bavaria, 1800–1860.* Ph.D. dissertation, Harvard University, Cambridge, Mass., 1967.

So Ruf Ich an Maria: Risse mit Wallfahrtsmotiven aus Schönstein. Exhibition catalog, Gäubodenmuseum Straubing, July 25–October 5, 1986.

Spamer, Adolf. *Das kleine Andachtsbild vom XIV. bis zum XX. Jahrhundert.* Munich, 1930.

Spamer, Adolf, and Mathilde Hain. *Der Bilderbogen von der "Geistlichen Hausmagd": Ein Beitrag zur Geschichte des religiösen Bilderbogens und der Erbaauungsliteratur im populären Verlagswesen Mitteleuropas.* Göttingen: Schwartz, 1970.

Sperber, Jonathan. *Popular Catholicism in Nineteenth-Century Germany.* Princeton: Princeton University Press, 1984.

Spindler, Max. *Handbuch der Bayerischen Geschichte, Vol IV, Das neue Bayern, 1800–1970,* part 2. Munich: C. H. Beck, 1975.

Staininger, Robert. "Sandl und seine Einwohner." *Heimatgaue* 9, no. 3 (1928): 148–56.

Stark, Rodney, and William Sims Bainbridge. *The Future of Religion: Secularization, Revival and Cult Formation.* Berkeley: University of California Press, 1985.

Statistik des Deutschen Reichs, n.s., 6, no. 2. Berlin, 1885.

Statistisches Jahrbuch 1987 für Bayern. Bayerisches Landesamt für Statistik und Datenverarbeitung, 1987.

Statistisch-topographische Beschreibung des Landgerichtes Wolfstein im Unterdonaukreise. 1830.

Steinbauer, Gaby. *St Ulrich—Patron des Bistums Augsburg: Untersuchungen zu Ulrichlegende.* St. Ottilien, 1981.

Stevens, Evelyn P. "Marianismo: The Other Face of Machismo in Latin America." In *Female and Male in Latin America: Essays,* edited by Ann Pescatello. Pittsburgh: University of Pittsburgh Press, 1973.

Stiss, Bedrich. "Hinterglasmalereien in Böhmen." *Bayerisches Jahrbuch für Volkskunde* (1972–75): 126–35.

Theilmann, John M. "Medieval Pilgrims and the Origins of Tourism." *Journal of Popular Culture* 20, no. 4 (Spring 1987): 93–102.

Theopold, Wilhelm. *Das Kind in der Votivmalerei.* Munich: Thiemig, 1981.
———. *Hab ein kostbar Gut erfleht: Ein Essay über Votivmalerei.* Munich: Thiemig, 1977.
———. *Votivmalerei und Medizin: Kulturgeschichte und Heilkunst im Spiegel der Votivmalerei.* Munich: Thiemig, 1978.
Thirsk, Joan. *Economic Policy and Projects: The Development of a Consumer Society in Early Modern England.* Oxford: Clarendon Press, 1978.
Thomas, Keith. "An Anthropology of Religion and Magic, II." *Journal of Interdisciplinary History* 6, no. 1 (Summer 1975): 90–109.
Trenner, Florian. *Der heilige Florian.* Regensburg, 1981.
Trexler, Richard. "Florentine Religious Experience: The Sacred Image." *Studies in the Renaissance* 19 (1972): 7–41.
Turchini, Angelo, ed. *Lo straordinario e il quotidiano: Ex voto, santuario, religione popolare nel Bresciano.* Brescia: Grafo, 1980.
Turner, Victor. *The Forest of Symbols: Aspects of Ndembu Ritual.* Ithaca: Cornell University Press, 1967.
Turner, Victor, and Edith Turner. *Image and Pilgrimage in Christian Culture: Anthropological Perspectives.* New York: Columbia University Press, 1978.
Twyman, Michael. *Lithography: 1800–1850: The Techniques of Drawing on Stone in England and France and Their Application in Works of Topography.* London: Oxford University Press, 1970.
Vasily Kandinsky: Painting on Glass (Hinterglasmalerei): Anniversary Exhibition. Exhibition catalog, Solomon R. Guggenheim Museum, New York, 1966.
Veit, Ludwig. *Historisches Atlas von Bayern: Teil Altbayern: Passau Hochstift.* Vol. 35. Munich: Kommission für Bayerische Landesgeschichte, 1978.
Veit, Ludwig, and Ludwig Lenhart. *Kirche und Volksfrömmigkeit im Zeitalter des Barock.* Freiburg: Herder, 1956.
Verzeichniß der bey der lithographischen Kunstanstalt an der Feyertags-Schule zu München erschienenen Kunstprodukte. 1818.
Vydra, Josef. *Die Hinterglasmalerei: Volkskunst aus tschechoslowakischen Sammlungen.* Prague: Artia, 1957.
Wagner, Carl. *Alois Senefelder, sein Leben und Wirken: Ein Beitrag zur Geschichte der Lithographie.* 1st ed. Leipzig: Giesecke und Devrient, 1914.
———. *Alois Senefelder: Sein Leben und Wirken und die weitere Entwicklung der Lithographie.* 2d ed. Leipzig, 1943.
Wallfahrt kennt keine Grenzen. Exhibition catalog, Bayerisches Nationalmuseum, Munich, June 28–October 7, 1984.
Ward, Mildred Lee. *Reverse Paintings on Glass.* Exhibition catalog, The Helen Foresman Spencer Museum of Art, University of Kansas, Lawrence, October 8–November 5, 1978.
Warner, Marina. *Alone of All Her Sex: The Myth and the Cult of the Virgin Mary.* New York: Vintage Books, 1983.
Washton Long, Rose-Carol. *Kandinsky: The Development of an Abstract Style.* Oxford: Clarendon, 1980.
Weber, Wilhelm. *Aloys Senefelder zum 200. Geburtstag, 1771–1971: Lithographien, Bücher, Noten, Dokumente.* Exhibition catalog, Stadtmuseum, Offenbach am Main, 1971.

———. *A History of Lithography.* London, 1966.
———. *Saxa Loquuntur.* Berlin, 1961.
Weber-Kellermann, Ingeborg. *Die Familie: Geschichte, Geschichten und Bilder.* Frankfurt am Main: Insel, 1976.
———. *Die Kindheit: Kleidung und Wohnen, Arbeit und Spiel: Eine Kulturgeschichte.* Frankfurt am Main: Insel, 1979.
Wegner, Wolfgang. "'Les Oeuvres Lithographiques' und ihre Entstehungsgeschichte: Ein Beitrag zur Erforschung der Inkunabelzeit der Münchner Lithographie." *Oberbayerisches Archiv* (1965): 139–92.
Weishaupt, Heinrich. *Bayern's erste technische Schule.* Munich, 1865.
———. *Theoretisch-praktische Anleitung zur Chromo-Lithographie oder zum lithographischen Farbendruck, so wie zum lithographischen Kunstdruck überhaupt, nach den neuesten, verbesserten Verfahrungsweisen, zur Herstellung des Vollendetsten, was diese Kunst zu liefern vermag.* Quedlinburg and Leipzig: Basse, 1848.
———. *Verzeichniss der lithographischen Incunabeln-Sammlung.* Munich, 1884.
Weiss, Peg. "Kandinsky und München: Begegnungen und Wandlungen." In *Kandinsky und München: Begegnungen und Wandlungen, 1896–1914,* edited by Arnim Zweite. Munich: Prestel, 1982.
Wilke, Gerhard, and Kurt Wagner. "Family and Household: Social Structures in a German Village Between the Two World Wars." In *The German Family: Essays on the Social History of the Family in Nineteenth- and Twentieth-Century Germany,* edited by Richard J. Evans and W. R. Lee. London: Croom Helm, 1981.
Wilson, Stephen. "Cults of Saints in the Churches of Central Paris." In *Saints and Their Cults: Studies in Religious Sociology, Folklore and History,* edited by Stephen Wilson. Cambridge: Cambridge University Press, 1983.
Winkler, R. Arnim. *Die Frühzeit der deutschen Lithographie: Katalog der Bilder von 1796–1821.* Munich: Prestel, 1975.
———. *Wie sammle ich Lithographien.* Munich, 1965.
Wrigley, E. A. "Marriage, Fertility and Population Growth in Eighteenth-Century England." In *Marriage and Society: Studies in the Social History of Marriage,* edited by R. B. Outhwaite. New York: St. Martin's, 1981.
Wuthnow, Robert. "Science and the Sacred." In *The Sacred in a Secular Age: Toward Revision in the Scientific Study of Religion,* edited by Phillip E. Hammond. Berkeley: University of California Press, 1985.
Wüthrich, Lucas Heinrich. *Ältere Hinterglasmalerei, 1520–1780.* Bern: Paul Haupt, 1976.
Zahn, Wilhelm. *Die schönsten Ornamente und merkwürdigsten Gemälde aus Pompeji, Herkulanum und Stabiae nebst einigen Grundrissen und Ansichten nach den an Ort und Stelle gemachten Original zeichnungen.* Berlin: Georg Reimer, 1829.
———. *Ornamente aller Klassischen Kunstepochen, nach den Originalen in ihren eigenthümlichen Farben dargestellt.* 20 volumes. Berlin, ?1832–48.
Zinnhobler, Rudolf. *Der Heilige Wolfgang: Leben, Legende, Kult.* Linz, 1975.
Zirngibl, Roman. *Geschichte des baierischen Handels.* Munich, 1817.

Index